FAMILIA

ULSTER GENEALOGICAL REVIEW

VOLUME 2 NO 8
1992

incorporating Ulster Genealogical & Historical Guild *Newsletter*

Ulster Historical Foundation
12 College Square East
Belfast
BT1 6DD

ISBN 0 901905 56 9

Printed by Graham & Sons (Printers) Ltd.
51 Gortin Road, Omagh, Co. Tyrone

This book has received support from the Cultural
Traditions Programme of the Community Relations
Council which aims to encourage acceptance and
understanding of Cultural Diversity.

Front cover illustration: S. T. Gill's The Irish Emigrant
(reproduced by permission of the Mitchell
Library, State Library of NSW, Macquarie
Street, Sydney, NSW, Australia).

Design by Wendy Dunbar

CONTENTS

EDITORIAL

Most of the articles in this issue of *Familia* are based on lectures given in Belfast in 1991 and 1992 at genealogical conferences organised by the Ulster Historical Foundation. The first gathering was about 'That Elusive Irish Ancestor' and David Harkness's inaugural lecture was published in *Familia* last year together with an address by Jack Magee. We did not know then that this was to be the first in a series of genealogical jamborees in Belfast. In September 1992 'Auld Lang Syne: Searching for that Elusive Scots Irish Ancestor' was held as part of the All-Ireland Homecoming Festival and plans for a 1993 conference are well advanced.

For those who were at the conferences the articles in this issue will revive, we hope, happy memories. For those who have not yet experienced a UHF genealogical conference they provide a glimpse of the range of subjects covered. But they are only a very small selection from a total of more than one hundred lectures given in 1991 and 1992 by almost as many speakers: a mere 10% sample.

In subject matter and geographical spread they reflect the range of the conferences: source material on Belfast balances immigrant records in USA; movement into Ireland from Great Britain is supported by a study of settlers' surnames; traditional immigrant areas of Canada and Australia contrast with the more bizarre story of Irish Argentina. The publication of Professor Maxwell's opening lecture in 1992: 'Canada and Ireland – Two Divided Countries – An Historical Perspective' gives those who heard it an opportunity to study the text of a solid survey in which facts and interpretation were presented to us by a very lively mind. The subject matter relates, alas, to a current and urgent problem in both countries and in varying forms and degrees elsewhere and thus has a topical and universal interest and application.

Gordon Forth's article on the Anglo-Irish and Australia also has a wider interest than its title may suggest; for when analysing Anglo-Irish attitudes it illuminates current Unionist modes of thoughts. He writes 'Though usually from relatively humble backgrounds themselves, the newly established Protestant gentry possessed the typical colonist's contempt for the native Irish. Regarding themselves superior on account of their proven military prowess, religious orthodoxy, English blood and more advanced culture, few Protestants mixed freely with the Celtic

3

Catholic population.' His article traces this squireen pathology into the wide spaces of Australia and underlines its contradictions: 'Though staunchly imperialist and monarchist, the Anglo-Irish remained ambivalent in terms of their national allegiances, not feeling fully Irish yet often disliking and being highly suspicious of the English.'

The continuity of Irish attitudes in colonial situations is also noted in the article on 'Irish Immigration to Canada . . .' where the joint authors write that 'Despite its great distance from Ireland, and the scattered nature of its population, Canada was in many ways a remarkably intimate place operating upon social values and connections directly traceable to particular situations in the Old World.'

By using material from the UHF genealogical conferences this issue of *Familia* has a slightly different tone from other years but we hope that there is that catholic and judicious mix of useful genealogical facts and serious historical perspective and judgement for which we strive each year.

Kenneth Darwin

TWO DIVIDED COUNTRIES: CANADA AND IRELAND

by M. Perceval-Maxwell*
Professor of History, McGill University, Montreal

The primary interest of those attending this conference is family history. This branch of the discipline has an obvious impact upon local history, but when accumulated, it also contributes to our understanding of the macro-historical trends which determine the nature of our world. Migration of population, for instance, consists in essence of a large number of individual and family decisions to move from one place to another, and migration, in turn, creates political and cultural minorities and majorities whose interaction has had a profound effect upon the civilization in which we live. As we observe current events, it is obvious that one of the major social challenges that we face is to find a way in which such cultural and political minorities and majorities may flourish and yet live in proximity with one another and in harmony. In providing an historical perspective on the current divisions within Canada and Ireland, I shall be looking at two case histories of attempts to deal with such problems in the past, and it is my hope that such a comparative exercise may shed some light upon the nature of those divisions today.

It is difficult in the space of one paper to do justice to the historical background of the division within one of these countries, and it is, therefore, probably foolhardy even to attempt to look at two of them together. It was estimated at the end of the 'eighties by John Whyte that a bibliography of studies on Northern Ireland since 1969 would contain 7,000 items, and it is probable that Canada's constitutional predicament has led to commentary of similar monumental proportions to the point that neither subject can be properly grasped by any one mind.[1] Indeed the wisdom of adding to this pile of literature may be questioned. My excuse, however, for even daring to embark on this venture is that only a few of the studies in the pile are comparative in nature, and most of them

---

* The opening lecture at the 1992 U.H.F. Genealogical Conference.
1. J. Whyte, *Interpreting Northern Ireland* (Oxford, 1990), p.viii.

observe only the very recent past. What I will try to do is look very briefly at the origins of the minorities and majorities in Canada and Ireland, the attempts made to devise workable arrangements between them during the nineteenth century, and finally, to look at the current situation in both countries.

It goes without saying that many pitfalls await the person rash enough to attempt such a comparison. There must be an almost complete dependence on the secondary literature, and the presence of as many differences as similarities between the two situations renders the task that much more complicated. A more serious difficulty is that one person's minority is another's majority. Irish nationalists are a majority in Ireland, but they were at times a minority in the nineteenth century British archipelago. The anglophones in Quebec (a term used to denote those whose first language in English) are a minority within the French Canadian minority, but they are, or like to think of themselves as, a part of the Canadian majority. This raises the question of which minorities or majorities should be compared. I have chosen to be more selective and flexible than consistent on this point and will make comparisons according to what seems to be appropriate within a particular context and time.

One striking feature of the major divisions within Canada and Ireland is that they both have their origins in the early seventeenth century. Meaningful English settlement of North America began with the foundation of Virginia in 1607. France began a settlement at Quebec in 1608, and it was in 1610 that the official British protestant settlement in Ulster was begun. It was the demographic patterns that followed this migration that gave rise to the minorities in both Canada and Ireland. The English population of North America very rapidly overtook the French. In 1622, for instance, the white population of Virginia was 4,000 whereas the French had settled only sixty persons in Quebec by the same date. By 1640, there were a total of 40,000 whites in the two English colonies of Virginia and New England, whereas the French population of Canada did not begin to reach this figure till a century later. During the century between the conquest and confederation the French-speaking population rose from 55,000 to 700,000, but migration from Britain and Ireland to both Upper and Lower Canada (that is Ontario and Quebec) during the same period was on a sufficiently large scale that by 1867 the French population had become a minority in the two Canadas. Only in Lower

Canada, that is the province of Quebec, did the French retain a majority.[2]

In Ireland, during the same period, a demographic pattern between catholics and protestants was being formed which in some ways resembles that between the English and French in North America although the manner in which this pattern was established was very different. During the first half of the seventeenth century, protestants from Britain migrated to Ireland at an even greater rate than they did to America, and by 1641 we may calculate that there were some 100,000 to 125,000 such settlers and their descendants in Ireland. These can have amounted to no more than ten percent of the total population of the island, but already, like the French along the valley of the St Laurence, they tended to be concentrated in one area. By 1641, some forty percent of the protestants in Ireland lived in Ulster, with the strongest settlements being established in the north-east. This distribution of population may be compared with that which prevailed at the beginning of the twentieth century. In 1911, Ireland had a total population of some four million, twenty-six percent of which (1·1 million) was protestant, but seventy-eight percent of these protestants lived in Ulster.[3]

There was, moreover, another similarity between the French in North America and the protestants in Ireland. Into the eighteenth century, both commanded a degree of political control out of keeping with their numerical strength. In the case of Canada, this was maintained by means of French arms, and in Ireland the protestant ascendancy was established and maintained by English and Scottish forces, yet, during this period both minority groups gained a sense of identity and cohesion, which, while strongly linked to the culture from which they emerged, looking back to their own particular history as a source of inspiration. As a modern French-Canadian historian has remarked, to the French who settled in North America after 1608, 'New France was their country.'[4]

2. M. Giraud, *Histoire du Canada* (Paris, 1971), p. 19; M. Trudel, *Initiation à la Nouvell-France: historire et institutions* (Montreal, 1968), pp. 45, 63, 91, 138; K. McNaught, *The Penguin History of Canada* (1988), pp. 23, 27; J. Douglas, *Old France in the New World; Quebec in the 17th Century* (Cleveland, 1905), p. 158.
3. The calculation of the seventeenth century figures is contained in: M. Perceval-Maxwell, *The Outbreak of the Irish Rebellion in 1641*, forthcoming, ch. 2. The 1911 figures are taken from J. J. Lee, *Ireland 1912-1985: politics and society* (Cambridge, 1989), pp. 1-2.
4. M. Brunet, 'The French Canadians' Search for a Fatherland' in P. Russell (ed.), *Nationalism in Canada* (Toronto, New York, London and Sydney, 1966), p. 48.

During the second half of the eighteenth century, the position of the two groups was transformed. In the case of the Irish protestants, the primary agent of change was the rise of democratic principles. Such principles, let it be said, were espoused particularly strongly by some protestant dissenters, but the protestants in Ireland as a whole did not immediately have to adjust to the application of such principles to Ireland because the issue was deferred by the creation of a parliamentary union under which the catholic majority in Ireland became, even after emancipation, the minority in a united kingdom of Great Britain and Ireland.

In the case of the Canadians, the most obvious source of change was the British victory over the French in 1759, and the American victory over the British two decades later, though, in the long run, the Canadians were to be as much affected by democratic concepts as were the Irish protestants. From this point, however, until the twentieth century, we see more divergence than convergence in the fate of these two particular minorities.

During the nineteenth century, the Canadians ultimately opted for a federation in which the French population would constitute a permanent minority. They did this in large part because, in contrast to the minority in Ireland, there was no political bond they could make by which they could become a part of a majority. They had three options: to become a separate and independent state, to join with the U.S.A. or link up with the North American colonies still owing allegiance to the British crown. The 1837 rebellion in Lower Canada indicates that the first option was not entirely dismissed, but the suppression of this rebellion and the subsequent imposition in 1840 by Britain of a union between Lower and Upper Canada indicates that it was not a viable option at the time. If annexation by the United States was to be avoided, therefore, partnership with the other British colonies in North America was the only option open to the French Canadians, but from the point of view of a comparison with the Irish situation, it is the nature of the partnership, not the identity of the partner, that is of significance.

To a large degree, the position of the French as a minority in North America in 1867 resembles more the position of the Irish catholics as a minority in the British archipelago than that of the protestants in Ireland. These last could, and after 1886 did, identify with the majority in the two islands, and the major difference between the political directions adopted by Canada and Ireland during the nineteenth century was that the French Canadians opted for a form of union with other colonies in which the majority was not only English-speaking but protestant, whereas those pursuing Home Rule in Ireland sought to leave a protestant and English dominated union in order to form a state in which catholics would be the majority. Here, however, a difference between the two situations needs to be stressed. The French Canadians enjoyed a substantial advantage over their fellow catholics in Ireland. Whereas the latter had to wait till 1829 for political emancipation, under the Quebec Act of 1774, catholics were accepted as members of the governing council, and when lower Canada obtained a legislature in 1791, the existing acceptance of catholic participation in the governing process was continued. Catholics in other British North American colonies were not as fortunate as those in Quebec, but the issue did not leave a residue of bitterness as in the main catholic Irish migration occurred after 1829. Moreover, in the open and generally egalitarian society of the colonies, catholic participation in government on lines already existing in Quebec quickly followed emancipation. Generally, therefore, catholics in Canada negotiated as political equals, and it cannot be doubted that this enormously enhanced the prospects for amicable negotiations.[5]

In looking at confederation, we may select three other issues in addition to catholic emancipation that are pertinent to the comparison at hand: the strategic situation, the attitude of the Irish in North America towards the federation and finally, the attitude of the French Canadians. One of the catalysts that helped form the federation was the strategic interest of both Britain and the colonies themselves. The only vital British interest in North America by 1860 was the harbour at Halifax, and with German power growing on the continent, the British wished to shed their American military responsibilities and persuade the colonies there to pay for their own defence. (By 1858 only four British battalions

---

5. D. Creighton, *The Story of Canada* (London, 1971), pp. 84-5.

were in garrison in America and there were no cavalry, though reinforcements were dispatched on the outbreak of the American civil war.) Similarly, it had been hoped in Canada, and particularly in French Canada, that the American civil war would produce two weakened states to the south instead of one strong one. As a northern victory became certain, and as Britain's interest in North America in North America declined, only in union could the colonies find security against annexationist designs within what had become a very powerful neighbour.[6]

The security issue was closely related to the attitude of the Irish in America towards the Canadian union. No sooner had assurance been obtained that the recently victorious American union would not move north than a new threat appeared from the same direction in the form of the American Fenians. Fenian efforts having failed in England and Ireland, one element within the American branch of the movement believed that, if a military presence could be established in British America, their friends in the U.S. congress could be used to turn Canada into a lever to force England out of Ireland. Preparations were made for an invasion of New Brunswick in 1865, and although this was thwarted before it began, the following year a force of some 800 men crossed the Niagara River and attempted to establish a position in Canada. The attempt failed, but what is of interest is the absence of support among the Irish in British America for the efforts of their American compatriots to liberate their common homeland.

Had the Irish north of the American border shared the attitudes of those to the south to any considerable extent, the colonial governments would have faced a very serious situation that might well have jeopardized the process of Canadian union. It is estimated that, at the time of confederation, just under one third of the population of the British North American colonies was of Irish origin. According to the 1871 census, the catholics constituted a minority of this population in

---

6. The discussion of the formation of the 1867 federation is based primarily on W. L. Morton, *The Critical Years: the Union of British North America 1857-1873* (Toronto, 1964).

Ontario and Nova Scotia (thirty-five and forty-two percent respectively), but in New Brunswick and Quebec they outnumbered Irish protestants.[7]

The Fenians made contact with a dissident French group and a store of their arms was discovered in Montreal, but their campaign received little support in either the Atlantic provinces or Canada. There was no Fenian martyr in Canada despite the capture of some of the invaders. Indeed, the only killing resembling a catholic martyrdom was that of D'Arcy McGee, the leader of the Irish in Lower Canada, who, despite a revolutionary past in Ireland, supported the government and died by a Fenian bullet.[8]

To explain the contrast in loyalties between the catholic Irish Americans and those in British America we have to look at their respective experience in the new world. It has been remarked that the Irish catholics who emigrated to America brought a nationalism derived from Wolfe Tone and the Young Ireland movement, but they also developed a sense of 'loneliness and alienation' in America, and it was from life in their new home that they derived what has been described as their most distinctive attitudes: 'a pervasive sense of inferiority, intense longing for acceptance and respectability and an acute sensitivity to criticism.'[9] The Irish catholics who settled in British America brought the same ideology, reinforced, no doubt, by bitter memories of their treatment in Ireland and by the appalling consequences of shipping fever. Hostility to protestants remained deep seated; indeed, the Irish in New Brunswick had strong reservations about joining in a federation with an Upper Canada represented by George Brown, editor of the Toronto *Globe and Mail*, who stood for no popery. Yet the experience of the catholic Irish in the colonies differed from that of their co-religionists to the south. This is best illustrated briefly by citing from a letter written by Archbishop Connolly of Halifax, who was responsible for all catholics in

7. Ibid., p. 183; C. J. Houston and W. J. Smyth, *Irish Emigration and Canadian Settlement* (Toronto, Buffalo and Belfast, 1990), p. 229.
8. *D.N.B.*, xii, p. 529.
9. T. N. Brown, *Irish-American Nationalism 1870-1890* (Philadelphia and New York, 1966), pp. 23-4.

the Atlantic provinces. Writing to the lieutenant governor of New Brunswick after the threat of the Fenian invasion had arisen, he remarked that Irish catholics in the U.S. were excluded from the executive, had no seat in the senate, enjoyed little representation in the house of representatives, and in no state commanded full equality in terms of appointment to public office. By contrast, 'In Canada, New Brunswick, Nova Scotia, Newfoundland, and Prince Edward Island, there has been no period since the days of emancipation, at which catholics have not possessed that influence in the community to which their number and position fairly entitled them . . . The great government of the United States has nothing more tempting to offer.'[10] The hierarchy not only opposed the Fenians; it also supported the formation of the federation in which catholics would constitute a minority, albeit a substantial one.

Given this emphasis upon the catholic Irish, perhaps it needs to be stressed that most of those involved in the negotiations to bring about a union of the colonies were not catholics. The man who is credited with having first conceived of a British American federation in a form very close to that which it ultimately took was Alexander Galt, whose father was a Lowland Scot. Canada's governors from 1861 to 1878 were all protestant Irish, but the generally positive attitude of the Irish catholics towards the creation of a state in which they would constitute a minority helps us to understand how the French, a minority in terms of language as well as religion, could also participate in the formation of such a state.

This is not to suggest that French Canadians were unanimous in their support of the new federation. There was strong opposition based on nationalist sentiment, which, in turn, was based on the claim that a French nation in North America had been recognized under the treaty of Paris, which, it is claimed by Quebec nationalists, was confirmed by the Quebec Act of 1774 and the Constitutional Act of 1791. [11] The Union of

10. Cited in Morton, *Critical Years*, p. 191.
11. Morton, *Critical Years*, p. 90; Brunet, 'Fatherland', p. 49.

Upper and Lower Canada into one political unit had, in a sense, preserved this claim to a separate French nationality in that it was not a complete union. What had been Lower, or French Canada, received equal representation both in the legislature and in the cabinet with what had been Upper Canada. Even the leadership of the government was split and the capital alternated between Quebec and Toronto. The British settlers had accepted this arrangement while they constituted a minority in both Canadas combined, but by 1860 their numbers exceeded the French and a demand arose for representation by population, or majoritarian rule. Understandably, the French felt threatened by this proposed change in the rules. As one of them remarked, any departure from equality meant civil war. Even Sir George-Etienne Cartier, later to be one of the prime architects of the federation, observed in 1861 through the pages of his journal, *La Minerve*:

> We will consent to no compromise whatever on a principle so closely bound up with the existence of our nationality, of our religion, of all that remains of our heritage from our fathers. Either [there must be] equality of representation for the two provinces [note the assumption that there were still two] or the dissolution of the union.[12]

There was, of course, a compromise, but it was one which did not threaten the principles laid down by Cartier. The federation of 1867 created a two-tiered system. This provided for a legislature in Quebec with a strong French and catholic majority. This controlled those matters linked to religion and nationality, though there were special provisions to protect the protestant minority in the province. As in Ireland, one of the areas deemed most crucial for minority control was education as it was the key to the preservation of faith and language. At the same time, the principle of representation by population was introduced in the formation of the central legislature, which meant that the French would constitute a permanent minority. However, this was balanced by the limitation of Ottawa's jurisdiction to matters that were, at that time, not crucial to

12. Cited in Morton, *Critical Years*, p. 93.

French Canadian survival, by the existence of the Quebec legislature and by other measures such as a strong representation of Quebec in the upper house.

Some English Canadians argued during the negotiations that the French nationality could be preserved within a unitary state. In doing so, they pointed to the British model within which the Welsh and the Scots had managed to preserve their separate identities. Cartier, however, was adamant on the issue of the double legislature because he had to persuade his compatriots that a federation with the English provinces could preserve the French nationality as fully as a separate state. He did, however, concede that two nationalities could be maintained within a single state, though he perceived the Canadian nationality as being political rather than cultural.

It is, of course, striking that a nineteenth century resolution to the majority-minority question was found in British North America, even in the presence of large numbers of Irish catholics and protestants, but not in Britain itself. Here is not the place to enter into the history of Home Rule, but it is instructive to compare the two situations with the help of John Kendle's recent book on *Ireland and the Federal Solution*.[13]

We do not need this comparison in order to see that delay in granting catholic emancipation poisoned the political atmosphere in which Anglo-Irish relations had to work, but we have in the Canadian experience the nearest thing to a control group that a historian can expect to receive, and this experience shows what could be done when emancipation, and perhaps more important, when discrimination was not a grievance. Similarly, we do not have to look to North America to see that one of the obstacles to granting Home Rule was that it did not serve England's strategic interests. Nevertheless the comparison is valuable in that it serves to show what an important factor the strategic issue was. If, declared Gladstone in 1871, Ireland were to be given Home Rule, then

13. J. Kendle, *Ireland and the Federal Solution* (Kingston and Montreal, 1989).

Scotland and Wales would have to receive it also, and then he continued: 'Can any sensible man, can any rational man, suppose that at this time of day, in this condition of the world, we are going to disintegrate the great capital institutions of this country for the purpose of making ourselves ridiculous in the sight of all mankind?'[14] Finally, given that French Canadian nationalism resembled that found in Ireland in opposition to the union, and in Ulster in opposition to the Home Rule (note that I am comparing the French as a minority to both components of Ireland), we may conclude that this type of nationalism did not necessarily preclude a satisfactory resolution to the majority-minority question during the nineteenth century.

When we look at the majority-minority issue in the context of Ireland, Ulster and the United Kingdom from 1840 to 1921, we find politicians who understood the possibilities of the Canadian solution to the problem. The first of these was Sharman Crawford, an Ulster landlord, who in the 1840s looked to the 1840 Canada act as a model for Anglo-Irish relations. One of the early leaders of the Home Rule movement. Isaac Butt, also a protestant, published *Home Government for Ireland, Irish federalism: its meaning, its objects and its hopes* in 1870. This work draws on the British North America Act, which established the Canadian union, and envisaged England and Scotland as well as Ireland operating on the lines of Canadian provinces, with a federal parliament in Westminster. Other Home Rulers, however, such as Parnell, had little interest in such schemes, and if they had a North American model in mind, it was of an Ireland with a relationship to Britain similar to Canada's, not that of one of the Canadian provinces to the federal government.

When Gladstone drafted the 1886 Home Rule bill, one of the more important influence on him was the B.N.A Act, his own copy of this Act being heavily marked, but his bill was not a federal proposal. Initially, it provided for an Irish legislature but no Irish representation at Westminster, although that parliament was to continue to legislate for

14. Cited in Kendle, *Federal Solution*, p. 32.

Ireland in many areas. Thus, in some respects Ireland was to acquire the status of the Canadian dominion, but in others it was to be treated as colony.

Later, in 1893, when trying to persuade a visiting deputation from the Belfast Chamber of Commerce that it had nothing to fear from the second Home Rule bill, he declared: 'I compare Ireland with Canada.' He then continued:

> The distinction of race in Canada, as you know . . ., is infinitely sharper than it is in Ireland . . . I recollect the days when the investiture of Canada with powers of self-government was accompanied with just the same prophecies on the part of those who differed from the proposal as you now most conscientiously make. What has been the result . . . with this population, with a revenue corresponding to your own and with internal division of race, language and religion sharper than exists in Ireland? Canada is happy, is contented, and is prosperous.[15]

What he omitted to say was that Canada enjoyed an entirely different type of constitution to that which he was proposing for Ireland.

There were those who urged that the arrangements being made for Ireland should follow a Canadian model. Earl Grey, for instance, who served for some years as Canada's governor general, wrote to the Conservative leader, Arthur Balfour, in 1910, to urge that the time had come to 'federate' the United Kingdom, 'which will make Ireland, not into a Canada or Australia, but into an Ontario or Quebec.' Later, in the Lords, he developed this idea by saying 'Ireland might possibly consist of two provinces under the federal system – the North-East of Ulster would form one Province, and the rest of Ireland another.'[16]

However, despite such influential adherents of the idea of governing the United Kingdom through a federal system, it never gained sufficient momentum to be included in a parliamentary bill because of three fundamental obstacles. First, whereas in Canada federation meant the union of separate elements into a larger whole, with benefits flowing to all the units as a result of the union, federation in Britain looked as

---

15. *Gladstone's speech to the Belfast Chamber of Commerce and the Chamber's Reply* (London, 1893) pp. 12-13.
16. Kendle, *Federal Solution*, pp. 117, 158.

though it might lead to the disintegration of an existing state which controlled an empire. The demands of Ireland did not seem worth running this risk. Second, whereas discontent with the union in Ireland was patently obvious, there was only a little support in Scotland and Wales for becoming provinces in a federal union, and virtually none in England. Few could be convinced that three parts of the state should have a system imposed on them that they did not want in order to deal with Irish discontent, particularly as the Irish themselves were not asking for a federal state. As a result, the Home Rule bills contained a mixture of systems – devolution, colonial and federal – and became open to ridicule when examined in detail. As Balfour remarked of the 1893 bill: 'A Federal Government may be good. Colonial government may be good. The British Constitution as it stands may be good; but this bastard combination of the three is ludicrous and impossible.'[17]

The third difference between Canada and Britain in this context was that in Canada there was no comparable entity to Ulster. The closest analogy would be the English minority in Quebec, but this had none of the cohesion that we find in the Ulster protestants subsequent to the introduction of the first Home Rule bill. Gladstone had an understanding that special conditions existed in Ulster, but his Home Rule bills made no particular reference to Ulster and gave only general protection to religious minorities by contrast to the B.N.A. Act which provided specific protection to the English in Quebec. Other politicians, both Irish and English, showed even less sensitivity to Ulster than Gladstone. We can understand this because, unlike French Canada which had always projected a distinct political identity, it was only during the 1880s that popular support for a distinct political entity in Northern Ireland began to develop for the very good reason that it had not been necessary before Home Rule became a serious possibility.[18] But develop it did, and the

17. Ibid., p. 76.
18. Whyte, *Northern Ireland*, p. 127.

Irish majority committed the same error as the English majority had committed against it of not taking the minority seriously.

As we know, after the threat of rebellion in the north of Ireland and actual rebellion in the south, Ireland was partitioned, most of it being given a status similar to Canada's while part of Ulster was retained in the union. At the same time, devolution, if not federalism, was added to the mixture in that Northern Ireland obtained an assembly of its own with limited internal powers. Since 1921, the southern portion of the island has followed a constitutional path similar to Canada's in that the ties with Britain have been severed one by one, including, in Ireland's case, that with the monarchy. On the other hand, Ireland has also begun to move into a type of federation in which the United Kingdom is one of a number of partners; thus the trend in terms of political ties is complex and not unidirectional. In Northern Ireland, for its part, because it too has now acquired a minority problem, union has taken precedence over devolution since 1974, when the assembly was suspended pending a workable arrangement between the two groups within the population.

As we look at Canada and Ireland today, there are again a number of different ways in which minorities and majorities can be compared. Quebec, for instance, might point to the Republic as an example of how its own independence could work, particularly if a North American area of free trade is formed. Once it looked at Ireland's economic performance as an independent state, it might find the analogy less attractive, but there are some obvious similarities in the political situations of the two regions. However, the most striking similarity between groups is that of the tension between Quebec and Canada on the one hand and that between the majority in Northern Ireland and the Republic on the other.

At the heart of the concerns of the majorities in both Quebec and Northern Ireland lies the fear of losing a treasured identity, and this, in turn, rests on the anxiety of being demographically overwhelmed. After Terence O'Neill left the premiership of Northern Ireland, he remarked that the 'basic fear of protestants in Northern Ireland is that they will be outbred by Roman Catholics.'[19] There is some substance behind this fear

19. Cited in Lee, *Ireland 1912-1985*, p. 426.

in that in 1911 twenty-two percent of the province was catholic, but by 1986 this proportion had risen to forty percent, and by 1981 among those under fifteen years of age the catholic proportion amounted to 46·5%. The fertility of catholics seems to be diminishing and their rate of emigration exceeds that of the protestants, but such possible influence on future trends do not diminish the protestant fears about existing ones.[20]

We find very similar fears among the French in Quebec based on similar trends. 'The fear of "disappearing"', remarked a Quebec columnist recently, 'is deeply ingrained in the French-Canadian psyche . . .'[21] At the time of confederation, the population of Quebec amounted to about a third of the total for Canada. By 1951 this proportion had dropped to 29%, and by 1991, the percentage had declined to a quarter. The French-speaking population of Manitoba declined from 40,000 in 1971 to 23,000 in 1986, and that in Saskatchewan from 16,000 to 6,000 during the same period. Moreover, the recent decline in the Quebec birthrate has been dramatic, from 4·3 in 1951 to 1·35 in 1987, the latter figure being well below the rate necessary for replacement. Again, we can find figures that should reduce the fears of Quebec's majority that it may soon disappear. In 1976, 16·6% of primary and secondary students in Quebec were studying in English. Ten years later, after the passage of legislation to direct students into the French stream of education, this figure had dropped to 10·4 percent. Thus, the rate of decline in the English-speaking population as a proportion of the total in Quebec is evidently going to be dramatic and this has been brought about by direct government action, but what ought to be reassuring evidence to the majority is slow to penetrate its collective psyche and allay its anxiety.[22]

Another similarity that we find within the communities of Ireland

20. Ibid., p. 413; Whyte, *Northern Ireland*, pp. 24-5.
21. *Globe and Mail*, 22 Aug. 1992.
22. Morton, *Critical Years*, p. 264; P. Fournier, *A Meech Lake Post-Mortem*, trans. S. Fischman (Montreal and Kingston, 1991), p. 84.

and Canada is the presence of a two-nation theory. The two theories differ from each other, but they serve the same protective purpose. Quebec's has a long history, is well articulated and is used in its relations with the other provinces to argue for special status within the federation as one of the founding nations. The federation, thereby, becomes more a treaty between nations (Quebec being one nation and the rest of the provinces and the federal government being the other) than an agreement between eleven governments. Quebec being one among equals. In Northern Ireland, the theory has more recent origins than in Quebec and was, in fact, first enunciated by Englishmen. However, as in the Quebec case, the theory is used to warrant a different status within a larger unit. The relevance of the comparison is borne out by the similar reactions of the two groups to which the theories are respectively addressed. English Canada on the whole has rejected the concept, as have nationalists in Ireland, at least until recently. The Alberta minister of intergovernmental affairs, for instance, remarked in July 1992: 'There are not two nations here, there is one country and its called Canada. There are ten provinces. Quebec is being recognized for its special responsibilities for language and culture which is different.' This comment may be compared with that of the final statement to emerge out of the 'New Ireland Forum' of 1983-4, which declared that 'the particular structure of political unity which the Forum would wish to see established is a unitary state.' Here there is even less concession to any special status for Northern Ireland than the Alberta minister was willing to grant to Quebec.[23]

Several other comparisons between the Irish situation and the Canadian could be drawn, for instance in the use of annual parades in Northern Ireland and Quebec to demonstrate popular support for the majority opinion in those provinces, but I will make only one more. The size of the protestant minority in the Republic, like the French one in Manitoba and Saskatchewan, has declined substantially over time. It is now half the size it was when Ireland became independent. This decline,

23. *Globe and Mail*, 11 July 1993. For a discussion of the two-nations idea in Northern Ireland, see Whyte, *Northern Ireland*, pp. 146-7 and N. Mansergh, *The Irish Question 1840-1921* (Toronto, 1965), pp. 182-95.

however, has been for reasons that are unrelated to government policy. Government-minority relations in this case have been harmonious, but the decline in the size of the protestant community in the south is used in the north as a warning of what would happen in a united Ireland just as the fate of the French minorities in Western Canada is seen as a portent of what is to come if Quebec remains part of the federation.

The question that may now be in your minds is: what conclusions should we draw from these comparisons? As a historian, I should evade the question as we know that a knowledge of the past does not necessarily lead to specific knowledge about the future. A series of events, after following what appears to be a trend, can change direction quite suddenly and take historians as much as others by surprise. We have only to look at recent events in Eastern Europe to prove the point.

At the same time, as we look back at what was achieved during the nineteenth century in British North America we may derive some hope that reasonably harmonious relations can be established between very different groups living in the same area. It may, of course, be objected that Canada's size and relative wealth gave it an unfair advantage, but this objection is answered by noting that size and wealth has not prevented the development of Canada's present precarious state. However, the example also shows that rather special conditions have to exist before such accommodation is possible. One of these is external pressure, and here there may be hope for Ireland in that the current trend in Western Europe, unless it is upset by the collapse of the Soviet Union, is towards reconciliation between differing nationalities. It is in the interests of both Britain and Ireland to develop harmonious relations between their respective populations. Yet there is another condition which emerges from the comparison which provides less grounds for optimism. You will recall Cartier's assertion in 1861 that an essential element within a union had to be equality for French Canadians. The loyalty of the Irish catholics in the colonies also depended on the same criterion. It is surely because, as Canada has grown, French Canadians have lost this sense of equality that the nineteenth century arrangement has become less and less satisfactory to the majority in Quebec, and the matter has become even more complex as the aboriginals in Canada have become a political force and, in turn, demanded similar recognition to that accorded the French minority.

The difficulty here is that equity and fairness to minorities is not always within the power of democratically elected governments to give. Such qualities within a community often depend as much upon grass-roots attitudes as upon legislation, and it is the grass roots who choose the politicians, not the politicians who determine the attitudes. Fear, isolation and a sense of threat at the local level is often immune to change by means of academic argument or political exhortation. John Whyte observed with some sense of disappointment at the end of his book, *Interpreting Northern Ireland*, that the enormous amount of research devoted to the province had made little social impact because those who create the climate for inter-community relations do not read the results, or if they do, reject the findings if they feel themselves challenged. We find the same phenomenon in Quebec. Polls suggest that there is gathering support for independence despite the numerous economic studies indicating that such a political change would lower the standard of living.

Such a rigidity of mind is probably a *sine qua non* of inter-community conflict, but Whyte's expectations, and his disappointment at their failure to be realized, seem to me to be based upon a fundamental misconception of the nature of the conflict. He seems to have assumed that it is essentially ideological in its nature and that once the flaws in the ideas are revealed, they will be abandoned. Yet, as A. T. Q. Stewart pointed out about Northern Ireland in 1977 in his book, *The Narrow Ground*, at the heart of the conflict lies an atavism which is often immune to change by argumentation and the same phenomenon is evident within certain groups of the population in Quebec and Canada.[24]

Nevertheless, in saying this, I do not wish to suggest that because such atavism exists we should adopt a sort of cynical pessimism that such situations will go on for ever. Even atavism, however resistant to the presentation of alternative evidence it may be, rests upon an intellectual foundation. This consists of a particular interpretation of the past, and we can see that popular interpretations of the past do change, if only at a glacial rate.

The atavism that contributes to the community conflict that we see

24. A. T. Q. Stewart, *The Narrow Ground: aspects of Ulster 1609-1969* (London, 1977).

around us rests to a considerable degree upon a perception of the past fostered during the nineteenth and early twentieth centuries which stressed both the sufferings and successes of particular groups, thus separating them from their neighbours and stressing the irreconcilability of traditions. Such an approach towards the past reinforces group solidarity, and by repeated emphasis upon isolation evokes the very external hostility that it predicts.

This brand of historiography is still with us to some extent and its adherents denounce those historians whose examination of the evidence leads in other directions. No doubt the distrust and recrimination that this perception of the past tends to engender will continue into the next century, but such attitudes will not stop historians in places where there are majority-minority conflicts from looking at the past in ways that have been developed in the profession as a whole. The very variety of papers being presented at this conference is a reflection of the many approaches to the past that are being cultivated simultaneously. It is hard to believe that these differing perceptions will not affect future generations in all communities, and if they do penetrate the popular mentality, they will almost certainly diminish the belief that any one group stands alone in isolation from the experience of the rest of humanity.

This paper has been a small exercise in comparative history, which is but one way of looking at the past. Such an exercise should not lead to the belief that what was done in one place at one particular time can be applied like some formula to other times and places. Each minority-majority problem is in some respects unique, but it is probable that if those problems, wherever they occur, are to find some degree of resolution, it will be through a combination of an internal analysis of the particular circumstances that prevail in a given situation, along with an outward-looking awareness by all those involved of the experience of others in similar situations.

THE ANGLO-IRISH TRADITION AND ANGLO-IRISH MIGRATION TO COLONIAL AUSTRALIA

by Gordon Forth
Deakin University

In December 1840, George Winter, a gentleman squatter, visited the recently founded settlement of Port Phillip. It was on this occasion that Winter clashed bitterly with a fellow Ascendancy colonist, Augustine Barton, in the presence of the diarist and leading member of the 'Irish Cousinage' Charles Griffith. In the course of an 'unpleasant altercation' Winter denounced Barton's conduct as 'very colonial', a statement which Griffith considered 'expresses what we call at home going very close to the wind'.[1] Some months later, Griffith and no doubt other Port Phillip gentlemen were struck by the appearance of George Winter's younger brother Samuel as he rode through the settlement. A confident and experienced bushman of twenty-five, full-bearded, tall and strikingly handsome, the younger Winter reminded Griffith of 'one of the knights errant in the days of chivalry'.[2] On such occasions it was apparently Winter's custom to have an Aboriginal page in livery mounted up behind him and to be escorted by several retainers on foot. In attempting to play the eighteenth century style grand seigneur, Winter may well have been influenced by romantic images from his Ascendancy background. In a modified colonial fashion, he was possibly striving to emulate the likes of John Fitzmaurice, later Earl of Shelburne, who a century earlier had received official guests resplendent in brilliant feudal regalia attended by mounted retainers. Such unusual as well as less remarkable behaviour on the part of Australia's Ascendancy colonists can often be linked to their Old World Irish background. As representative of a separate national subgroup, these Anglo-Irish brought with them to Australia distinctive and commonly held attitudes and customs. Both consciously and unconsciously, this Anglo-Irish tradition influenced the responses of these Ascendancy to their new and changing circumstances in the Australian colonies.

1. Charles Griffith, Diary, 1840-41, 8 December, 1840, La Trobe Library, State Library of Victoria. This brief journal by one of Port Phillip's Irish cousinage and a younger son of Richard Griffiths M.P. provides an Ascendancy view of early Melbourne Society.
2. Ibid, 1 February, 1841.

As a small, scattered and rapidly assimilated migrant group, it is hardly surprising that Anglo-Irish colonists in early Australia have received so little recognition from historians. Yet at least during the first half of the nineteenth century, the Anglo or Ascendancy Irish were an influential as well as distinctive element in Australian colonial society. An Anglo-Irish presence was particularly noticeable in pre-goldrush Tasmania and the Port Phillip District (later Victoria) of New South Wales during the 1840s. As senior government officials; military officers in charge of penal settlements; Anglican clergyman; gentlemen pastoralists and founding members of the professions, the collective influence of the Anglo-Irish on early colonial society was considerable. Often outspoken and independently minded, these colonists, though not always identified as Anglo-Irish, featured prominently in the establishment of Australia's legal, political, religious, educational and cultural institutions. Influenced by their distinctive Old World tradition, generally speaking the Anglo-Irish in early Australia strove enthusiastically and with a fair degree of success to improve the crude and often brutal penal-pastoral society in which they found themselves. By examining the ways in which the Anglo-Irish tradition influenced the aspirations, attitudes and behaviour of a small but influential group of colonists this paper seeks to reconcile a generally positive assessment of the Ascendancy Irish in Australia with the widely accepted view of Ireland's Protestant gentry as a particularly selfish and reactionary class.

The Anglo-Irish tradition had its origins in the particular situation of the Protestant landed class established in Ireland following Cromwell's defeat of the Catholic Loyalist forces. Though the English (Norse-Welsh) had established a foothold in Ireland by the end of the eleventh century, the Anglo-Irish were largely the descendants of English settlers who took advantage of Cromwell's victory to acquire the defeated Catholic's confiscated estates. Based on entries in Burke's *Landed Gentry of Ireland*, Curtis concludes that the overwhelming majority of this class settled in Ireland during this period.[3] Under the 1652 Act of Settlement a majority of Catholic landowners were deprived of their estates and required to move to designated areas west of the Shannon. Cromwell's soldiers who had fought in Ireland, and adventurers who

---

3. L. P. Curtis, Jnr. 'The Anglo-Irish Predicament', *Twentieth Century Studies*, Nov. 1970, p.37.

helped finance the campaign, were entitled to apply for grants of land from the Catholics' forfeited estates. With the greater part of Ireland's more fertile lands distributed amongst them, the Act of Settlement saw the creation of a new class of Protestant gentry, the Irish Ascendancy.

The violent manner in which this Protestant élite was established in Ireland greatly influenced the kind of landed society that developed subsequently. By the early eighteenth century the descendants of these settlers, the Anglo-Irish, held attitudes and had developed a lifestyle regarded as typical of their class. Though having much in common with the longer established English gentry, whom they strove to emulate, their situation as an alienated and isolated ruling class and their exposure to Gaelic culture resulted in important differences. As well as unconsciously held beliefs and attitudes the Anglo-Irish brought to Australia a conscious awareness that they were the descendants of a conquering military caste: that their family's gentry status had involved the defeat, dispossession and continued suppression of the Catholic majority. The behaviour of the Anglo-Irish in Australia was also influenced by their knowledge of the Ascendancy's historic role as civilising colonisers both within Ireland and abroad. The nature of the British occupation of the Australian continent provided the Anglo-Irishwith little by way of opportunity for military conquest. Distance and a harsh environment rather than armed resistance from a scattered native population proved the main obstacles to the expansion of European settlement. However as influential members of the ruling elite in what was generally a brutal society where Aborigines and convicts were often subject to cruel abuse, Ascendancy colonists had ample scope to play their part as civilising colonisers.

Though usually from relatively humble backgrounds themselves, the newly established Protestant gentry possessed the typical colonist's contempt for the native Irish. Regarding themselves superior on account of their proven military prowess, religious orthodoxy, English blood and more advanced culture, few Protestants mixed freely with the Celtic Catholic population. With most Catholic gentry having either fled abroad or been exiled to Ireland's barren west, the victorious Protestants presided over a demoralised and largely leaderless native population. This was still basically the situation a century and a half later when the first Ascendancy Irish began arriving in Australia. In Ireland and abroad, these Anglo – or establishment Irish possessed the deeply ingrained attitudes of an established ruling class and were thus well suited, at least in this respect, for membership of pre-goldrush Australia's penal-pastoral hierarchy.

The first generations of Cromwellian settlers in Ireland though far from secure assumed the arrogant and self-confident stance of a dominant landed caste. In spite of Cromwell's crushing victories and the fact that the Catholics had largely been deprived of their capacity for effective armed resistance, the newly established Protestant gentry faced the prospect of losing their estates. Following the restoration of Charles II in 1660, former Catholic proprietors confidently applied to the English court to have their estates returned. As a concession to his Catholic supporters Charles required certainProtestants to give up a portion of their estates to former Catholic proprietors who had been judged innocent of involvement in the initial insurrection of 1641. Though Charles eventually confirmed the great majority of Protestant landowners in the possession of their estates, the possibility remained of a future English monarch making further concessions to Catholic claims. Hated and feared by the Irish they had dispossessed they also faced losing their lands and lives in the event of a future uprising. Isolated on their estates, resident Protestant landlords, their families and employees remained vulnerable to attacks upon their persons and property.

Not until after the comprehensive Williamite victory over the resurgent Catholic forces at the Boyne in 1690 were Ireland's Protestant gentry really free from the threat of dispossession by military or legal means. The Ascendancy's dominance now acquired legal sanction through the passing of penal laws designed to prevent the possibility of a future Catholic uprising. Rather than seeking to retain their landed property by conforming, many influential Catholics responded by seeking service with sympathetic rulers abroad. The completeness of their victory and the fact that the Catholic peasantry were deprived of their natural leadership enabled the Protestants to consolidate their position of dominance over a demoralised Catholic population. Yet even then the Protestants, though well armed and organised into local militia, relied heavily on continued British military support. Unwilling or unable to assimilate with the native Irish, these Protestants remained colonists psychologically, permanently attached to English culture and institutions. Though staunchly imperialist and monarchist, the Anglo-Irish remained ambivalent in terms of their national allegiances, not feeling fully Irish yet often disliking and being highly suspicious of the English.

Insecurity resulting from their position as an imposed ruling caste led to the adoption of a garrison mentality amongst the Protestant gentry: an attitude which persisted long after the reasons for it had ceased to be important. More than anything else, it was the fierce desire to retain their landed property which united these Protestants into a particularly close-knit and resilient community. The Anglo-Irish then came to Australia not only with the usual gentry emigrants' desire for land, but with particular sensitivity to any move which threatened their continued possession of it. Though eventually secure in the possession of their estates, Ireland's Protestant gentry recognised that few amongst the Catholic majority recognised the legitimacy of their position. Memories of the violent fashion in which they had been dispossessed, continued religious persecution and exploitation as cheap labour maintained the Catholics' deep sense of grievance and ensured that the Protestants remained isolated and alienated. Though masked by outward displays of pride and arrogance, suspicion and guilty fear of the oppressed Catholic population remained features of the Anglo-Irish tradition. Apart from its sharp division on religious lines, the most striking feature of Irish society at the beginning of the eighteenth century was just how successful the Protestants had been in the struggle for land and power. As well as dividing most of Ireland's better farming land between themselves, the Protestants monopolised public offices, higher education and the professions. In the Irish countryside, Protestant landlords, often magistrates as well as the major local employers, were virtually a law unto themselves. During the eighteenth century rapid population increase and extensive enclosure of agricultural land for pastoralism meant that while more labour was available in Ireland, significantly less was required. In much of Ireland an increasingly desperate peasantry had to pay exorbitant rents and provide low-cost labour for a few acres on which to grow potatoes, or face the prospect of beggary and starvation. The power of landlords over the Irish peasantry was total. According to one contemporary observer, the Ascendancy wit, lawyer and politician, Jonah Barrington, 'no English nobleman could have ruled so absolutely over his tenantry as did any Irish gentleman'.[4] The liberal-minded

---

4. Jonah Barrington, 'Personal Sketches' in *The Ireland of Sir Jonah Barrington:* Selection from his 'Personal Sketches', ed. H. B. Staples, Peter Owen, London, 1968, p.6.

Arthur Young, appalled by the power of Irish landlords, claimed that 'a landlord in Ireland can scarcely invent an order which a servant, cottar or labourer dares to refuse to execute. Nothing satisfies him but unlimited submission'.[5]

In pre-goldrush Australia, Ascendancy settlers on their remote holdings also found themselves subject to little direct government control. Yet they were for the most part not as free as Protestant landlords in Ireland to treat 'inferiors' (Aborigines, assigned convicts and free farm servants) as they wished. For a start the law in Australian colonies,being centrally administered, was more impartial in its applications than in Anglo-Ireland. Those who assumed immunity from the law on account of their status as Irish gentlemen and openly flouted government regulations were likely to find themselves deprived of official favour or facing prosecution. One such case involved William Bryan, formerly of Spring Valley, County Meath who during the 1820s managed to establish himself as a large landowner in north-eastern Tasmania. Overly confident of his standing as an 'Irish gentlemen' and magistrate, Bryan attempted to establish his own pastoral tenantry by entering into an illegal agreement with two of his assigned convict servants. As a consequence of this action and his subsequent intemperate behaviour, Bryan was singled out by senior officials including Governor Arthur, and in April 1834 was forced to flee to England to avoid arrest.[6] More importantly, Ascendancy settlers who sought to oppress their farm servants in the worst traditions of Irish landlordism faced possible retaliation, or at the very least the potentially ruinous desertion of workers. This is precisely what happened in the case of George Winter whose failure as a pioneering squatter was largely due to the fact that 'no man would stay with him for more than a week owing to the way he treated them'.[7] For while chronic unemployment and widespread poverty produced a large and servile workforce in Ireland, labour remained scarce and independently-minded in the colonies.

5.Arthur Young, *A Tour of Ireland in the Years 1776, 1777 and 1778*, Vol. 1., London, p.2.
6. For a detailed account of the Bryan case see G. J. Forth, Chapter 3 'The Brothers Bryan: Irish Origins and colonial careers' in *Winters on the Wannon*, Australia Felix Series, Deakin University Press, Warrnambool, 1991.
7. Thomas Murphy to Samuel Pratt Winter, 31 October 1848 in *Winter Cooke Papers*, La Trobe Library.

Throughout the eighteenth century Ireland's southern Protestants justified their continued domination of the Catholic native Irish by proclaiming the superiority of their Anglo-Saxon culture, the orthodoxy of their Anglican faith and the innate inferiority and unreliability of the native Irish. Far from involving any denial of Irishness, the Ascendancy saw themselves as the true Irish. Yet in spite of the often arrogant and self-assertive manner in which such claims were made, the Anglo-Irish were never free of the guilty fear that those they had so brutally oppressed would eventually rise andrevenge themselves for past humiliations. Wellington's biographer Phillip Guedalla suggests that because 'Anglo-Irish magnates knew themselves observed by long rows of Irish eyes . . . the silent watchers made and kept them prouder than ever'.[8] This deep-seated sense of insecurity influenced the manner in which the first generations of Protestant landlords utilised their Irish estates. Owing to the uncertain bases on which members of this class initially held their grants, many looked to their Irish estates for short term profits rather than as longer term investments. Seeking quick returns, many Irish landlords granted tenants perpetual leases following the payment of a cash sum. As well as gaining a quick return from an as yet uncertain investment, Irish landlords were influenced by the need to have a tenant in possession to consolidate their claim to ownership. During the eighteenth century, perpetual tenants, who were in fact landlords themselves, took advantage of increased land values to raise rents paid by sub-tenants on short-term fixed or determined leases. Deeply etched into the Ascendancy's psyche was the view that land was an asset to be exploited, rather than developed or improved, to provide them with the means of a genteel, leisured existence. Their short-term aspirations as emigrants plus the speculative nature and general insecurity of landholding in pre-goldrush Australia reinforced this view amongst Ascendancy colonists. Like their Cromwellian forebears in Ireland, Australia's Ascendancy settlers initially viewed their colonial holdings and stock as short- term investments: speculations with the potential to provide a quick and substantial return on capital invested. For most, landholding in Australia represented the most promising

8. Phillip Guedalla, *The Duke,* Hodder and Stoughton, London, 1921, p.3.

option available that would enable them to achieve financial independence and eventually resume their place in Ascendancy society.

If landlordism was the basis of Anglo-Irish landed society, absenteeism was one of its more distinctive features. The difficulties and dangers of living and travelling in Ireland and the fact that many landlords owned more than one estate contributed to the extent of absenteeism. While most English gentry permanently resided on, or at least regularly visited their country estates, many major Irish landlords never or only rarely visited theirs. Though probably not as widespread or damaging as had often been claimed, absenteeism contributed to the depressed living standards of the peasantry and seriously undermined the reputation of Ireland's Protestant gentry. Large scale absenteeism in Ireland resulted in the flow of much-needed capital from the Irish countryside often to support the absentee's extravagant lifestyle in London, Bath or Dublin. Yet there is no conclusive evidence that the absentee's tenants were, generally speaking, worse off. Some were excellent landlords, with others only absentees because economic circumstances forced them to close up their large country houses and find cheaper accommodation elsewhere. Though certain notable absentees spent substantial amounts improving their estates, the practice overall deprived Ireland's backward agriculture of desperately needed capital. The absentee mentality also encouraged many of Ireland's most able people to live and work abroad. Allegations concerning the greed and indifference of Ireland's absentees, (many were of course English) has done much to damage the Ascendancy's reputation. Ireland's Protestant gentry have consistently been portrayed as a class of irresponsible landlords who ruthlessly exploited Ireland's fertile lands and people for their own selfish ends.

Absenteeism also encouraged the practice, common amongst Irish landlords, of successively subletting and subdividing their estates. Generally the greater part of an estate was let to substantial tenant farmers or agents (middlemen) on long term leases at moderate, fixed rents. Middlemen subdivided their leased land into small agricultural holdings sublet for the highest possible rents. This practice obviously reduced an individual landlord's sense of responsibility for the proper management of an estate and the welfare of people who lived and worked on it. Lack of alternative employment and a chronic shortage of agricultural land meant that many Irish peasants were forced to pay exorbitantly high rents for small potato plots. The ruthless practices of 'rackrenting' middlemen has done much to damage the general reputation of the Irish gentry. That most astute observer of rural Ireland in the late eighteenth century, Arthur Young, angrily denounced 'middlemen' as ' . . . the most oppressive species of tyrant who not satisfied with the screwing up of rent to the uppermost farthing . . . are rapacious and relentless in the collection of it'.[9] Young is highly critical of these 'squireens' for their seedy, pretentious lifestyle, referring to them as 'the masters of a pack of wretched hounds with whom they wasted both time and money'.[10]

Colonial Australia offered few opportunities for large landholders to establish themselves as landlords. Consistent labour shortages, relatively high wages and the availability of cheap farmland made it difficult for landowners to attract and retain agricultural tenants. Ascendancy colonists seeking to replicate the Irish land rental system in Australia such as William Bryan in Northern Tasmania and William Rutledge at Port Fairy were unlikely to succeed, at least in the longer term. Perhaps the most successful of Australia's Anglo-Irish landlords was William Rutledge, formerly of Bawnboy, County Cavan who between 1843-1865 had many tenants on his 'Farnham Park' estate near Koroit in Western Victoria.[11] Yet for those who did become large landholders, conditions of pastoral pioneering in the colonies certainly encouraged absenteeism. For as in Ireland a century before, Ascendancy settlers on their remote farms and pastoral runs in early colonial Australia, frequently experienced loneliness and harsh living conditions, difficulties in travel and the threat of native or outlaw attack. Not surprisingly, those who could arrange it, like Samuel Pratt Winter at Murndal in Victoria's Western District, employed resident managers while remaining for the most part in more civilised locations. Samuel Pratt Winter for example, only visited his Spring Valley run for about a month each year during the 1840's, preferring to live mainly on his small Cluan estate in northern Tasmania.

9. Arthur Young, op. cit., p.303.
10. Ibid, p.26.
11. M. Rutledge, 'William Rutledge - pioneer', *Victorian Historical Magazine*, no.36, 1965.

Irish laws and customs relating to the rental of farming land also contributed to the backward state of Irish agriculture and the low living standard of the Irish peasantry. Unlike England, where landlords were responsible for basic improvements, Irish tenants, Ulster excepted, received their lands bare, and most were not compensated for improvements completed during their lease. Those who undertook substantial improvements faced the prospect of paying increased rent as a result. For when a fixed term lease 'fell in', the tenant in possession had no special claim and the lease was auctioned to the highest bidder. An obvious disincentive for much needed improvements, this practice resulted in some tenants deliberately wasting their plots towards the end of a lease to make it less attractive for competitors. Lacking education, capital and the incentive to improve their holdings, Ireland's peasant farmers remained poor and ignorant. In most accounts it is Protestant landlords rather than the Irish land rental system which have been singled out as the principal cause of the peasantry's distress.

The second half of the eighteenth century, saw a marked deterioration in the situation for the poorer classes of Irish peasantry. Widespread degradation of land due to poor farming practices and the greater profitability of pastoralism resulted, in some counties, in the wholesale eviction of smallholders as leases expired. Denied legal redress and with little prospect of alternative employment, desperate Irish peasantry increasingly turned to systematic agrarian terrorism as their sole defence against evicting or otherwise oppressive landlords. In Munster and parts of Leinster, resident landlords, their families and employees and even non-conforming tenants became subject to attack. The terrorist activities of Catholic guerilla bands such as the notorious Whiteboys and Steelboys and the savage retaliation these attacks provoked, formed part of Ireland's still unresolved tradition of mutilation and murder.

Only a small proportion of Australia's Anglo-Irish would have themselves been the victims of agrarian terrorism in Ireland or have actively participated in punitive expeditions against suspected Catholic terrorists. However, many who had grown up on country estates had experienced a turbulent, violent atmosphere with 'the bullet, the sabre and bayonet lash and halter, being met by the pike, the scythe, the blunderbuss, the hatchet and the fire-brand'.[12] Few questioned the

12. Jonah Barrington, op. cit., p.303.

necessity of rigorously suppressing outrage whenever it occurred. During the first decades of white settlement in Australia, settlers and officials in remote regions also faced the prospect of native or out-law attack. With their Old World background, Anglo-Irish colonists such as William and Samuel Bryan in Tasmania, were as one might expect prominent in local initiatives to repel such attacks and punish those responsible. However should such measures involve illegal actions which became public knowledge, Anglo-Irish colonists were more likely to face prosecution than Protestant gentry in Ireland undertaking similar reprisals. For example when George Winter and several of his men fired on and killed five Aborigines and then failed to report the incident, Superintendent La Trobe did everything he could to have Winter arrested and charged with murder.[13]

Though he might with relative impunity apply his whip to the backs of peasants blocking his path or burn the wretched cabins of suspected Catholic rebels, the Ascendancy landlord usually enjoyed only limited rights over 'his' landed property. As well as being bound by the detailed provisions of existing mortgages and leasehold agreements, most had to abide by the complex feudal style arrangements governing property rights within Ascendancy families. Having inherited rather than acquired estates, Irish landowners were normally required to make specific provisions for both living and future family members. The standard, traditional provisions of settlement and wills were designed to keep landed property intact within families. About half of the Irish estate owners were in fact mere life tenants with limited powers over what was in reality family property. Having acquired land themselves, Anglo-Irish landowners and landholders in Australia were free of many of the legal and customary restraints which traditionally governed land ownership and utilisation in Ireland.

In Ireland, disputes over property matters between and within Ascendancy families were sufficiently common to be a feature of the Anglo-Irish tradition. Legal complications and the general confusion which accompanied the Cromwellian resettlement of Ireland often led to

---

13. Superintendent Charles La Trobe to Colonial Secretary, 3 April 1840, Further correspondence relating to the incident is contained in Governor Gipps dispatches 1841-42, Mitchell Library, Sydney.

protracted and often quite senseless property litigation. The Bowens of Bowen's Court, County Cork were one Ascendancy family whose fortunes suffered due to one family member's penchant for property litigation for quite futile ends.[14] Fortunately, not all such disputes involved recourse to the courts. Where wiser counsel prevailed, quarrels could sometimes be more economically and amicably settled by referring disagreements to a trusted relative or mutual friend for arbitration.

Most Anglo-Irish who arrived in Australia would have possessed some detailed knowledge of Old World property laws and customs and probably an inclination towards litigation. In colonial Australia, the rapid and largely unsupervised nature of the pastoral expansion resulted in a high incidence of property disputes between landholders and stock-owners. As settlers or officials in remote areas, the Anglo-Irish were involved in often bitter and protracted disputes over such matters as the proper location of boundaries, the ownership of unbranded stock and the employment of 'runaways' (absconding workers). Though in general, the principles of British law applied, knowledge of Old World property laws and procedures was often of little use in such situations. Without appropriate local laws and customs to guide them, most settlers also lacked reasonable access to senior officials, courts or even trusted mutual friends to whom they might refer disputes. To succeed in the competitive and largely unregulated world of pastoral pioneering, these Ascendancy colonists had basically to rely on their own resources.

Proud, close-knit and litigious, the situation of the Protestant gentry in Ireland also encouraged an indolent and indulgent lifestyle. Lacking education and with little opportunity to exercise civic responsibility, the Irish gentry acquired a reputation for dissipation and extravagance. John Loveday in 1732 observed that 'The Irish gentry are an expensive people continually feasting one another'.[15] Lord Chesterfield, Viceroy of Ireland claimed that 'nine gentlemen in ten in Ireland are impoverished by the vast quantities of claret which from mistaken notions of hospitality they think it is necessary should be drunk in their houses'.[16]

14. Elizabeth Bowen, *Bowen's Court and the Seven Winters: Memories of a Dubin Childhood,* Virago, London, 1984 (first published 1942) p.218.
15. Constantia Maxwell, *Country and Town in Ireland Under the Georges,* Tempest, Dundalk, 1949.p.27.
16. Ibid, p.21.

Arthur Young, later in the century, criticised the 'numbers of brothers, cousins and younger sons found swarming in gentlemen's houses with nothing better to do than to chase after hares and horses'. Young roundly condemned these ' . . . fellows with round hats edged in gold who hunt in the day, get drunk in the evening and fight the next morning'.[17]

This leisured gentry lifestyle was possible for a high proportion of the Ascendancy because of relatively lower costs in Ireland. With land cheap and servants plentiful, even the pettiest squireen could supply his own basic provisions, including illegally distilled whiskey. For many, entertainment consisted entirely of feasting and field-sports. A high proportion of Australia's Ascendancy would have experienced firsthand, even if only as guests or dependent relatives, the Irish gentry's privileged lifestyle. In this respect the Old World background of Ascendancy settlers contrasted sharply with that of the Scots' experience of frugality, piety and hard work.

In pre-goldrush Australia, though wages were higher and servants much harder to find, circumstances were similar to those which encouraged the Irish gentry to lead such wasteful and dissolute lives. In both societies alcohol provided a ready palliative to isolation and boredom. Like Anglo-Ireland, oppression and brutality were common-place in penal-pastoral Australia. However while a large and servile peasant population supported an essentially parasitic gentry in Ireland, shrewdness and consistent endeavour were usually required in Australia for material success. Though a gentry background provided important advantages, considerable adjustment was required on the part of most Anglo-Irish if they were to succeed as colonists in Australia.

Whether grand magnate or petty squireen, the Ascendancy's lifestyle depended on the continued possession of landed estates. Though many landlords neglected or mismanaged their estates, the importance of land-ownership in Ireland can hardly be over-stated. Even more than for the rest of Britain, the continued possession of landed estates was virtually a requirement for gentry status in Ireland. Where this was not possible, the Anglo-Irish responded enthusiastically to opportunities offering in the New World to acquire cheap farming land. Career and other investment opportunities were important, but the prospect of acquiring pastoral land

17. Arthur Young, op. cit., p. 71.

was central to the motivation of those Ascendancy who chose pre-goldrush Australia as their New World destination.

The possession of a landed estate as well as providing status and a rising income, conferred important benefits on Ascendancy families. Life on a well situated country estate provided family members, their relatives and friends with ample opportunities for hunting, fishing and shooting. Experience with horses and guns, of outdoor life generally, proved useful training for the sons of Irish gentry intent on a military career. Such experience and a lack of employment opportunities in Ireland (rather than the Ascendancy's alleged inbred fighting qualities) resulted in a high proportion of Anglo-Irish officers in British regiments. Pre-emigration experience of country life may have encouraged Ascendancy emigrants to take up pastoral pioneering in Australia. Yet on balance these apparent advantages were more than offset by Ascendancy settlers' softgentry origins. As members of a rural leisured class, young Irish gentlemen may well have developed rare skill in riding over fences at breakneck speed in pursuit of a fleeing stag or in winging woodcocks in rapid succession. However should his hunter lose a shoe or his gun jam, most such young gentlemen had little idea and less inclination to effect even minor repairs. Similarly, while living on a country estate provided ample opportunities for observing Old World farming practices, few of the young Irish gentlemen who arrived in Australia brought with them any detailed knowledge or practical experience of the work involved. In spite of the obvious advantages of an Ascendancy back-ground, which usually included some access to family capital, influential connections and experience of country life, the average young Ascendancy gentleman was hardly a prime candidate for success as a settler in pre-goldrush Australia.

Another highly prized aspect of estate ownership in Ireland was the extent to which it conferred a sense of intellectual and social inde-pendence on individual landlords. With a general lack of customary and legal restraint, estate ownership in Ireland encouraged independence of thought and action which in the case of certain Irish gentry took the form of outspoken and eccentric behaviour. Isolated and on their country estates with relative freedom to speak and act as they pleased, the Irish gentry were less selective in their choice of acquaintances than their more class-conscious English counterparts. With little by way of constructive activity to occupy their time, some Irish gentlemen indulged in wayward or even violent behaviour. Though tolerated in eighteenth century Ireland, such behaviour, as certain Anglo-Irish colonists were soon to discover, was far less acceptable in early nineteenth century Australia.

Mindful of the extent to which their future economic security and gentry status depended upon the continued possession of landed estates, Ascendancy families sought at least to preserve and where possible extend their holdings. To this end the rule of primogeniture strictly applied. The negotiation of satisfactory marriage alliances with other Ascendancy families involving mutually acceptable financial and property arrangements was also vitally important. As heir to at least the family's principal estate, the eldest son or nominated male relative was expected to acquire additional property through marriage. Though designated owner of certain estates, the terms of inheritance usually limited the heir's powers over 'his' property. Under the provisions of his parents' marriage settlement and wills, the favoured eldest son was usually required to adhere to specified financial arrangements for other legitimate family members and his own future issue. Anglo-Irish colonists who acquired rather than inherited landed property in Australia were obviously not bound by such family and dynastic considerations. Many had come to Australia in the first place because of their position as younger, potentially property-less sons. Through emigration they had effectively removed themselves from their extended family circle and direct moral responsibility for other, less well-off family members. Most were therefore free to dispose of their colonial property as they thought fit. Even so, as members, albeit long absent ones, of extended Ascendancy families, many still felt obliged somehow to assist less fortunate relatives and friends at home. For certain Anglo-Irish in Australia this meant encouraging and financially assisting friends and relatives in Ireland to take full advantage of better employment and investment opportunities in the colonies.

Eligible young Ascendancy besides marrying within their own propertied, Protestant class, were under some pressure to marry close relatives and neighbours. The Irish gentry's somewhat belated concern over racial purity, logistics and even property considerations all con-tributed to this practice. According to Curtis ' . . . it was because the Anglo-Irish suspected a degree of ethnic mixture in their veins, yet prided themselves on purity of race that they paid themselves the highest possible compliment by marrying cousins'.[18] Commenting on the extent of intermarriage between neighbouring usually interrelated families, Edith Somerville explains that "each estate was a kingdom and with the impossibility of locomotion, each neighbouring potentate acquired a relative importance quite out of proportion to his merits; for to love your neighbour – or, at all events to marry him was almost inevitable when marriages were made by a map".[19]

Religious and ethnic considerations were important, while difficulties involved in wider travel certainly encouraged intermarriage between neighbouring families. Both parties would also have been aware of the advantages of linking adjacent estates to form larger, more economic units. For whatever reasons, this tendency of the Irish gentry to marry neighbours and relatives meant that "Anglo Ireland was not just a class of landowners strewn over the countryside . . . It was a congeries of familiar families, tied together by marriage, by mortgages, history, creed and a myriad of mutual interests".[20]

Individual Anglo-Irish came to Australia as members of close-knit, extended families to which most intended returning as soon as financial circumstances permitted. Such powerful kinship ties meant that once established, many Anglo-Irish in the colonies sought to persuade friends and relatives at home to join them. Multiple chain migration of related Anglo-Irish was to result in the formation of several Ascendancy enclaves in Australia, the most notable being the 'Irish cousinage' of Port Phillip in the 1840s.

Life for most Irish gentry by the late eighteenth century had become more comfortable and secure following a period of persisting peace and relative prosperity. In many cases their rambling fortress-style houses had been replaced by elegant Georgian or Italianate mansions, sited with prospect rather than defensive capability in mind. As well as serving as family residences, these impressive 'Big Houses' and the surrounding demesne represented an outward expression of the Protestant gentry's sense of power and permanence. Usually accommodating numerous staff,

18. L. P. Curtis Jnr., op. cit., p. 40.
19. Edith Somerville and Ross, Martin, *Irish Memories*, Longmans, Green, London, 1918, p. 71.
20. L. J. Curtis Jnr. op. cit., p. 40.

guests and dependent relatives, the Anglo-Irish 'Big House', as T. R. Henn points out, served as 'a centre of hospitality, of country life and society, apt to breed a passionate attachment'.[21] In rural Ireland the local Big House also served as an administrative and legal centre where rents were paid, quarrels reconciled and old debts arbitrated. For Henn, the construction and maintenance of such impractical and often ruinously large expensive houses represented the Ascendancy's 'search for beauty and stability in the midst of poverty and defeat'.[22] As with the possession of landed estates, the ownership of such country houses was necessary to establish a family's status within the ruling Protestant hierarchy. For an impoverished peasantry in their smoke-filled, ramshackle cabins the Big House became a reference point and source of envy. Most of Australia's Anglo-Irish colonists aspired to become eventually master or mistress of their own Big House, preferably in Ireland, but alternatively in Australia. Circumstances in pre-goldrush Australia were hardly con-ducive to the replication of this distinctive feature of Anglo-Irish society. Their own initial short term aspirations as colonists, the uncertain profitability of pastoralism, and the general lack of surplus labour or a potential tenantry discouraged attempts to recreate the physical and social environment of the Irish Big House.

With the Big House, the other focal point for an often scattered Southern Protestant community was their local Church of Ireland. How-ever, for many, active membership of the Church of Ireland by the end of the eighteenth century had become more of an expression of Protestant solidarity than genuine religious commitment. During the eighteenth century Ireland's Southern Protestants looked less to their Anglican orthodoxy to justify their continued domination of the Catholic majority. Having failed to convert the Catholic masses through systematic coercion, there followed a marked softening of attitudes amongst the Anglo-Irish. Unlike Ulster's hardline Presbyterians, the Ascendancy's collective memory of massacre and pillage faded with the passing of the generation that experienced it. Many now recognised the absurdity and in-justice of continuing to persecute countrymen whose sole crime consisted of maintaining a different doctrinal interpretation of Christian theology.

---

21. T. R. Henn, *The Lonely Tower*, second edition, London, 1956, p. 3.
22. Ibid., p. 5.

It was significant that Catholic Emancipation was supported by a majority of Anglo-Irish members years before it was eventually passed in the British Parliament.

Increased toleration was also reflected in growing apathy and religious indifference amongst the Ascendancy. Elizabeth Bowen commenting on the Ascendancy's need to '. . . make a social figure of God' suggests that because of their circumstances 'nothing. . . gave the soul any chance to stand at its full height'.[23] As far as Ireland's Protestant gentry and religion were concerned Bowen argues 'that to enjoy prosperity, one had to exclude feeling, or keep it within prescribed bounds'.[24] By the end of the nineteenth century apathy and emigration had resulted in a moribund Church of Ireland attended by a dwindling and ageing congregation of drably respectable, often nominal Protestants.

This gradual drift towards spiritual impotence was interrupted by the evangelical revival which spread from England to Ireland following the Act of Union. By zealously propagating the study of the scriptures, ardent evangelicals sought to revitalise their fellow Protestants as well as convert Catholics. Though not particularly successful in either area, the movement provided Anglican laity with new opportunities to become actively involved with the work of their Church. The Church of Ireland remained the natural channel for airing the views of the Anglo-Irish community as a whole. McConville suggests that due to evangelical influence, 'rakes, bucks and eccentrics . . . faded as a subspecies' during the first half of the nineteenth century when 'the Anglo-Irish knuckled under to the conformist respectability that flowed from Victorian England'.[25] Though many clergy remained ineffectual and indifferent, the Church of Ireland produced its share of effective evangelical reformers.

The Anglo-Irish who arrived in Australia however, were more likely to be nominalAnglicans or freethinkers than inspired evangelicals. In colonial Australia as in Ascendancy Ireland the Anglo-Irish benefited from their association with a privileged Anglican Church. In both societies Catholics, though eventually no longer subject to penal

---

23. E. Bowen, op. cit., p. 248.
24. Ibid, p. 248.
25. Michael McConville, *From Ascendancy to Oblivion: The Story of the Anglo-Irish*, Quartet, London, 1986, p. 154.

sanctions, were distrusted and openly discriminated against by the dominant Protestants. Bitter sectarian feeling remained a feature of Australian colonial society yet few prominent Ascendancy colonists became active in the anti-Catholic cause. In Ireland theAscendancy's guilty fear of the long suppressed Catholic majority had produced an insular and aggressive Protestantism. In Australia, the Anglo-Irish could become part of the religious, cultural mainstream. In any case, by the time the Anglo-Irish began arriving in Australia strident anti-Catholicism was no longer such a distinctive feature of their tradition.

Though a majority generally supported the gradual repeal of anti-Catholic penal laws, few Ascendancy seriously questioned the morality of their continued domination of Ireland. Most Ascendancy intuitively recognised that any substantial move towards wider political representation or the more equitable distribution of land threatened the very bases of their society. For this reason Nora Robertson believes that 'the Anglo-Irish could not recognise that deep down, the normal native Irishman was obsessed by his longing for national freedom and the ownership of land'.[26] Because of their situation in Ireland, many Ascendancy who in England would have been Whigs or even liberals, remained staunchly and inflexibly Tory.

In Australia, individual Anglo-Irish were obviously less threatened by moves towards more democratic forms of government or a more equitable distribution of farming land. However, it was not simply the changed circumstances of their colonial situation that encouraged prominent Ascendancy emigrants in Australia to support progressive causes. Though mostly unwilling to make significant concessions to the Catholic majority in Ireland, within their own ranks the Anglo-Irish practised a kind of aristocratic egalitarianism. In an inherently unstable Anglo-Irish society, land ownership and achievement rather than lineage determined status. To ensure their survival, the ruling Protestant minority saw the need to foster talent among their own caste. Ambitious young Protestants from humble backgrounds could gain admission to Trinity where sizar-ships were available to assist the most able. With students

26. Nora Robertson, *Crowned Harp. Memories of the Last Years of the Crown in Ireland,* Allen, Figis, Dublin, 1960, p. 99.

coming from a wider range of backgrounds, Trinity was something of a liberal institution compared with the Tory backwaters of Oxford and Cambridge. Though it remained largely Protestant, Trinity in 1793 became the first British University to readmit Catholics. Trinity's liberal atmosphere was reflected not so much in the formal courses of study but in the nature of the College's student societies.

Within Ireland's resident gentry class, isolation, interdependence and the need for company discouraged class distinction. Necessity also encouraged the adoption of democratic practices in the Ascendancy's civilian militia, the Yeomanry. Formed in the late eighteenth century as a response to a threatened French invasion, the Yeomanry elected their own officers, a practice then unthinkable for the rest of Britain. Within both the civilian and military sphere, the possibility of such advancement for Protestants of humble origin was characteristically Anglo-Irish.

The idea of Ireland's Protestant gentry being somehow liberal minded or democratically inclined hardly tallies with the widely held view of this class. In the traditional picture of Anglo-Ireland, 'the most familiar figure' according to J. C. Beckett, ' . . . is that of the greedy tyranical landlord squeezing the last penny out of a starving tenantry and spending the proceeds in the fashionable world of London or Bath or in riotous living at home'.[27] At the wider level, the more extreme Irish nationalists have generally dismissed the Ascendancy as West Britons, agents of a foreign power and apostles of a foreign culture. Historians have for the most part supported the nationalists' view that the Anglo-Irish were somehow responsible for much of pre-republican Ireland's often violent and miserable past. For example, in commenting on the Cromwellian resettlement of Ireland, Paul Dubois asserts that 'never has a more savage design been put into execution . . . than the project of destroying one nation and putting another in its place'.[28] In 1945, T. J. Kiernan, a former Irish ambassador to Australia, went so far as to liken Anglo-Irish landlords to the Nazis. Referring to the disastrous consequences of the Great Famine, Kiernan held the Ascendancy responsible for the legalised extermination of one million people.[29]

---

27. J. C. Beckett, *The Anglo-Irish Tradition*, 1600-1921, Faber, London, 1976, p. 73.
28. Paul Dubois, *Contemporary Ireland*, Dublin, 1908, p. 46.
29. T. J. Kiernan, *The Irish Exiles in Australia*, Burns & Oats, Melbourne, 1954, p. 46.

Recent scholarship provides a more balanced, less emotive view of the historical role of the Ascendancy. In *The Anglo-Irish Tradition* J. C. Beckett suggests that where the Anglo-Irish are concerned, 'historians have been inclined to accept at face value allegations which have long been accepted as self evident truths'.[30] Revisionist histories of the Anglo-Irish refer to misuse of contemporary sources to provide an unjust and basically inaccurate view of the Protestant Ascendancy. Some of the most damning criticism of Ireland's Protestant gentry has taken the form of quotations by leading Ascendancy writers. For example, frequent use has been made of Swift's assertion that in Ireland 'every squire, almost to a man, is an oppressor of his tenants, a jobber of all public works, very proud and generally illiterate'.[31] What the Ascendancy's critics rarely mention is that Swift was writing in a highly satiric fashion. Similar use has been made of carefully selected passages from Jonah Barrington's *Personal Sketches*. Essentially a wit and satirist, Barrington, a lynx-eyed observer of eighteenth century Ireland, offers a basically comic view of his fellow Ascendancy. Yet his desultory mélange of recollections has obviously misled many into supposing that these were the common characteristics of his class. Maria Edgeworth's fictional account of a particularly unattractive Ascendancy family, the appropriately named Rackrents, has provided even richer fare for those who would condemn without qualification Ireland's Protestant gentry. In spite of the writer's unambiguous assurance when Castle Rackrent was first published in 1800 that 'the race of Rackrents has long been extinct in Ireland'[32] it has widely been assumed that the fighting Sir Kit, the slovenly Sir Condy and the drunken Sir Patrick were contemporary, representative figures. In all, eighteenth century Ascendancy writers with their satire and colourful characters have helped perpetuate the misleading impression of a society 'compounded of whiskey, rot, decay, guttering candles, damp, horses and dust: or in more abstract terms of improvidence, stupidity, cupidity, pride, subservience, animosity, sentimentality, brutality and perversity'.[33]

30. J. C. Beckett, op. cit., p. 73.
31. Cited in J. C. Beckett, op. cit., p. 73.
32. Maria Edgeworth, *Castle Rackrent,* first published 1810, G. Watson, ed., London, 1964, p. xxi.
33. J. Newcomber, Maria Edgeworth. The Novelist, Texas, 1967, p. 155.

To entertain and possibly appeal to the anti-Irish prejudices of their English readers, leading Ascendancy writers have frequently emphasised the humourous and colourfully distinctive aspects of the Irish gentry's lifestyle. In Edgeworth's case, it should in fairness be pointed out that she was a sincere reformer who sought to shame less responsible members of her own class into following the example of her own worthy father. The model of an improving landlord and sincere country gentleman, Richard Lovell Edgeworth was reputed to have 'honestly and unostentatiously used his utmost endeavours to obliterate all that could lead to perpetual illwill in the country'.[34]

This tendency to portray the Ascendancy as a basically irresponsible and rather eccentric class is present in several recently published works on the Anglo-Irish. Barrington's jaundiced view of his fellow Ascendancy re-emerges in coarser form in J. P. Donleavy's bawdy novel, *The Destinies of Darcy Dancer, Gentleman*, which describes the amorous escapades of an impetuous young Ascendancy rake. While having an obvious and valued place in comic literature, such exaggerated accounts of Ascendancy life are less acceptable in otherwise scholarly histories of the Anglo-Irish. In seeking to entertain as well as inform, Michael McConville's *From Ascendancy to Oblivion* and Mark Bence Jones's, *Twilight of the Ascendancy* reinforce misleading stereotypes.[35] Concentrating mainly on the eighteenth century, McConville seeks to offer a 'welcome counter to the polemicists who try to reduce Ireland's inherited complexities to us and them, good and bad'.[36] Viewing the Anglo-Irish as 'a rich source of comedy' McConville describes the eccentric, often violent behaviour of such certifiable misfits as the infamous 'Fighting' Fitzgerald, 'Fireball' McNamara, and 'Hairtrigger Dick' Martin. As well as murdering several of his peers, Fitzgerald once chained his elderly father to a live pet bear and later imprisoned him, (the father), in a cave on the family estate. Explaining Anglo-Ireland's seemingly endless supply of eccentrics, McConville refers to the effects

34. Maria Edgeworth, op. cit., p. ii.
35. Michael McConville,op. cit., and Mark Bence-Jones, *Twilight of the Ascendancy*, Constable, London, 1987.
36. Covernote M. McConville, Ibid.

of persisting peace and a bored gentry's need to find outlets for energies previously expended on warfare. Bence-Jones's description of the decline and eventual demise of the once powerful Ascendancy is liberally spiced with gossipy anecdotes describing the often quite bizarre antics of a decaying and impoverished gentry. Again the overall impression is misleading. Insufficient attention is paid to less colourful but more representative landlords such as the Martins of Ross and Pakenhams of Pakenham Hall.

Yet in seeking a more balanced view of the Irish gentry, too great a reliance should not be placed on the memoirs and family histories produced by some of the more literate members of the Ascendancy. Such basically sympathetic accounts of this class include the genteel, witty reminiscences of Somerville and Ross[37] the novelist Elizabeth Bowen's thoughtful history of her own Cork family, and Nora Robertson's often astute account of Anglo-Irish society this century. Usually humorous and sharply observant, such accounts are frequently tinged with a deeply felt sense of regret for the passing of the world they describe. Written when the Ascendancy's once-impregnable world was beginning to crumble or had all but disintegrated, these writers express a subtle yearning for times past when life for Ireland's gentry consisted of a more or less continual round of social and sporting events. Happier times are recalled when a devoted tenantry lit bonfires (outside rather than inside the Big House as was to become the custom) to celebrate the birth of a male heir or the landlord's long awaited return from abroad. In her account of what were in 'most ways . . . fairly ordinary Anglo-Irish country gentry' Elizabeth Bowen refers to 'a lively and simple spontaneous affection between the landed families and the people around them'.[38] She attributes the strength of this bond partly to the foster system which involved the gentry's children being wet-nursed and mothered by Catholic servant women. Violet Martin commenting on the landlord-tenant relationship at Ross wistfully recalls that the 'personal element was always in it and the hand of affection held it together'.[39]

---

37. As well as *Irish Memories,* see Edith Somerville's novel, *The Big House of Inver,* Longmans, Green, London, 1925.
38. Bowen, Elizabeth, op. cit., p. 126.
39. Somerville, E., and Ross, M., op. cit., p. 26.

Yet, though thoughtful and insightful, rarely do the authors of such cosy rural reminiscences rise above the privileged, insular world they describe. Most avoid confronting the unpleasant truth that the maintenance of the Ascendancy's lifestyle necessarily involved the continued exploitation and suppression of the Catholic majority. Brian Inglis in *West Britain* reflects on the nature of the landlord-tenant relationship in Ascendancy Ireland. He suggests that 'we loved them as a landowner in the Deep South loves his negro servants – because they knew their place and stayed in it'.[40] The rising tide of Irish nationalism experienced at the local level is described in terms of tenant disloyalty conveniently attributed to the influence of a few, misguided extremists. Lacking the zeal, aggressive militarism and ruthless acquisitiveness of their Protestant forbears, these writers seem unwilling to concede that the position of their class, now untenable, was never morally defensible. As with most of their fellow Ascendancy, they seem unable to recognise Ireland as a nation of people capable of governing themselves without the supervision of an hereditary ruling caste. This view of themselves as a class born to rule may help explain why so many Anglo-Irish sought and obtained positions as governors and other senior positions in Australia.

The truth concerning the common attitudes and behaviour of Anglo-Irish, during the century when representatives of this class emigrated to Australia, remains elusive. Identifying the important features of the distinctive Old World tradition which the Ascendancy brought to colonial Australia involves somehow reconciling contrasting accounts of the Anglo-Irish: the exaggerated, highly coloured accounts offered by satirists and novelists; the politically motivated, polemical accounts of the nationalists; the romanticised, nostalgic accounts of the apologists; and recently published revisionist histories of the Ascendancy period.

Perhaps it is sensible to begin by rejecting extremes. Improving land lords were not as common as members of the Kildare Street Club like to think, or rare as the nationalists would have us believe. On balance,

---

40. Brian Inglis, *West Britain*, London, 1962, p. 15.

available evidence seems to support the view that Ireland's Protestant gentry were neither as unpopular or as wickedly irresponsible as depicted by the nationalists. Anecdotal evidence, and the fact that a relatively small number of Protestants were able to retain power with minimal military force, support Professor Maxwell's carefully qualified conclusion "that on the whole, setting aside the general and often theoretical dislike of the people for English and Anglo-Irish, and for particular landlords who definitely ill-treated them, it would seem that the Irish gentry were not so very unpopular".[41]

Though, as Beckett readily admits, 'the Anglo-Irish were not good managers', neither were they '. . . cruel and grasping tyrants, wringing the last penny of rent from a starving and terrified tenantry'.[42] While the Protestant gentry in Ireland as a class have much to answer for, it is simply unjust to hold them primarily responsible for the impoverished state of the Irish peasantry. In the first place the situation of most Irish peasants during normal times was not particularly grim when compared with the conditions of other rural populations in the poorer parts of Europe. In this respect it was England, not Ireland, in the late eighteenth century that was singular and phenomenal. During the second half of the eighteenth century agricultural prices rose more sharply than rents, with the increase going mainly to the tenant. In spite of their monotonous diet of potatoes, their appalling housing and ragged dress, Irish peasants were often observed to be happy and capable of considerable exertion. In fact, the backward state of the Irish peasantry had more to do with Ireland's lack of natural resources and the depressed state of the Irish economy than the rapacious practices of Protestant landlords. The landholding system in Ireland (as in much of Europe) was patently unjust, involving the mass exploitation of a hungry peasantry, yet other factors were more significant. A potentially disastrous rate of population increase coupled with the peasantry's dangerous dependence on a single crop; England's restrictive policies which effectively discouraged the growth of Irish trade and manufacturing, all contributed to a deteriorating situation which culminated in the disastrous famine of 1846-48. Probably more than any other single factor, it was the Great Famine which fixed in the

41. C. Maxwell, op. cit., p. 183.
42. J. C. Beckett, op. cit., p. 92.

minds of the Catholic population as a whole the idea that the Protestant landlords were somehow the major enemies of Ireland. Yet despite evidence to the contrary, the nationalist myth persists that 'English' landlords (the Anglo-Irish) were directly responsible for the deaths and suffering of millions of Irish Catholics. In fact, the great majority of Irish landlords, whether resident or absentee, were relatively powerless to cope with a disaster of the magnitude of the Great Famine. Many faced ruin themselves, due not only to a sharp reduction in income as rents remained unpaid, but also as a result of their own considerable efforts to assist a stricken population.

The Anglo-Irish tradition was neither stable nor uniform. Like their Catholic Celtic countrymen, each generation of Anglo-Irish emigrants brought with them a different experience of Ireland to the New World. On the whole the Ascendancy Irish who emigrated to Australia were better educated and more liberally minded than generations that preceded or succeeded them. By the late eighteenth century when the first Anglo-Irish began to arrive in New South Wales and Tasmania, a period of prolonged peace and prosperity had resulted in Ireland's Protestant gentry becoming more civilised and tolerant. The Anglo-Irish who arrived in Australia during the first century of European settlement represented a society that had peaked intellectually and culturally but was soon to enter a period of stagnation and decline. By the late nineteenth century when Anglo-Irish emigration to Australia had all but ceased, the Ascendancy had become classbound and intellectually rigid. Reflecting on Anglo-Irish attitudes at this time, Nora Robertson recalls that 'the heads of leading Protestant families were, generally speaking less intellectually minded than their grandfathers'.[43] Commenting that fewer Ascendancy families now sent their sons to Trinity, Robertson attributes the Irish gentry's intellectual decline to the increased influence of the British military in Ireland.

To conclude – it is possible to reconcile the generally favourable impression of the Anglo-Irish in early Australia as able and energetic and on the whole liberal minded colonists with far less flattering descriptions

---

43. Nora Robertson, op. cit., p. 101.

of Ireland's Protestant gentry as a class. As well as taking a balanced view of their Old World Anglo-Irish tradition, one also needs to take into account the ways in which their changed circumstances in pre-goldrush Australia influenced the aspirations and behaviour of these Ascendancy Irish. In Australia there was little opportunity or need for these 'establishment' Irish to attempt to recreate what many recognised as a patently unjust and inequitable system in Ireland. At the same time, inspite of their soft gentry origins, many Anglo-Irish were well equipped to take advantage of specific employment and investment opportunities offering in penal-pastoral Australia. Largely because of their Old World tradition and Ascendancy background, the Anglo-Irish were particularly well suited to take on the role of civilising colonists in these remote outposts of Empire.

A WORLD STAGE FOR IRISH MUSIC

by Labhras O Murchu
Director General of Comhaltas Ceoltoiri Eireann

One is tempted to quote statistics ad infinitum accruing from the world-wide popularity of Irish traditional music. I have met young French students who, with very broken English, enquire about the Doolin tin whistle player Miko Russell as if Doolin were the capital of France and Miko one of its leading citizens. A young Swede came on a short visit, heard our music and now wishes to make his home here. A German fiddler comes each year to improve his repertoire of Irish tunes. Bill Ochs, a Jewish piper, has mastered the uilleann pipes, one of the most difficult of our instruments; while American-born Tomas Standevan won the Oireachtas on the same instrument and then added a bonus by becoming a fluent Irish speaker.

Film and television crews of many countries have come to capture the simple magic of the Clare concertina player; the uniqueness of the Dublin piper; the native richness of the Connemara singer; the vitality of the traditional Kerry dancer; or the melodious and peaceful strains of the Northern Presbyterian fiddler. All are adherents of a fine cultural heritage: they are links with the past which, surprisingly, in these days of haste and progress, can still command attention. They go against the tide and reject the glitter and shifting sands of this instantaneous age. They prefer the more stable and comforting sounds which have lulled generations of babies to sleep; satisfied centuries of dancing feet; or tell tales of love and hope. People come from the most 'advanced' countries of the world to record this simple philosophy of life and re-transmit it as an example for their own people.

While at home the huge upsurge of interest in ou. own native music may be explained or traced back to the founding of Comhaltas Ceoltoiri Eireann in 1951, a similar development outside of the country is, indeed, an unexpected success.

There are numerous classes throughout Britain (some of them officially sponsored by the Education authorities) where young people may learn the fiddle, accordion, whistle, flute and other instruments suitable for traditional music. The fruits of these classes are obvious in the All-Ireland Fleadh Cheoil results each year. And Britain has its own fleadhanna cheoil with the All-Britain Fleadh attracting attendances of up to 6,000. Because of the close proximity of Britain to Ireland, and the regular commuting, it is understandable that the cultural impetus at home would be mirrored and emulated by our emigrants across the sea, but it must be recorded that in many cases it is even surpassed! At a Comhaltas concert in the Albert Hall, London, there was an attendance of 4,000 enthusiastic and committed patrons.

If we look further afield, we find that there were five chartered flights from the United States for the Fleadh Cheoil in Listowel: this would account for almost 900 people. The American contestants topped the list in many of the competitions and this is no mean achievement when one considers that this, in many cases, was their first time setting foot in Ireland and add to this the high standards of performance which now prevail at home. The influential *New York Times* declared that 'the Fleadh Cheoil is the year's most popular musical gathering' and adds that 'it is a music festival unlike any in the world, with thousands of vocal and instrumental musicians gathering from all parts and for three days the Summer air is drenched with traditional music.'

In reverse, Comhaltas sends a Touring Group to America and in the course of three weeks their concerts attract over 25,000 people. There is a great feeling of pride in the realisation that what in less enlightened days was termed "peasant" entertainment can raise the "fullhouse" signs in Chicago, New York, Detroit, St. Louis and other cosmopolitan centres. The *Rocky Mountain Journal* put it like this: 'The programme unfolds in measured cadence revealing the rich variety that lies at the motherlode of the Irish consciousness. It is clear that this band of traditional performers are motivated by more than the traditional appeal of the roaring crowds and the smell of grease-paint.'

One is led into many cul-de-sacs in trying to analyse this new found appeal of our musical past. Analysing the popularity of a soap powder, a brand of cigarettes or a political leader is a relatively simply task but not so the popularity of a centuries-old music in a hyper-progressive world. There are many valid opinions but none all-embracing enough to be convincing. Many have attested to the beauty of the music itself; others have pointed to its environmental attributes; then there are the connotations of fraternity; and perhaps worthy of mention is a desire to cling to an identifiable and well-tried safety plank in a choppy sea of change. One cannot apply statistical criteria to something which is an element of the spirit.

There is an accompanying philosophy with our folk music which takes cognizance of the source of origin, its people, its welfare and its aspirations. There is a comradeship which is crystallised at the "session", concert or fleadh cheoil – a comradeship which transcends all community divides; age, sex, religion, occupational status or politics. The mere mention of this consideration tends to make it clinical and calculating: to experience it is like a shared secret requiring no verbose recognition or assessment. In the entertainment world much emphasis is placed on image-building through syndicated publicity; the trappings of performance become exaggerated and sometimes take priority over the performance itself. This is not the case with Irish traditional music.

The combination of talent and natural flair is the criterion of success, and it was this uninhibited and simple approach which brought 2,000 people in Hunter College, New York, to their feet in a sustained ovation during a Comhaltas concert. One thing on which there is general agreement is that our music is not the possession of any one section of the community: it is not confined to Gaeltacht or rural areas; it is not the exclusive domain of an arty class or the sole right of the less pretentious. It is the music of all the people, young and old; it has its exponents in Carna and Ballyfermot, in Belfast and Cork, in the itinerant community and business circles.

The bearded and long-haired ones; the conservative conservatives; the rebel and society's pillar, all can find common ground midst the strains of an old Irish air or a rollicking dance tune. The universality of the music is echoed in the tune titles: 'The Maid behind the Bar', 'Off to California', 'My love is in America', 'The Rambling Pitfork', 'The Hut in the Bog', 'The flags of Dublin', 'The Glenroad to Carrick', 'The Hare in the Heather', 'The Liverpool Hornpipe', 'Over the Moor to Maggie', and, of course, thousands of others. As the titles show, the music is an expression of the people and their environment: it is not something doctrinaire or academic, it is fresh and elating, emotional and artistic.

What is the movement which has spearheaded this cultural revolution? Comhaltas was founded back in 1951 by a small group of traditional music lovers on the promptings of the Pipers' Club, Dublin. This Club is today one of the most active branches of the movement and still continues its Saturday night session at the Culturlann in Monkstown, Co. Dublin.

Comhaltas has now extended through the 32 counties of Ireland and also to Britain, America and Australia. There are 400 branches in all and among the achievements are 45 fleadhanna cheoil each year; 600 classes; courses for beginners, teachers and adjudicators; a regular magazine and tutors; weekly radio programme and involvement in 25 television programmes per year; records, cultural tours abroad, music collection. It is estimated that over 1,000,000 people attend Comhaltas functions annually. Branches of Comhaltas are to be found worldwide from Japan to Italy; Luxembourg to Australia; Canada and the United States; Britain and every county in Ireland. Another achievement of the movement was the establishment of an Irish Cultural Institute, Culturlann na hEireann. This is a nerve centre of cultural philosophy and activity; identifying and promoting Ireland's distinctiveness as a nation.

There was a fine response for this project but none so moving as that of Dr. and Mrs. J. Richardson Usher of St. Louis. They wrote: 'On October 27, 1973, our second son, Scott, age twenty, was killed in an automobile accident while riding home from college with a close friend. Our family's decision to establish a Scott Usher Memorial Fund to benefit the proposed Cultural Institute must come as a bit of a surprise to our Irish friends . . . Less than two weeks before Scott died he had made a special trip home from college to be with us for the Comhaltas concert in St. Louis. He was enchanted with our stories of the fun we had had with our Irish house guests. Scott went back to college the next day, intent on mastering the fine art of Irish fiddling. His brother, Dave, and his friends at school said he was absolutely ecstatic over the whole Irish encounter. He even mentioned to his roommate that when he died he wanted his friends to gather and have an "Irish wake" '.

And so, after his death, we celebrated his short life on this earth as he wished. Instead of the usual visiting in a cold sombre funeral parlour, our home was the warm setting for our friends to come offering their love and condolences . . . Soon the instruments were taken from their cases and the music began. 'Such beautiful music – heartfelt and soaring – our friends had never played so well. By the light of candles and roaring hearth fire, we sipped hot spiced apple cider, and nibbled all the good things the church ladies had brought in, and ended the evening with arms encircling one another singing some of the old traditional folk hymns. We were wrapped in a blanket of warmth and comfort, a tender balm to the aching pain in our family heart.'

'Now perhaps you understand', said Dr. and Mrs. Usher, 'why we, his family, designated Comhaltas as the recipient of his memorial fund, since there is no similar organization in our country. In music there are no geographical boundaries – only a love for beautiful music. It gives us joy that this tribute to Scott will be used to further the thing that he loved best. In his own life he brought much joy to all who knew him through his fiddling. He lived long enough to inspire his little brother to take up the art. As Chris wistfully said, heading off to his fiddle lesson several weeks after Scott's death, "Well, I guess I'm the fiddler in the family now." And so the tradition goes on, passing from one musician to the next.'

Yes, indeed, it is a continuing tradition bringing joy to generations of Irish people and their friends throughout the world.

ORDNANCE SURVEY MEMOIRS OF IRELAND (1830-40)

by Patrick McWilliams
Institute of Irish Studies, Q.U.B.

To understand the origin and development of the Ordnance Survey 'Memoirs', which provide the fullest descriptive survey of pre-Famine society in the northern half of Ireland, we must first examine the organisation through whose agency the scheme evolved, almost accidently. I refer of course to the Irish Ordnance Survey, which was established in Dublin in 1824.

Ever since their first involvement with Ireland many centuries before, the island had remained a mystery to most Englishmen. Whether through her people, history or customs, little was known about that troublesome island across the water. Indeed, in official circles, it was thought that more was known about India than Ireland, and this, combined with the subconscious effect of the Irish rebellions of recent centuries, may have contributed to the decision taken in 1824 to authorise a geographical survey of·Ireland, with the object of equalising taxation at the local level.

This led to the establishment of the Irish Ordnance Survey, under the command of Colonel Thomas Colby of the Royal Engineers. Its priority was to undertake a minute survey of Ireland for the preparation of maps on the scale six inches to one mile. So well was the task done that an English nobleman was to complain, if that be the correct term, that Ireland, the most disagreeable part of the three kingdoms, had the best Ordnance map. The Memoirs were to evolve through the surveys of the Royal Engineers, though the mapping proper always took precedence in the Ordnance Survey and in higher circles.

The corps of the Irish Ordnance Survey were officers of the Royal Engineers. Colby's first act, which was of great significance was to appoint a remarkable man as his deputy. In 1826 Lieutenant Thomas Aiskew Larcom was recruited to the Survey from the headquarters of the Ordnance Survey in Southampton. He was to spend a quarter of a century with the Survey, before becoming a principal in the administration at Dublin Castle. For his services he was to receive the Order of the Bath. Few Englishmen can have left such a mark on Ireland as Larcom. He was an early 'friend of Ireland'. He was the guiding hand behind the Memoir scheme, leading by example with his great energy and attention to detail and by the interest he showed in the work of his subordinates.

The heads of the Survey decided to use the parishes of the Established Church in each county as the main unit of reference for the officers employed in the field. Yet if an index of names on the six inch map was to be compiled, a more suitable and smaller unit of area would be needed. Larcom's engineer eye immediately settled on the townland, a denomination peculiar to Ireland, of which there were more than 60,000 in the whole country, averaging 330 acres each. As he reported, retrospectively, to the Treasury in 1851,

> '. . . clearly it ought to be the smallest space which pervades the whole country, and has a fixed recognised name and boundary. The townlands . . . possess all these requisites. Their boundaries can only be altered by act of parliament. They are recognised and used in all public transactions and assessments for county purposes, and various other public objects, and the Ordnance Survey is the authority on which their boundaries and designations rest.'[1]

Thus it could be said that if the parishes comprised the hull of the mapping and Memoir scheme, the townlands formed the compartments.

We now come to the genesis of the Memoir scheme itself. The term 'Memoir' comes from the French *aide-memoire* 'an aid to memory'; the Memoirs as we know them evolved as follows. The engineers had a custom of keeping a journal in which to record such matters of interest and *common use*, as well as their surveying notes, as were uncovered during the course of their work. It was also customary for them and others employed on such work to furnish with every map or plan a report or *Memoir* explaining the subject at hand and containing such information as could not be exhibited on the maps. One such example can be found in the Field Name Books for Co. Antrim, compiled by the Irish scholar John O'Donovan.

"Parish of Aghalee, barony of Upper Massareene. Received name: Aghalee townland, *acadh laoigh* 'field of the calf'; orthography and authority: Aghalee – custom; Aghalee – *Statistical Survey of County Antrim*, the Revd J. Dubourdieu; Aghalee – Lord Hertford's office map,

---

1. Larcom Papers (henceforth LP) 7512, National Library of Ireland.

1792; Aghalee – map of Lough Neagh attached to *Statistical Survey of County Armagh*; Aghalee – the Revd E. Cupples; Aghalee or Aghanalee – Shaw Mason's parochial survey; Aghalee – Lendrick's county map. Situation: it is situated at the north-west part of the parish. Descriptive remarks: this townland is chiefly under cultivation. It contains the small village of Aghalee, which has no fairs or markets. There are the ruins of an old church situated on the road from Aghalee to Ballinderry, and at the east extremity of this townland there is a remarkable fort called Robinson's fort."[2]

The earliest Memoirs were thus the reports submitted by the officers in the course of their main duties of surveying. As the six inch mapping scheme was a townland by townland survey, a substantial amount of information was available to and uncovered by the officers, much of which was included in their reports. As 'equalisation of taxation' was the primary tenet of the survey, any material likely to be of use in this field would have been desirable.

This practice of submitting a Memoir developed only gradually, yet by the time Memoir writing was halted in 1840, over 23,000 pages of material had been accumulated. From its original limited scope the scheme had developed into a huge social survey.

As the reports of the officers filtered into Larcom's office from 1830 onwards, it was decided that these would be better written to a prescribed form. Already the brief descriptive remarks on townlands and other notable features were being expanded to include information on social, economic and antiquarian matters. In 1832 therefore Larcom drew up his 'Heads of Inquiry', a document which codified the headings to be used by the Memoir writers in compiling their reports. The Memoir was to follow three main headings: Natural State comprising natural features and natural history; Topography Ancient and Modern; and Social and Productive Economy. If we examine the introduction to this document, we can see the light it casts on Larcom's own view of the Memoir scheme.

2. Ordnance Survey (henceforth OS) of Ireland, Name Books, Co. Antrim. Royal Irish Academy.

"In proposing the following inquiries, the object is to collect and diffuse general information for the benefit of every class in society; for no class of persons can advance their real and permanent interests, without at the same time conferring a general good on society at large."[3]

The main benefit accruing from these inquiries, it was hoped, would be a more even distribution of taxation.

The Heads of Inquiry gave a considerable boost to the Memoir scheme, as the men in the field now had an 'official' document to follow in compiling their reports, and it gave an even greater impetus to all to contribute to the scheme, not all officers having bothered previously to submit reports. It is after this date, and from 1834 onwards in particular, that the best of the Memoirs are written, and the Heads of Inquiry necessitated the creation of a separate department within the Ordnance Survey. As Colby was to say in 1837:

> "To carry on a minute survey of all Ireland so as to meet the various objects proposed by the Heads of Inquiry . . . it became indispensable to train and organise a completely new department for the purpose. Officers and men from the corps of Royal Engineers formed the basis of this new organisation, and very large numbers of persons possessing various qualities were gradually added to them to expedite the great work."[4]

The first non-military men recruited to Memoir writing were the hill sketchers, to be joined later by other civil assistants and men of antiquarian expertise, as well as soldiers with geological or botanical experience. As the remit of the men involved in the scheme was never actually laid down, the nature of the research undertaken was able to be expanded without undue difficulty, especially as it mirrored and contributed to the detailed townland survey being carried out for the six inch maps. Larcom himself later admitted that the need for the maps to include the most accurate and authoritative townland names had led to a great deal of investigation on this topic, in the course of which much of an antiquarian nature had been collected. Thus we can see how the scheme mushroomed: who was to say what was useful or not; little in

3. LP 7550.
4. Ibid., 7552.

fact was ever excluded; and as compliance with instructions from headquarters, in the form of the Heads of Inquiry, involved a broad degree of research, the Memoir writers were obliged to include as much material as possible.

Many of Larcom's subordinates shared his enthusiasm for the scheme. The following letter to him from James Boyle in November 1837 may serve to illustrate this.

"I am very happy to find by your letter to Mr Dawson that you approve of my Antrim Memoir. In about 9-10 weeks I hope to have successively completed rather more than half of the county, when I shall send you 26 at least equally good Memoirs. Even already a spirit or taste for information has been excited among the country people, merely by enquiries made among them and collecting information."[5]

One of the most remarkable of Larcom's assistants was the eminent geologist Captain, later Major-General, J. E. Portlock, who produced a series of incredibly detailed Productive Economy tables for Co. Londonderry. He in turn instructed those under his command to go well beyond the field of natural history, as shown by the following letter.

"No-one is to consider that because his services are principally directed to some particular object, he is on that account to neglect every other. On the contrary, all are labouring to promote the general interests of a great work, and each person should note all he sees and all he hears, whether in reference to his own immediate inquiries, to the social condition and habits of the people, to antiquities and traditionary recollections of all kinds, or to natural history in all its branches, naming at the same time his authority for each statement."[6]

Larcom's expanded department had its own hierarchy; ranking below him were officers like Lieutenants J. Rimington and J. Chaytor, the latter of whom produced the superb Memoir for Enniskillen. From 1834 onwards the hill sketchers and other civil assistants came to the fore. Men like C. W. Ligar, J. B. Williams, J. Boyle, J. Stokes and J. R. Ward contributed many of the very best examples of Memoir writing,

5. Ibid.
6. OS Memoirs of Ireland, Box 48 I.

while junior assistants like T. Fagan and J. Bleakly collected much material on a more personal, but no less valuable, level. Topographical and antiquarian expertise was supplied by the distinguished pairing of G. Petrie and J. O'Donovan. With so many people available to him, Larcom was at least able to ensure coverage of a substantial area, in varying degrees of detail.

The writing of the Memoirs continued until 1840. It covered the province of Ulster primarily, with only fragments for areas further south. Counties Londonderry and Antrim were particularly well surveyed, with Down, Fermanagh, Tyrone and Donegal next in line in terms of coverage. Armagh, Monaghan and Cavan were the least well recorded, as allocation of resources necessitated occasional revisions of earlier work.

What survives is a marvellous wealth of information on life during the years 1830-40, parish by parish, townland by townland. It is doubtful if any country possesses a source comparable to the Memoirs in terms of casting light on the way of life of ordinary people. It provides that which the census cannot hope to achieve: it puts flesh on the bones of statistics; it defines the attitudes and character of the people; it records the traditions and antiquities of the period. We are also fortunate regarding the era encompassed by the Memoirs, for it was a period of great change in Ireland: a religious awakening was taking place in many parts, communications were about to be revolutionised by the advent of the railway and life was as yet unaffected by the Great Famine just around the corner. Whether it be the crop in the field, the textbooks used at school or the daily wage of the farm labourer, there is something of interest for everyone in the Memoirs.

While the scheme *was* progressing at a fair speed, it had always its detractors amongst those who were worried that it might spark off a rebirth of Irish nationalism or who considered it a waste of public money for research to go beyond the fields of geography and natural history. Plans to publish a Memoir for a chosen area of Co. Londonderry were mooted at an early stage, and in 1833 the Treasury agreed that a Memoir relating to this county alone might be published as an experiment, to see if it would pay for itself. The area chosen was the parish of Templemore, comprising the west bank of Derry city and its surrounding area. This was an unfortunate choice, as the city occupied a special place in the political history of the country, and whatever was published was certain to offend many. In the event, the preliminary volume submitted to the

British Association in 1835 did indeed contain much on the history of the city, and from a largely Irish viewpoint; and this, allied to the book's bulky and statistical nature, confirmed the fears of those who had always been suspicious of the scheme. Larcom was later to admit that this volume had been 'hastily put together',[7] and the failure to publish it until 1837, 'was very unfortunate',[8] and jeopardized the scheme. Even though the Templemore volume broke even, its appearance sounded the death knell for the project.

Contemporary reactions to the scheme were, however, in the main very favourable. After the appearance of the preliminary Templemore volume in 1835, the following appeared in the *Dublin Evening Post* and in the English periodical *Athenaeum*, respectively.

"We would add, also, a hope that the numerous opportunities the surveyors must have possessed of discovering the resources of the country and tracing the causes of their comparative disuse or mismanagement, may lead to much valuable illustrative matter in the form of geological, statistical and historical Memoirs."[9]

"... if the remainder of the work be executed with the same diligence and accuracy, Ireland will possess a record of its resources unparalleled in Europe, and the conductors of the Ordnance Survey will, in the strong words of Mr Babbage, 'have earned a right to the lasting gratitude of their countrymen, as national benefactors'."[10]

As word of 'official' knives being sharpened reached the public, reaction was hostile. The *Irish Press* declared in 1838 that "this is no party question", however in 1840 the Master of Ordnance gave instructions for the suspension of Memoir writing. Work was to continue on natural history only, and Larcom's plans for the publication of the Memoirs in their entirety were postponed. Those committed to the scheme proposed limiting future publications to two Memoirs per county, but this was rejected. The paymasters refused to budge even though it was pointed out that if work on Memoir writing was not resumed immediately, the six inch maps would be incomplete as features

7. LP 7552.
8. Ibid.
9. Ibid., 7558.
10. Ibid.

contained thereon would not be explained. They also refused to entertain a proposal from Larcom that his department should be retained to correlate and work on census returns, as well as continuing work on statistical Memoir material. He claimed that the expense of both would be reduced as experience and efficiency increased, and that there would be no need for annual, expensive parliamentary commissions to investigate statistical matters, as these would already be be incorporated in Memoir material and census returns. The counter argument which prevailed, however, was that Memoir statistics and census returns over-lapped anyhow, and that statistical material needed constant revision.

The final attempt to revive the scheme came in 1843 when Sir Robert Peel, faced by a delegation of distinguished Irishmen, agreed to set up a commission to inquire into the facts relating to the Ordnance Memoir of Ireland. The issues were examined at great length and various proposals made, such as that the antiquarian material collected could be published by individuals or societies. Those deepest involved in the scheme, however, expressed the view that all publications, being of public benefit, should come from the public purse, and the result was that the commissioners appointed agreed unanimously that the scheme should be continued. However, the administration was not convinced, and on 1 July 1844 the order came through that further research was to be confined to geology and that nothing else was to be collected. The civil assistants returned to their previous duties and the Memoir papers were gradually deposited in the Royal Irish Academy, where they still remain.

The most remarkable fact relating to the Memoir scheme is that it was ever allowed to develop to the extent it did. That this was the case says much about the character of Thomas Larcom. How fitting then that the proposed Memoir publication project was to have a title from Cicero's *De Officiis*. For Larcom, a soldier and officer of Engineers, the Memoir scheme was a duty, albeit a pleasant one. In later years he was to express regret that the work of many years never came to fruition, in the form of publication.

The value of the Memoirs is that they are the first recorded example of a systematic survey of Irish life, and that they amount to a Domesday of the period.

APPENDIX

The three main types of material comprising the Memoirs were Main Memoirs, Fair Sheets and Tabulated Information. Examples are given below verbatim to illustrate the form and detail of the text on representative places.

1. *MAIN MEMOIRS*
   (a) *Officers' Statistical Reports*: The earliest accounts, written by officers of the Royal Engineers.

      (i) Parish of *Enniskillen*, County *Fermanagh*
          Written by Lieutenant John Chaytor, October 1834
          Town of Enniskillen
   The town of Enniskillen is very peculiarly situated on an island in Lough Erne, nearly in the centre (and is the assize town) of the county of Fermanagh, in the south-west circuit of assize and within about 12 miles of the western extremity of the province of Ulster; 80 Irish miles from Dublin, 22 from Belturbet, 19 from Clones, 32 from Sligo, 22 from Ballyshannon and 19 from Belleek. The island is somewhat of a triangular form, with its base or longest side extending from south-east to north-west and its vertex south-south-west, in area 68 acres. It forms 2 little hills, the larger of which is situated on the south-east end of the island. A drain passing through the hollow lying between forms the boundary of the baronies of Magheraboy and Tyrkenedy.

      (ii) Parish of *Drumlomman*, County *Cavan*
          Written by Lieutenant Andrew Beatty, November 1835
          Cattle: the breed of cattle is mixed and of an inferior sort but is improving, the shorthorned cattle having lately been introduced. The horses are of every breed. The pigs have been improved by a cross of the Dutch breed. Cattle and pigs are bought up by jobbers and taken to Drogheda for exportation to England. Green feeding is not practised in this parish.

   (b) *Memoirs/Draft Memoirs by civil assistants:* These were often more detailed than the officers' reports and comprise the bulk of the text of the Memoirs.

(i) Parish of *Balteagh*, County *Londonderry*
Written by J. Butler Williams, July 1835.

Balteagh Old Church: the date of its erection or the name of its founder is not preserved by tradition. It only mentions that it was the first in this parish after the introduction of Christianity into it. It is built of stones averaging from one to one and a half feet in length, irregular in their shapes and not very closely fitted; the interstices between them being filled with small stones and mortar mixed with shells, which is now exceedingly hard and tenacious. A great part of the walls are yet covered with plaster. Of the windows, only 2 remain at present, viz. the west window and one in the south gable. The first of these is of a large size and ornamented with sandstone artwork, but has been filled up since its construction, the mortar with which the interior of the window was built differing from the other in being without shells. The second window is of that style, in which if the sides were produced to the outer surface of the wall, they would touch each other.

This church was in a tolerable state of repair up to November 1777, at which period a violent storm took place which carried off many of the slates of the roof and otherwise injured it. Repairs were neglected and in a short time the church was becoming every day more unfit for service, and some of the inhabitants began to steal away the timber of the pews and roof, all of oak. About 1780 the Rev. Robert Magee, then rector of the parish, finding its parts of the roof and other fixtures rapidly disappearing, had the roof taken off the church altogether and thenceforward officiated in the Glebe House on Sundays. All the clergymen who succeeded him officiated in Newtownlimavady and other places of the neighbourhood, until the erection of the present church. To this there was an exception, i.e. that the first Sunday after his installation each incumbent officiated in the roofless parish church, which act was necessary to make his appointment valid. The ruin is preserved with care and the churchyard is enclosed by a wall on side next to the road, and good fences on the remaining sides. It continues to be used as a burying place, chiefly by the Roman Catholic inhabitants.

(ii) Parish of *Carnmoney*, County *Antrim*
Written by James Boyle, April 1839

Character and Morals of the farmers: in their morals they are on a par with the inhabitants of the surrounding parishes. They are rather fond of whiskey drinking, and there is another species of immorality to which from habit they are quite reconciled, and which among themselves does not bear the same character or appellation as is most applied to it. It is by no means an unusual circumstance that intercourse should have taken place between two parties previous to their being united by the bonds of matrimony. In this custom, strange as it may appear, there is an ulterior motive on the part of both: on the woman's that she may compel her father, to avoid exposure, to make such a settlement on her as will ensure her marriage, and on the man's, who frequently for some time refuses to consent, that he may obtain from her father a larger dowry. It is alleged that this is the common motive which in most cases of the kind influences both the parties, nor is such an affair by any means held as disreputable.

(iii) Parish of *Newry,* County *Down*
Written by J. Rodrigo Ward, October 1836

Reading Room: Newry commercial reading room is underneath the assembly room, Hill Street. It is afforded by subscription from the members. Strangers are most liberally allowed to read the papers in the room for three months, after which period they must become subscribers or pay 2s 6d for every time they enter the room. (Military are excepted from this fine). There are a great variety of Irish and British papers, the *Army List*, *Navy List* and *Lloyds' List*.

2. *FAIR SHEETS*

"Information gathered in the field" by lower ranking civil assistants. While this material often supplements the main Memoirs, it is on occasions the only source.

Parish of *Blaris* (Lisburn), County *Antrim*
Written by Thomas Fagan, 1837

Fort and derivation of Lisnagarvey: in the north rear of Castle Street, Lisburn, and in the grounds now occupied by Dean Stannus, there formerly stood a circular fort which was called in the Irish language Lissnakarvagh, and from which Lisburn derived its original name, Lisnagarvey. Lissnakarvagh signifies the "gamblers' fort", a term to which this fort was justly entitled under the following circumstances. Previous to the battle and burning of Lisnagarvey in 1641, the only hotel then in town was situate contiguous to the fort above mentioned and on the site where the Messrs Richardsons' office now stands in Castle Street. At the rear of the hotel and adjoining the fort there was an eminent bowling green. The fort itself, which was then sheltered by lofty oaks, was also a theatre for various amusements such as card play, dice play.

Hundreds of persons from various districts assembled here at seasons of the year set apart for amusements and enjoyed themselves at bullet play in the aforesaid bowling green, also at cards and dice and various other games in and about the fort, and had their liquors both in the hotel before mentioned and in the fort and bowling green occasionally. However, from the concourse of people from different districts assembling at the place at different periods of the year for gambling purposes, the fort was in consequence called in the Irish language Lissnakaruagh but subsequently corrupted and changed to Lisnagarvey and gave name to the town, which was in them times only in an infantine state of improvement. Either of the above two names signifies the "gamblers' fort". This fort was levelled some years back. There is a neat tea-house that was built at some former period now standing on its site.

Parish of *Montiaghs*, County *Armagh*
Written by Thomas McIlroy, December 1837
General appearance and scenery: the appearance of the country is wild and dreary. The immense tracts of bog which extend along the shore of Lough Neagh down to high water mark, with only a few islands far distant from each other, give the country a dreary and lonely aspect.

3. TABULATED INFORMATION.

This kind of material is found consistently throughout the reports, often as an appendix to the main Memoir or scattered through the Fair Sheets. Two main types, emigration lists and school statistics, are featured here.

(a) Parish of *Magherafelt*, County *Londonderry*
Written by Thomas Fagan, June 1836
Emigration to America in 1835: the following is a list of the persons that have emigrated to America from the above parish during the year

1835. It will show the name, age and religion of each person, the townland in which they resided, the year emigrated and ports to which the different persons have gone.

Name	Age	Townland	Religion	Destination
Elenor Bradley	20	Killyneese	Roman Catholic	New York
David Morton	18	Ballynocker	Presbyterian	Philadelphia
ElizabethChambers	30	Glenmacuil	Established Church	New Orleans
Joseph Keesie	26	Aghagaskin	Roman Catholic	New York
Henery McQuaid	27	Magherafelt	”	”
Murtagh McKeown	19	”	”	”
John Smyth	20	”	Established Church	”
Maryann Lunnon	20	”	Roman Catholic	Quebec

Total 10. Information obtained from Edward Walsh, William Love and many others. Finished 28th June 1836.

LOS IRLANDESES EN LA ARGENTINA

by Pat Nally

Secretary, Longford-Westmeath Argentina Society

The above title will surprise many readers. Even more surprising is that places in Argentina like Buenos Aires, Pergamino, San Antonio de Areco, Salto and Arrecifes are not only household names in certain parts of Ireland, but are places with relatives of people in Ireland in such places as Ballymore, Ballynacargy, Castlepollard, Moyvore in Co. Westmeath; Ballymahon and Carrick-Edmund in Co. Longford; Kilrane, Co. Wexford and Castletownbeare, Co. Cork. All their Argentine relatives, of course, speak Spanish, the language of Argentina and most of Latin America.

So how has this exotic family connection come about? To find the answer, we must take ourselves back to the beginning of the 19th century when Spain was the imperial power in Argentina. In this period of the early 1800s, a wave of wars of independence swept Spanish America, led by Simon Bolivar, Bernardo O'Higgins, Jose Artigas and Jose de San Martin. San Martin was the hero of the Argentine War of Independence which was achieved in 1816. Admiral William Brown from Foxford, Co. Mayo, played a prominent role in that war of Independence, being the founder of the Argentine navy. Another Irish man, John Thomond O'Brien from Co. Wicklow, also was prominent in the war of Independence, being adjutant to San Martin. It is said that San Martin asked O'Brien to go back to Ireland for 200 emigrants. Argentina was then a country of vast unclaimed lands. O'Brien spent the 1827/28 period trying to recruit emigrants in Ireland, but without success. However, he met a John Mooney of Streamstown, near Ballymore, Co. Westmeath. This was to be the start of the Irish emigration to Argentina from the Westmeath/Longford/North Offaly area because Mooney went to Argentina in 1828 when O'Brien was returning. In addition to John Mooney, his sister, Mary Bookey (nee Mooney) and her husband, Patrick Bookey, went with O'Brien. They were to achieve rapid success in farming in Argentina and, due to this success, Mooney wrote home to Westmeath for emigrants to come out and help him farm the vast lands they had found. People in Westmeath responded in large numbers, from the 1820s onwards, and right through the 19th century, and even up to

69

1914, emigrated to Argentina. As it was John Mooney and Patrick Bookey who started off this emigration from the Irish Midlands, a few words about both of them is appropriate at this stage.

John Mooney was born in 1803 in Streamstown, Co. Westmeath, and arrived in Buenos Aires in 1828, where he became involved in farming. In the 1869 census in Buenos Aires, he was described as a bachelor but was actually a widower. The records show that he had children but no names are shown nor is his wife's name recorded. He died in Buenos Aires in 1873. His brother-in-law, Patrick Bookey, was born in Ireland about 1810 and arrived in Buenos Aires in 1828, and his name appears in the 1869 Buenos Aires census. It is mentioned that, soon after his arrival, he was the owner of 900 acres containing magnificent gardens and plantations containing no less than two million trees. This became a model farm and is now the property of the University of La Plata. Bookey had a respected position among the Irish community in Buenos Aires. He was treasurer of the Irish Hospital. In 1835, he married Mary Mooney (sister of John Mooney) in Argentina. They had six children, Catalina, Margarita, Maria, Patricio, Guillermo and Tomas. Bookey died in 1883, and Mary Bookey in 1873 in Buenos Aires.

Let us now move to the Wexford connection with Argentina. The shipping firm of Dickson and Montgomery had a man named John Brown from Wexford representing them in Buenos Aires. In 1827, this Liverpool based firm appointed Patrick Brown, a brother of the Brown already mentioned, to be their representative, to succeed his brother. Patrick Brown was born in Wexford in 1806. He went to Liverpool to work for Dickson and Montgomery, and moved to Buenos Aires in 1824. He got involved in the meat industry and became prosperous enough to live in the San Isidro area of Buenos Aires which is an exclusive part of the city. In 1874, he returned with his family to Wexford. He returned to Argentina in 1888 on the death of John Brown there in the same year. He became a highly respected member of the Irish emigrant community in Argentina where he died in 1893. The arrival of Brown in Argentina in the 1820s was the start of Wexford emigration to Argentina which, though significant, was nothing like the numbers that went from the Longford-Westmeath area.

Indeed prior to this emigration there were a small number of Irish in Argentina who arrived as part of the abortive British invasions of 1806 and 1807. The first one was commanded by General William Beresford and both expeditions had Irish officers, Duff, Browne, Nugent, Kenny, Donelly and Murray. Some Irish members of both expeditions deserted and settled in Argentina such as Patrick Island, Michael Hines and Peter Campbell.

So one of the most amazing emigrations had started 'travelling in humble carts, drawn by donkeys carrying a whole family with their modest household goods and headed to Cobh, Liverpool and Southampton, looking for the dreamt of Argentinian Pampas.' The journey took many months travelling by sailing ship.

It is reckoned that there were around 300 Irish emigrants in Argentina by 1830, enough to see the first Irish Roman Catholic priest, Rev. Patrick Moran, arrive as chaplain to the emigrants in 1829. He was succeeded by Rev. Patrick O'Gorman in 1830. A survey of the male emigrants in 1827 shows the following sources of the new arrivals:

        60% from Westmeath/Longford/North Offaly

        15% from Wexford

        3% from Cork

        3% from Clare

        19% from the rest of the country

The emigration started by John Mooney saw Westmeath providing two thirds of all the emigrants throughout the 19th century. In 1844, a William McCann, during a 2000 mile ride through Argentina, said 'at least three quarters of the emigrants are from Co. Westmeath.'

During the 1830s, there was a continued rise in emigration to Argentina, coming from three sources: Ireland, Irish coming down from the United States and Irish coming in from Brazil. Some Irish had gone to Brazil but, on not receiving a great welcome, crossed into Argentina. Argentina gave them a great welcome as it did to all Irish and other emigrants. Some such as Brown and Mooney became involved in the meat trade, but it was the sheep trade that attracted most of them. Irish and Basque emigrants became the mainstay of the sheep trade, and helped develop a wool based economy. Indeed, a Peter Sheridan from Cavan, who emigrated in the 1820s, became one of the largest sheep farmers in Argentina, and was instrumental in introducing the Merino sheep which today are to be seen all over Argentina. The Irish achieved great success with sheep, especially because the native gauchos preferred cattle and had no interest in sheep. Labourers earned up to ten shillings a day. A system of halves operated, i.e. the owner of land supplied the land

and flock, and the tenant was responsible for all other expenses. In time, many became owners of large estancias (ranches). By 1880, there were 58 million sheep in Argentina.

The first stage of emigration can be dated from the late 1820s to early 1840s. The famine of the mid 1840s saw another stage develop. Names which occur in the first stage include Duggans, Murrays, Hams, Gahans, Kennys, Dillons, Mooneys and Brownes. People in this stage prospered enormously and achieved greater success than later emigrants. The emigrants of that early period would have been influenced by Daniel O'Connell, and were less nationalistic than emigrants of the post-famine era. By the time of the famine, many of the early emigrants had become part of the Argentine establishment.

The famine of the 1840s in Ireland boosted emigration to Argentina from Westmeath and Wexford. This movement continued into the 1850s. 1844 saw the appointment of Rev. Antonio Fahy as chaplain. He was a native of Galway who had spent two years in Ohio in the United States. There he had seen the problems among Irish emigrants in cities, so when he arrived in Argentina, he urged Irish emigrants to avoid the cities and head for the vast countryside. He has been described as the adviser, banker, matchmaker and administrator of a welfare system for the newly arriving emigrants. The records of the port of Buenos Aires for 1849 show 708 emigrants arriving from Ireland. Church building became part of the Irish scene around this period, with new churches built in Buenos Aires, Barracas, Coronel Brandsen, Carmen de Areco, Rojas, Arrecifes, Mercedes and Venado Tuerto.

The 1850s show a lot of Irish owned estancias which in turn employed new emigrants. Women began to arrive in greater numbers in the 1850s. They worked often as cooks, maids and governesses. Many married sheep farmers. At this stage, women comprised half of the emigrants. Irish married Irish, and marriages with Argentines were rare. Indeed, up to the third generation they rarely married outside the Irish community. English was the household language of emigrants throughout this period. The arrival of Edward Mulhall in 1852 was significant. Born in Dublin in 1832, he emigrated first to the United States and then moved to Argentina. His brother Michael also arrived in Argentina. Mulhall went into the sheep trade, and in 1861, together with his brother, founded *The Buenos Aires Standard* newspaper which was the first English language paper, and was published for the English speaking community which, at this stage, comprised Irish, English and Scottish emigrants. He disposed of his farming interests and settled in Buenos Aires city. He became a friend of Presidents Roca and Avellaneda and also a city councillor. He was a great promoter of the farming industry, through his own 40,000 acre estancia. He died in 1888, having been married in 1856 to Eloisa Eborall from England.

Another wave of emigrants arrived in the 1860s, bringing names like Ryan, McCormick, Mullally and Casey. At this stage, some people were arriving to join their relatives already in Argentina, while others arrived after the Fenian Rising in Ireland. As the 1870s approached, there was a clear political division among emigrants, with the early wealthy emigrants pro-Home Rule in Ireland, with this expressed through *The Buenos Aires Standard* newspaper. The new arrivals of the 1860s, like the post famine 1840s arrivals, tended to be more nationalistic. This led to the foundation of another English language paper, *The Southern Cross* (La Cruz del Sur) in 1875, with Monsignor Patricio Jose Dillon as its first editor. He was born in the Diocese of Tuam and reached Argentina in 1863. *The Southern Cross* saw itself as somewhat greener than *The Standard*. Perhaps its most famous editor was William Bulfin, author of the famous book *Rambles in Erin*. He was editor from 1869-1906, being originally from Co. Offaly. *The Southern Cross* appeared as an English paper and remained so until 1964 when it changed to Spanish. The interesting aspect about the early days of *The Buenos Aires Standard* is that not alone was it the first English language paper, but it was also bi-lingual - English and French. An interesting picture of the Irish community in Argentina appeared in the first *Southern Cross* of January 16th, 1875, stating 'In no part of the world is the Irishman more esteemed and respected than in the Province of Buenos Aires, and in no part of the world, in the same space of time have Irish settlers made such large fortunes. The Irish population in the Republic may have set down at 26,000 souls. They possess in this province 200 leagues of land or 1,800 miles or 1,500.000 acres. Almost all of this land is of the very best quality. They own about 5,000,000 sheep and thousands are worth 5,000,000 sterling. This vast fortune has been acquired in a few years.'

The 1880s witnessed a further influx from Ireland, many of whom were joining an earlier generation of relatives in Argentina. During the 1875-1890 period, there was a great development of organisations and educational institutions by the Irish community. Newman College, St.

Brendan's College and St. Brigid's College were established and still exist. Branches of the Gaelic League and Sinn Fein were formed. The Irish Catholic Association was formed and hurling clubs were organised in Buenos Aires and Mercedes. Hurling continued to be played until the second world war. The hurling club of Buenos Aires still exists and now has rugby and hockey. However, the amazing news is that moves are currently afoot (July 1992) to revive hurling in Argentina, based in the Buenos Aires Hurling Club.

By the 1890s, there were only limited opportunities for new emigrants. The sheep industry was in decline and cattle and tillage were taking over. With the decline in the sheep trade, Irish emigration declined. Sheep had been the goldmine for Irish emigrants. The emigrants had been country people with agricultural skills who adapted easily to farming life in the great pampas of Argentina. So when, in 1889, 1,800 emigrants from the cities of Cork and Limerick arrived, they met disaster and ended up settling in the Bahia Blanca area in the province of Buenos Aires.

A trickle of emigration continued from Westmeath until 1914. Two of my own grand-aunts, Julia and Ellen McCormick, emigrated from Westmeath as recently as 1910. Italy was the great 20th century source of emigration to Argentina. Viva Irlanda y Viva Italia.

So, such wonderful sounding places in Argentina as Rojas, Carmen de Areco, Salto, San Antonio de Areco, Monte, San Andres de Giles, Mercedes, Venado Tuerto (founded by Edward Casey), Chascomus, Canuelas, Realico (founded by Tomas Mullally), Mar del Plata, Pergamino, Villa Gral, Belgrano, Loberia, Tucuman and Bahia Blanca are household names in places in Ireland, like Ballymore, Streamstown, Moate, Moyvore, Bishopstown, Ballynacargy, Castlepollard, Walshestown, Athlone, Ballymahon, Carrick-Edmund, Kilrane and Castletownbeare.

As readers will have noticed, I have relations in Argentina. In fact, a multitude of relatives. All originated from Westmeath, and the family name was and is McCormick. My maternal grand-mother was McCormick. The first to go to Argentina was William McCormick who was born in 1844 in Bishopstown, Co. Westmeath, and went to Argentina in 1866. It took him months to get there by sailing ship. He settled in Salto in Buenos Aires Province, married Margaret Maxwell in 1883, who was from Ballilnagore, Co. Westmeath. They had five children, Juan

Jose, Julian, Santiago, Lucia and Brigida. Juan Jose visited Ireland frequently and also visited the United States. Lucia married a Bernardo Kenny. I have met a daughter of theirs, Margarita Kenny who has been a well known Argentine singer. William McCormick died in 1904, never having returned on a visit home. Margaret Maxwell, who had been born in 1855, died in Argentina. Her sister, Mary, and brother, Patrick, also went to Argentina. The next McCormick to emigrate was James, a cousin of William, in 1882. He also was born in Bishopstown, Co. Westmeath, in 1852, and married Ana Casey in Argentina, who was also from Bishopstown. James became an estanciero in Roque Perez in Buenos Aires Province, an area where few Irish people went. They had a family of nine, Juan Tomas, Catalina, Santiago, Daniel, Ana Maria, Guillermo, Patricio, Cornelio and Leon Bernardo. Three of their children were sent to Ireland to be educated with Juan Tomas and Santiago going to Rockwell College, Co. Tipperary, and Catalina to Dublin. The boys are to be seen on the rugby and cricket teams of Rockwell College in photos taken in 1914. Their brother, Daniel, became head of the Radical Party in Roque Perez, and also a member of the Provincial Parliament of Buenos Aires. Ana is still alive, aged 91, and living in Roque Perez. There are very few of this generation still alive, whose parents went from Ireland. In 1910, as already mentioned, two of my grand-aunts, Julia and Ellen McCormick, left for Argentina to join their cousins, the McCormicks, mentioned above. Julia married George Ronayne in Argentina. He was from Cork and she was from Walshestown, Mullingar, Co. Westmeath. She returned on two occasions. They had three children, Con, Bridie and John. All are dead. I was at John's funeral last October, while in Argentina. Ellen married Louis Cloud (a French name). Their children were Horacio, Enrique, Beba and Roberto, with only the latter living. I met him for the first time in January 1992.

I have met descendants of most of my relatives who emigrated, while on three visits to Argentina since 1989. That was the year of my first visit when I went to see the country I had heard so much about for as long as I can remember. Lots of letters and photos from Argentina through this century had maintained contact. I encountered enormous warmth, affection and friendliness from all my relatives, only one of whom I had ever met, as well as great friendliness from everyone I met. This is typical of Latin Americans. Today, there are about 350,000 Argentines of Irish descent. Many of the younger generation have moved to the cities and are to be found in all walks of life. Of course, many still work their estancias. Ireland has diplomatic relations with Argentina, and its current ambassador is Mr Bernard Davenport who is also accredited to Venezuela which also has Irish connections. Names like Kavanagh and Rossiter crop up there. Back in Argentina, I met lots of people of Irish descent. Some names I encountered were McCabe, Wade, Murphy, McCormick, Fitzsimons, Healy, Cunningham, Rush, Richards, McLoughlin, Fay, Ronayne, Kenny, Ennis, Leyden and Kearney.

The population of Argentina is currently 32 million, with 40% of Italian origin, followed by people of Spanish origin, and the third largest grouping of Arabic descent. Indeed, there are people of just about every racial background, and it has one of the largest Jewish populations in the world. Some people have kept in touch with their Irish relatives, but for many people contact has been lost twenty, forty, sixty and eighty years ago. Now, there is the added difficulty of language for people wishing to resume contact. *The Buenos Aires Standard* ceased publication in the 1960s, but the English language daily *The Buenos Aires Herald* marked its 115th anniversary in 1991.

One Spring day, September 21st, 1991, I visited the town of San Antonio de Areco in the Province of Buenos Aires, north of the city of Buenos Aires, to see its famous Gaucho Museum. The parish priest is a Palatine padre from Galway who took me to a big remate (auction). It was a cattle auction of 500 cattle on the estancia San Ramon of the Duggan family (originally from Ballymahon, Co. Longford). There is a town named Duggan in the same area, as well as one named Diego Gaynor. Prior to the auction, there was a big asado for a few hundred people comprising workers on the Duggan estancia, folk from neighbouring estancias, prospective buyers and visitors. Seated opposite me at the asado was a woman named McDermott of Wexford origin. Indeed, at that remate, there were others of Irish descent like Oliver Clancy, Michael Cox and Guillermo Keilliff. Elsewhere in San Antonio, I met another person of Wexford origin, Anselmo Devereux. To visit the nearby cemetery was like visiting an Irish cemetery with tombstones showing Longford names like Farrell, Geoghegan and Campbell; Brennan from Wexford; O'Farrell and Morgan from Cork and Brady, Geraghty, Murray, Mooney and Kelly from Westmeath. Of course, the intense heat reminded one that one was not in an actual Irish cemetery. It was hot enough to be bitten by mosquitos.

Argentina is equal in size to all the Common Market countries, and the Province of Buenos Aires is the size of France. It has four climates. It stretches from the spectacular Iguazu waterfalls of the North to Tierra del Fuego in the South. Its vineyards, tea plantations, fields of sugar cane, oil fields, pampa grasslands, millions of cattle and sheep, potato fields, skiing resorts, seaside resorts and magnificent Buenos Aires, with eleven million people, give it resources beyond our wildest dreams, and made Argentina one of the richest countries in the world between 1870 and 1950. It is the country which warmly welcomed Irish emigrants from the 1820s onwards, and is always assured of a special place in the hearts of people in Ireland, with relatives there.

TRACING YOUR LEITRIM ANCESTORS

by Sean O Suilleabhain
Leitrim Co. Librarian

COUNTY LEITRIM - LOCATION AND SIZE

Leitrim, one of Ireland's thirty-two counties, is in the province of Connacht,in the North-West of Ireland. It is exceptionally rural with it's biggest town, Carrick-on-Shannon, having no more than 2,000 population. It is shaped like a figure eight and at it's greatest length it stretches for almost 70 miles from the Co. Longford border to Tullaghan village on the Atlantic Ocean.

Even by Irish standards it is an exceptionally beautiful, unspoilt, unpolluted and friendly county. The lack of any major industry, a problem in other ways, has helped to maintain it's legendary heritage and character.

DIVISIONS

Leitrim has 17 civil parishes, these are divided up into a total of almost 1,200 townlands. The townland is the smallest division of territory in Ireland. The County is also divided into 24 Roman Catholic parish divisions. These are more frequently used than the civic parish divisions and are the basis for most organisational activities within the County.

POPULATION - A SAD STORY

Leitrim is truly a land of legend, story and song, but the saddest story of all is the continuous depopulation of the County since the days of the "Great Famine" of 1845-51. For two centuries Ireland, as a whole, has been badly effected by emigration but nowhere, has the scourge of emigration ravaged and pillaged so desperately as in County Leitrim. Just look at the Census figures since 1841:

YEAR	POPULATION
1841	155,297
1851	111,897
1871	95,562
1891	78,618
1911	63,582
1936	50,908
1956	37,056
1971	28,360
1991	25,297

Emigration has decimated Leitrim. What started at the time of the Famine has continued right down to the present day, and there are no indications that it is likely to be reversed in the near future.

The result is that Leitrim sons and daughters are scattered throughout the globe but particularly through the English speaking world. Estimates suggest that there are at least 40 million people in America of Irish descent. If that is so, then there has to be about one million people there with Leitrim ancestry. It is hard to comprehend how there can be one million people with Leitrim roots in the United States alone, yet there are only 25,000 native Leitrim people living in the historic county of Leitrim. With figures like that it's no wonder Leitrim needed a genealogical service as large numbers of the descendants of these emigrants want to re-establish their ancestral links with Leitrim.

STARTING A GENEALOGICAL SERVICE FOR LEITRIM
Until the early 1980s trying to trace ancestors in Leitrim, like all other Irish counties, was like trying to find the proverbial needle in a reek of hay. Records were scattered in various locations and, worse still, there were no indexes to facilitate ease of access. Leitrim County Library, where many of the enquiries ended up, decided to try to get all the records in the one place and to index them. The key to producing indexes to vast stores of records was the use of youth training schemes under FAS, the national training authority.

INDEXING SCHEMES
So far, five major indexing projects have been organised:

1. CHURCH RECORDS

    All records of baptism, marriage and death for all parishes, all religions, were indexed up to 1900. This work finished in 1985 and dealt with about 250,000 records.

2. NEWSPAPERS

    A project to index Leitrim newspapers has been in progress since 1987. All newspapers from 1850 to 1882 have been indexed and others are in progress.

3. GRAVEYARD INSCRIPTIONS

    All inscriptions in cemeteries in Leitrim were transcribed and indexed.

4. COMPUTERISATION

The major project in progress at present is transferring the index of church records from cards. Some smaller groups of records such as the printed valuation of all properties in the 1850s have already been computerized.

5. INTERVIEWS

Leitrim Co. Library has also organised a project to interview old residents of the county about local history, folklore and related subjects.

LEITRIM HERITAGE CENTRE

While the above projects were in progress and as the number of genealogical enquiries increased, it became obvious that a full-time, professionally staffed genealogical service was required. In 1986 Leitrim Heritage Centre was set up to provide such a service. The service is based in the County Library in Ballinamore and operates full-time all the year round. Being attached to the Library means that staff have access to a wide variety of local studies material like newspapers, archives, original registers on microfilm, estate papers, directories etc, as well as advice on matters requiring local knowledge and expertise.

GETTING A SEARCH DONE

In 1992 the cost of a basic search with Leitrim Heritage Centre is £45. A full report costs £60. A basic or short search is designed to establish the essential details of the family required while a full report means checking and providing information from every available source. It is fair to say that Leitrim Heritage Centre provides one of the most advanced and well-organised County genealogical services available in Ireland.

MAIN SOURCES

There are five main sources which are the backbone of genealogical research in Ireland, and their order of importance could probably be given as follows:
(1) Church records of baptism, marriage and death.
(2) Civil Records of birth, marriage and death 1864-. Protestant marriages 1845-.
(3) Griffith's Valuation, (1857).
(4) Tithe Surveys 1823-38.
(5) 1901 and 1911 Census.

OTHER SOURCES

There are numerous other records which can, in certain cases, be useful. Some available in print are:

'Census' of Ireland 1659: a poll tax return.

Flax Growers' Bounty List 1796: nearly 1,500 names of farmers in Co Leitrim arranged by parish.

Town Directories c.1824-.

Encumbered Estates Court Rentals and particulars of sale c.1850-.

Burke's Landed Gentry of Ireland.

Histories of particular families.

Documentary sources mainly available in the National Archives and National Library of Ireland are:

1. Religious census returns 1740 and 1766; searches in 1841 and 1851 census (done in the Public Record Office of Ireland c.1910-22 before the destruction of the records) for determining age for old age pension. The first national census returns available for the whole of Ireland are for 1901 and 1911.
2. Copies of Hearth Money Rolls 1660s (none available for Co Leitrim).
3. Memorials in the Registry of Deeds 1708-.
4. Field books of townland valuations 1830s, tenement valuation 1857 and annual revisions of this valuation; also valuation maps 1830-.
5. Election poll books and lists of free-holders entitled to vote.
6. Workhouse records: admission registers and minute books of the Boards of Guardians of Poor Law Unions c.1840-.
7. Wills: copies of wills probated in the local District Probate Registry available from 1858.
8. Court records.
9. National Board of Education: salary books and registers of correspondence with schools c.1832-.
10. School roll books and pupils' registers.
11. Irish Land Commission sale papers c.1880-.
12. Estate maps, rent rolls and leases.
13. Records of the Royal Irish Constabulary: recruits serving in British Army regiments and professional records.
14. List of individuals holding dog licences.
15. Registers of convicts.
16. Outrage papers.
17. Shipping records.

Sources without indexes are of limited value.

COMMON NAMES IN LEITRIM

The most common surnames in Leitrim are, in order of numbers:
McGowan   Reynolds   Rooney   Flynn   Kelly   Gallagher   Moran
Dolan   McLoughlin   McMorrow

LEITRIM NAMES

Most of the above names are not essentially Leitrim names but can be found in other counties as well. Surnames which are found almost exclusively in Leitrim, are:
Bohan   Clancy   Conefrey   Darcy   Duignan   Guckian   Heslin
McGloin   McKeon   McTiernan   Mulvey   O'Rourke   Shanley

ANGLICISED NAMES

Leitrim has numerous anglicised surnames and in most cases the Irish form and the anglicised form can be found in use, side by side. The origin of these anglicised surnames was that when an English official came across an Irish name he was unfamiliar with he gave it an English language equivalent. For example Guihen or Gooheen is a common name in Leitrim. In the Irish language "Gaoth" means "wind". At some stage some gam of an official decided that Guihen should be translated to the English name Wynne. Thus some families began to call themselves Wynnes and others retained the original Guihen.

Numerous other examples can be found in Leitrim; such as:

IRISH	ANGLICISED
Mulvanerty	Blessing
Gildea	Benison
Guckian	Hackett
McSharry	Foley
Colreavy	Grey
McNama	Creamer
Fahey	Green
McCusker	Cosgrave

HOW FAR CAN YOU GO BACK

If you can trace your ancestors back to the 1820s, you are doing well. That is certainly the case in Leitrim at least. Of Leitrim's 24 Catholic parishes, only 7 have records back to the 1820s. A further 8 have records to the 1840s. The final third has records which do not begin until the

1850s at the earliest. Church of Ireland (Anglican or Episcopalian) records are poorer still. (For two thirds of the parishes in Ireland the pre 1870 baptismal and burial registers and pre 1845 marriage registers were destroyed in the Public Record Office Dublin in 1922). Most Church of Ireland parish records only begin in the 1870s for baptisms and burials; there are few marriage registers surviving before civil registers begin in 1845. Civil registration starts in 1864 for all births, marriages and deaths and for Protestant marriages from 1845. It is important to note that in some instances the Leitrim Heritage Centre have had earlier registers made available for indexing than those filmed by the National Library of Ireland and the Public Record Office of Northern Ireland. For example for the Catholic parish of Bornacoola registers have been indexed from 1824 and Outeragh from 1841 and for the Presbyterian Church of Drumkeerin baptismal registers have been indexed from 1797 (only filmed from 1834).

Roman Catholic church registers indexed by Leitrim Heritage Centre:

Parish	Baptisms	Marriages	Burials
Annaduff	1849-1900	1849-1900	1849-1900
Aughavas	1845-1900	1845-1900	1845-1900
Ballyaghameehan	1851-1900	1844-69, 1875-1900	
Ballinaglera	1883-1900	1887-1900	
Bornacoola	1824-37, 1950-1900	1824-1900	1824-1900, 1854-1900
Carrigallen	1829-1900	1841-1900	1841-60 (Missing 1860-99)
Cloonclare	1841-1900	1850-1900	
Cloone	1823-1900	1823-1900	1823-77, (gap 1878-1900)
Drumlease	1859-1900	1859-1900	
Drumreilly Upp.	1878-1900	1870-1900	
Drumreilly Lowr.	1867-1900	1893-1900	
Fenagh	1825-1900	1826-1900	1825-94 (gap 1895-1900)
Glenade	1867-1900	1866-1900	
Gortletteragh	1830-39, 1841-1900	1826,1831-34, 1849-1900	1826-38,1852-68 (gap 1869-1900)
Inishmagrath	1834-38, 1881-1900	1834-38, 1881-1900	1834-38, 1881-1900
Killargue	1853-1900	1852-1900	
Killasnet	1852-68, 1879-97	1852-70, 1879-97	1852-65 (gap 1866-1900)

Killinummery	1828-45,	1827-45,	1829-45
	1849-1900	1849-1900	(gap 1846-1900)
Killtoghert	1826-1900	1832-1900	1832-53,
			1867-88
			(gap 1889-1900)
Killtubrid	1841-1900	1841-1900	1847-72
			(gap 1873-99)
Kinlough	1835-1900	1840-1900	1867-1900
Mohill	1836-1900	1836-1900	1836-1900
Murhaun	1861-1900	1867-1900	
Outeragh	1841-1900	1841-1900	

Church of Ireland church registers indexed by Leitrim Heritage Centre:

Parish	Baptisms	Marriages	Burials	PRONI Microfilms
Annaduff	1879-1900	1845-1900	1879-1900	
Ballaghameehan	1877-1900	1859-1900	1877-1900	MIC 1/232
Carrigallen	[1883-	1845-	1874-]	MIC 1/290
Cloonclare	1816-1900	1816-1900	1816-1900	MIC 1/268
Cloone	1880-1900	1845-1900	1880-1900	
Dowra	1877-1900		1877-1900	
Drumlease	1827-	1828-	1827-11,	MIC 1/265
			1879-	
Drumreilly	1877-1900	1840-1900	1877-1900	
Drumshando	1886-1900	1845-1900	1885-1900	
Farnaught	1883-1900		1892-1900	
Fenagh	1883-1900	1854-1900	1883-1900	
Inishmagrath	1877-1900		1877-1900	
Kilargue	1879-1900	1894-1900	1879-1900	
Killasnet	1877-1900	1846-1900	1863-1900	MIC 1/269
Killegar	1878-1900	1845-1900	1878-1900	MIC 1/222
Killinummery	1884-1900	1845-1900	1856-1900	MIC 1/264
Kiltubrid	1883-1900	1845-1900	1883-1900	
Mohill	1783-1813,	1783-1813,	1804-1809,	
	1832-1900	1832-1900	1836-1900	
Newtowngore	1877-1900	1846-1900	1877-1900	
Outeragh	1833-1900	1833-1900	1833-1900	
Rossinver	1876-1900	1845-1900	1876-1900	

Presbyterian church registers indexed by Leitrim Heritage Centre:

Parish	Baptisms	Marriages	Burials	PRONI Microfilms
Carrigallen	1829-1900	1835-1900	1880-1900	MIC 1P/163
Creevelea		1854-1900		
Drumkeerin	1797-1900	1835-1900	1880-1900	
(Co Cavan)				

Methodist church registers indexed by Leitrim Heritage Centre:

Parish	Baptisms	Marriages	Burials	PRONI Microfilms
Ballinamore	1882-			MIC 1E/55
Drumshando	1840-1900	1866-1900		
Inishmagrath		1886-1900		
Manorhamilton	1876-1900	1865-1900		
Mohill	1882-1900	1882-1900		
Newtowngore		1882-1900		
Boyle & Ballyfarnon		1883-1900		
(Co Roscommon)				

* Ballinamore & Newtowngore Wesleyan Methodist Circuit (known as Mohill Circuit before 1914; united with Killashandra Circuit 1929) with churches at Mohill, Ballinamore and Newtowngore.

WHERE DO ENQUIRIES COME FROM

In 1990 our statistics show that enquiries came from the following countries:

> U.S.A.   53%
> Ireland   21%
> England   11%
> Australia 6%
> Canada   6%
> Others   3%

Of those who called in person to the Centre the figure is even higher from the U.S.A. at 62%. It is interesting to note that Leitrim exiles and their descendants are now scattered throughout the U.S.A. In 1990 a breakdown of enquiries showed that they had come from 31 different states, with New York, New Jersey and California being the most prominent.

FAMOUS EMIGRANTS

Many of Leitrim's emigrants became famous in their country of adoption. Robert Strawbridge, born in Drumsna, Co. Leitrim, was the first man to take Methodism to America. Two Australian Prime Ministers of this century, Stanley Melbourne Bruce and Francis Forde, were both sons of Leitrim exiles.

THE FUTURE

With computerisation of records in progress the final phase in a major undertaking will ensure that Leitrim ancestors can be traced, if it is at all possible. Leitrim Heritage Centre, which operates as a non-profit making body, is pleased to be able to assist those of Leitrim ancestry who may be anxious to re-establish their long lost contact with their ancestral homeland.

Leitrim Heritage Centre can be contacted at The County Library, Ballinamore, Co. Leitrim, Phone (078) 44012.

PATTERNS OF MARRIAGE
IN NINETEENTH AND TWENTIETH-CENTURY IRELAND

by Dr. Sean Connolly
University of Ulster

Marriage is a subject of central importance to the family historian. Without it there would in fact be no family history – or at least not of a kind that most people would wish to enquire into too closely. Today marriage, in America and Europe at least, is primarily a personal matter, an arrangement between two individuals. But in Ireland, up to the relatively recent past, that has not been the case. This was a predominantly rural society, where land, parcelled out into small family farms, was the central resource. As a result marriage, with all its implications for the transmission of such land from one generation to the next, was something to be carefully planned and organised, and often a source of jealousy, apprehension and conflict.

The most important and powerful form of control exercised over the marriage of individuals was that of the family. This took the form of the arranged marriage or match. Families with a marriageable son or daughter entered into negotiations with other families of the same social status. The purpose of the negotiations was to determine the size of the dowry the bride would bring with her. This would consist of livestock or other goods, or most commonly of cash, and would be expected to be proportionate to the size of the farm her husband-to-be held or expected to inherit. The negotiations were sometimes conducted through a professional matchmaker. If the parents of both parties were still alive, they took the leading part in the negotiations: there are well documented cases of couples who met one another for the first time at the church on the day of their wedding. If a man had already taken over the farm on the death of his father, he negotiated his own match, and also that of his sisters.

It used to be believed that the arranged marriage or match was a new development of the second half of the nineteenth century. This belief was based mainly on the comments of the wide range of tourists, political commentators and self-appointed experts who visited Ireland in the decades before the Famine of 1845-50, and who attributed a large part of its social problems to the free and easy attitude to marriage that supposedly prevailed among the rural population.

Low expectations and an inherent fecklessness, it was repeatedly claimed, left the children of the rural lower classes free to marry as and when they pleased, often in their mid or late teens. The large numbers of children that inevitably resulted were reared in hastily erected sod huts, on a diet of potatoes grown on whatever small patch of land the family could acquire. Parents assisted in the process by repeatedly subdividing holdings to allow as many as possible of their offspring to set up their own households, covering the landscape with a proliferation of tiny patches of land. Such comment, however, was misconceived.

In part it reflected the panic induced by the runaway growth of Irish population, from around 4 million in 1780 to over 8 million sixty years later, as well as the universal desire to find someone, most commonly the poor themselves, to blame for the problem of poverty. In part it reflected a failure to appreciate the complexity of Irish rural society, with its complex gradations of large farmer, farmer, small farmer, cottier and labourer. In reality, we now know, the arranged marriage was already well established in early nineteenth-century Ireland. With the landless labourer, who had nothing much to lose and whose family could offer no inducements to enforce obedience, it may well have been that, as was reported from County Clare in the mid-1830s, 'an acquaintance begun the night before at a wake or a dance is sometimes consolidated the next morning into matrimony'. On the other hand, as the same government enquiry was told by witnesses in Queen's County, 'the small farmer's son, who has a little money, expects and seeks for as much, at least, in a wife, and the negotiations on this score with the girl's parents become a complete "Smithfield bargain", every shilling in money or stock, on either side, being carefully brought into the account, and set against the other party's means'.

Bargains were concluded, according to another account, 'by sitting up the whole night, talking over the terms, drinking whiskey and smoking tobacco'. The small holdings that multiplied so rapidly in the years before 1845, it is now recognised, were mainly on the poorer land, bog or mountain side. The most fertile land remained in substantial holdings, passed on intact through a succession of single male heirs who were expected to arrange their marriages in accordance with the family's overall economic strategy.

If the arranged marriage was already well known in early nineteenth century Ireland, however, there is no doubt that from the middle of the century family control became considerably more restrictive. This was partly due to a change in social structure: the Famine swept away above all the landless labourers and small holders, whose attitude to marriage had been relatively easy going, leaving behind the farmers among whom the mercenary match was already well established. (A horse kept on a middle sized farm in 1845, it has been pointed out, had a better chance of surviving the next few years than a labourer working for the same farmer.) But there were also other changes. Rising prosperity brought new expectations, pushing up the level of resources expected before a couple could undertake marriage. A move from tillage farming to pasture meant that there were fewer employment opportunities for those who did not inherit the family farm. Parents lived longer, so that sons and daughters had to wait longer for the inheritance that would enable them to marry. In the 1830s and 40s farmers had typically married at around 28 or 29, already four years later than labourers. By 1911 the average age at marriage for all men was 33, for women 28.

Rural Ireland in the early and mid-twentieth century was not just a land of middle-aged brides and grooms. It was also a land of lonely bachelors and spinsters. Census statistics suggest that more than one person in four never married at all. Some of these were sons and daughters for whom the farm or dowry had come too late to change the habits of half a lifetime. But most were the real victims of the arranged marriage system: those who were not chosen to inherit the family land, or to receive the single dowry which was normally the most a farming family could afford. For them the prospects were bleak. A fortunate few could be set up in other careers: as priests, shopkeepers, publicans, nurses. But these were generally the children of the best off families. For most the choice was between a life of permanent celibacy at home, or emigration. There is thus a direct connection between the arranged match and the huge outflow of emigrants which by the end of the nineteenth century had taken two out of every five Irish-born people then living to other parts of the world.

What sort of family relationships did marriages entered into in this calculating and mercenary spirit give rise to? The general image is a fairly harsh one. The Irish husband, it was claimed in 1812, 'considers his wife as his slave . . . [and] assumes over the partner of his bed an authority which is seldom claimed or submitted to in England'. The lower status of women, another visitor noted twenty years later, 'may be inferred from her being worse clothed, and from her being the first to suffer privations . . . She is made the drudge and the slave. The man's pride will not suffer him to ask alms, but he sends forth his wife and children as beggars. In an improving district, shoes and stockings are first seen on the men'. Even in the more prosperous second half of the nineteenth century it is clear that women bore the brunt of any hardship. Women normally live longer than men; but in late nineteenth-century rural Ireland their life expectancy was actually less, and this has been attributed to poorer diet. Women also continued, especially in the west of Ireland, to perform heavy physical work. A saying from Dingle, in County Kerry, recorded in the early twentieth century, was: 'If I don't get married this year, I'll have to buy an ass.'

The second important form of control exercised over marriages was that of the church. In the first place all of the churches sought to enforce their own moral laws, forbidding extra-marital sexual activity and also bigamy. Secondly there was the ecclesiastical prohibition on marriages between close relatives. The Catholic church, responsible for three quarters of the population, forbade marriage between first, second and even third cousins. This regulation proved difficult to enforce. In a society where marriage was looked on as an important bond between whole families, there was considerable pressure to cement existing relationships by negotiating the union of persons who were already related. Most clergymen also sought to discourage marriages between couples who did not have the consent of their parents, or who in their opinion did not have the resources to support a family, as well as marriages with persons of other religious denominations. The central mechanism for enforcing these different regulations was the requirement that couples should be married only by the clergyman of their place of residence. If they sought to be married elsewhere, they would require a licence from the church authorities, and a letter from their own priest or minister certifying that they were free to marry. It was above all to ensure that such information was accurate that each clergyman was expected to keep a register of the births and marriages at which he officiated.

The overall supervision which the churches exercised over sexual behaviour worked quite well. Illegitimacy rates – especially among Catholics – were half or less the level recorded in England at the same period. The proportion of Irish brides pregnant when they came to the altar was also considerably lower. But there were problems. It was not always possible to keep track with any confidence of persons who moved from place to place: soldiers and servants were for this reason regarded with particular suspicion by the church authorities.

Catholics and Presbyterians, thwarted by their own clergy, sometimes applied instead to the Church of Ireland incumbent, who as the minister of the established church could not refuse them. Couples of all denominations also resorted to 'couple beggars': suspended or unlicensed clergymen who, taking advantage of various loopholes in ecclesiastical law, were willing, for a fee, to marry anyone who applied to them. In other cases again couples denied marriage simply eloped together. To resort in this way to the minister of another denomination, to a couple beggar or to elopement was of course to risk being ostracised by family, community and church. In many cases, however, what was involved was a form of moral blackmail. Faced with the threat of conspicuous and long running scandal in family or neighbourhood, parents and clergy were generally willing to compromise, allowing the rebellious couple to make their peace by an act of public penance and receive official sanction for their union.

The third form of control exercised over marriages was that of the community or neighbourhood. Marriage, in a close knit rural society, could not be a purely individual, or even a family affair. Decisions affected too many others. At any one time, for example, there were likely to be only a limited number of men and women of the right age to marry. If an elderly man or woman married a much younger partner, therefore, they were using their superior economic power to 'steal' the bride or groom intended for a member of the younger generation.

Second marriages also raised serious problems of interest to the whole community: a man who married twice either disinherited the children of his first wife, or else left a second family likely to be turned out by his heirs after his death. Either way the scene was set for conflict, disharmony, and the burdening of the neighbourhood with destitute children. Hence marriages where there was a major disparity in age between the partners, or where one of them had been married before, were commonly met with noisy demonstrations – the Irish equivalent of the 'rough music' or 'charivari' of England and continental Europe – where crowds surrounded the house of the offenders to sound horns, fire guns, and otherwise make clear their disapproval of what had taken place.

Less easy at first sight to interpret than the 'horning' of the partners in unpopular unions are the displays of aggression that frequently greeted marriages that did not in themselves give any apparent cause for offence. In the late eighteenth and early nineteenth centuries, for example, there were numerous complaints regarding the custom of groups of men going round on the 1 May each year to demand a tribute – decorated 'May Balls' accompanied by money for drink – from couples married during the preceding year. A later custom of similar character was the attendance at weddings of the Strawboys, men dressed in straw, women's clothes or other disguises who turned up uninvited at the wedding feast to claim drink, food, and a dance with the bride. At times both practices were no more than a piece of colourful folk custom. But in other cases the demand for May balls, or the incursion of the uninvited Strawboys, led to serious violence. Recent studies of the Strawboys suggest that what was involved here was a ritualised letting off of steam: young men whose own turn at marriage had not yet come and indeed, particularly from the mid-nineteenth century onwards, might never come, were given the chance to express the jealousy and resentment they inevitably felt towards the more fortunate couple whose union was being celebrated. The real but controlled aggression of the May ball collectors and Strawboys, in other words, was a price worth paying, in order to defuse tension that might otherwise fester with unpredictable consequences.

All this may seem to present a rather bleak picture of marriage in Ireland over the past two hundred years: a picture dominated by images of the tyranny exercised over individuals by family, churches and neighbours. But it would be wrong to be too pessimistic. Some individuals clearly found the restrictions imposed on them burdensome, and sought to escape, by emigration, elopement or clandestine marriage. The majority, however, seem to have accepted the conventions of their society without question. We have to remember, after all, that the same individuals who in one generation were forced to submit to the choices made by their parents were later to claim a similar authority over the marriages of their own offspring. Nor was the mercenary spirit in which marriage was entered into something imposed on unwilling young lovers by tyrannical elders. Landless labourers, whose parents had no dowries or inheritance to bestow or withhold in order to extort obedience, may have married younger than farmers. But they did not do so in any radically different spirit. Servant boys in County Kerry, it was reported in the mid-1830s, married 'in order to have a person to attend them, and to wash their clothes etc; and the servant girls in order to have a provision for their old age.' There is even a case for saying that marriages entered into with such limited expectations have at least as good a chance of working out as those embarked on in a rosy glow of romantic expectation. But the real point is that there was no alternative. Rural societies in which the family unit is central to the working of the land have always had to require their members to conduct their personal lives in a way that safeguards the common good. If the marriage habits of rural Ireland came to seem unusual it was only because, in the absence of significant industrialisation outside the north-east corner, it remained such a society longer than most of its neighbours.

NOTE ON FURTHER READING

For a fuller account of the issues covered here, including source references for all quotations, see S. J. Connolly, 'Marriage in Pre-Famine Ireland', in Art Cosgrove (ed), *Marriage in Ireland* (Dublin: College Press, 1985). For the role of the Catholic church see S. J. Connolly, *Priests and People in Pre-Famine Ireland 1780-1845* (Dublin, 1982). There is an excellent short survey of the status of women in the opening chapter of Catriona Clear, *Nuns in Nineteenth-Century Ireland* (Dublin, 1987).

THE MOVEMENT OF BRITISH SETTLERS INTO ULSTER DURING THE SEVENTEENTH CENTURY

by Dr W. A. Macafee
University of Ulster

The aim of this paper is to examine the movement of British settlers into Ulster during the seventeenth century and their spread throughout the province. The first part of the paper discusses the sources which are available to reconstruct the numbers at various times throughout the century. The second part of the paper considers the various phases of colonisation between 1600 and 1700 looking at the numbers involved, why they came, and where they settled. Table 1 gives details of the numbers of Scottish and English households in each of the nine counties of Ulster during the 1660s and Table 2 gives estimates of Ulster's population, particularly the British component, at various times throughout the period. Figure 1 is intended to give a general idea of the various parts of the province allocated to English and Scottish undertakers and Figure 2 outlines the counties and baronies of the historic province of Ulster.

SOURCES

As far as the first half of the seventeenth century is concerned there are several surveys extant for those areas of the province affected by the official Plantation e.g. Carew's Survey of 1611, Pynnar in 1619 and Phillips and Hadsor in 1622. However the first source available for virtually the entire province are the Muster Rolls for c.1630. There are a number of problems associated with the use of this source. Firstly the figures refer only to adult males. Various ratios have been suggested to convert these into families and households. Robinson in his study of the Plantation in Co. Tyrone found that, in those instances where both the number of families and adult males were given, the number of adult males per family ranged from 1.8 to 2.7. Perceval-Maxwell used a conversion factor of 2. It is difficult to choose between these ratios mainly because we know very little about the size and structure of households at that time. Morgan's study of Blaris in the late seventeenth century indicated a completed family size of approximately 5 and early eighteenth-century statistics suggest a mean household size of 4.7. It is unlikely that household size during the seventeenth century was greater. For the purposes of this paper a conversion factor of 2 and a mean household size of 4.7 have been chosen.

The second problem associated with the Muster Rolls is the fact that, in common with all statistical sources for the seventeenth century, they seriously underestimate the actual population. It is of course difficult to assess the full extent of this underestimation. In some cases figures do not exist for certain areas: in Donegal, for example, no muster is available for the barony of Kilmacrenan, yet an earlier report of the Provost-Marshal indicated some 128 Scots and English in the barony. In Co. Londonderry there is no muster extant for the lands of the Salter's Company. Even in the case of those musters which are extant it is fairly clear that under-recording is a serious problem.

The extant Muster Rolls produce a total of 13,147 adult males in Ulster in 1630, a figure consistent with Wentworth's contemporary estimate of 13,092 British men aged between 16 and 60 in the province during the 1630s. Using the conversion factor of two, mentioned above, this produces a figure of 6,671 British households in the province of which 3,879 were Scottish and 2,792 English. This suggests a total population in excess of 30,000, with the Scots forming just over 60% of the total. This figure of 30,000 has to be seen as representing the minimum number of British settlers in the province by 1630; obviously there were more than this. An estimate nearer to 40,000 might be more appropriate and indeed even a British population of 50,000 would, by the standards of the later seventeenth century, have been relatively small.

The first source available for the seventeenth century which provides some evidence of the total population of Ulster is dated 1659. This source is generally known as Pender's Census because Pender, who was responsible for its publication in 1939, regarded it as a count of the whole population and, therefore, as a census. More recent opinion, however, considers it to have been a Poll Tax which listed adults over the age of fifteen. Once again a multiplier is required to convert it to a proper census. As mentioned earlier, any evidence we have for the later seventeenth and early eighteenth centuries points to a household size of 5.0 or even less. This would suggest a multiplier lying somewhere between 2.0 and 2.5. When allowance is made for underestimation and evasion, the 'census' suggests a total population for Ulster of around

TABLE 1

British Population in Ulster by County, 1630-1660s

COUNTY	Households 1630			Households 1660s		
	ENG	SCOTS	TOTAL	ENG	SCOTS	TOTAL
ANTRIM	159	665	824	2903	5512	8415
ARMAGH	354	108	462	865	212	1077
CAVAN	296	123	419			
DONEGAL	204	430	634	416	1237	1653
DOWN	553	1570	2123			2973
FERMANAGH	242	244	486			818
LONDONDERRY	677	288	965	1069	703	1772
MONAGHAN				177	47	224
TYRONE	298	460	758	337	842	1179
TOTAL	2783	3888	6671	5767	8553	18111

English and Scots have been identified by surname. Since there are some names which could be either Scots or English, the division can only be approximate.

SOURCES: The 1630 figures are based on the Muster Rolls. These list adult males and these have been converted to households by dividing them by 2.0. The 1660 figures are based on the Hearth Money Rolls, except Down and Fermanagh. The latter are based on S. Pender, *A Census of Ireland* circa 1659, Dublin, 1939. In the case of the 1659 census the household figures were obtained by dividing the number of adults by 2.2

TABLE 2

Population Estimates for Ulster and Ireland 1600-1712

Year	British	Irish	Ulster Total	Ireland Total
1600		180000?	180000?	1100000?
1630	40000*	200000?	240000?	
1670	120000**	230000**	350000**	
1687			1700000+	
1712	270000+	330000+	6000000+	2200000+

* These figures are based on the Muster Rolls for circa 1630

** These figures are based on the Hearth Returns for the 1660s and Pender's Census circa 1659.

\+ These figures are based on the Hearth Returns

300,000.It is difficult to estimate the size of the British in 1659 but given the circumstances after 1641 and the estimates available for later in the century it is unlikely to have been much more than 100,000.

There is a major source, the Hearth Tax Returns, available for the period 1664-69 which does give us a clearer idea of the numbers and geographical distribution of British settlers in the province around the middle of the century. The Hearth Money Tax was introduced into Ireland in 1662 as part of a general revision of the Irish fiscal system. A sum of 2/= per annum had to be paid on all chimneys, stoves and hearths unless the occupier of the house was exempt from payment. Persons whose house and land were worth less than 8/= per annum and whose personal property was worth less than 4 were exempt. Fragments of the Hearth returns are extant for the counties of Antrim (1669), Armagh (1664), Donegal (1665), Londonderry (1663), Monaghan (1663-1665), and Tyrone (1666 and 1670).

Assessment of the accuracy of these returns is very difficult because not only is there the problem of evasion but also that of exemption and there appears to have been considerable confusion among collectors regarding exemption in the early years of the tax. Comparison, by the author, of the Hearth Returns and Poll Tax Returns for the parish of Donagheady in Co. Tyrone suggests that they probably underestimate the British population in the province by 30-40%. Overall it must be said that these early Hearth Returns are probably more useful in giving some impression of the regional spread of the immigrant British population than in producing, even after adjustment, reasonably accurate estimates of total population in the middle of the seventeenth century. Since the Hearth Returns are a count of households a multiplier is necessary to convert them to a census. Once again a factor of 4.7 has been used.

1600-1641

The major thrust of immigration was initiated by the Plantation of Ulster which covered six of the nine counties of the province, Antrim, Down and Monaghan being excluded from the official scheme. This scheme made land available to undertakers and servitors from England and Scotland who were required to settle their estates with tenants from the mainland. Initially colonisation was slow and many undertakers were prepared to let their lands to the native Irish. Perceval-Maxwell in his study of Scottish migration to Ulster during the reign of James I pointed to an acceleration in the rate of Scottish migration between 1613 and 1619. Gillespie's study of settlement in east Ulster also agreed that settlement appeared to have expanded at a greater rate in the second decade of the century. Robinson's study of the Plantation in Tyrone suggested that the influx of British settlers into Tyrone in the period 1618-1622 was possibly greater than, and at least on the same scale as, the entire influx in the preceding seven years. Such a pattern of migration is consistent with other movements of population from the mainland, e.g. the number of English settlers migrating to Virginia was low during the period 1607-17 but by 1618-24 their numbers had increased sevenfold.

Despite this initial influx of settlers, their numbers do not appear to have been as great as the architects of the Plantation scheme would have desired. The Muster Rolls suggest a total British population of some 40,000 persons by 1630 with the Scots forming just over 60% of the total. Clearly, with a settler population at 40,000 the official Plantation was just beginning to make some impact on the ground.

The areas where the colonists chose to settle were influenced by two major factors. Firstly, there was the distribution of the estates of English and Scottish undertakers to which landlords and their agents encouraged or brought over settlers. The majority of settlers arriving in the province during the early years of the Plantation were probably of this type. However, as the century progressed more unaided settlers began to come. The places they chose to settle were often related to their point of entry which, usually, was one of the major ports viz. Derry, Coleraine, Carrickfergus, Belfast, and Donaghadee.

Figure 1 shows the general distribution of the areas where Scottish and English undertakers dominated. In general, with the exception of Co. Down, the Scots were more numerous in the north of the province with the English more predominant in the area of the province stretching from the Lagan valley, through north Armagh, and the Clogher valley. The granting of the county of Londonderry to the London Companies gave them a substantial foothold in the north of the province. Table 1 gives details of the estimated numbers of Scots and English households in each county by 1630. This data show that Scots were most dominant in Antrim and Down where they formed 81% and 74%, respectively, of the settler population. Within Co. Antrim two-thirds of the Scots were to be found on the lands of the Earl of Antrim in the north of the county. In Donegal three-quarters of the Scots were in the barony of Raphoe and in

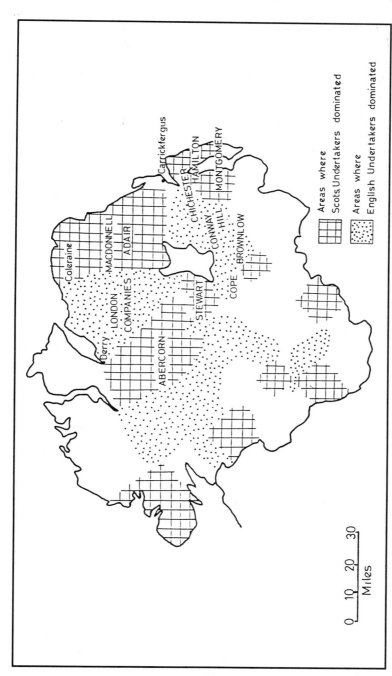

Figure 1: Province of Ulster: Settlement of Scottish and English Undertakers during the Seventeenth Century.

Tyrone they were concentrated in the baronies of Strabane and Mountjoy. In the north of the province the main centres of English colonisation were in Co. Londonderry. Here, the major settlements in the north of the county were around the new towns of Coleraine and Londonderry. In the south of the county in the barony of Loughinsholin there were some 149 households, of which 128 were English.

As mentioned earlier, the great majority of the estates of English undertakers were concentrated in the mid and southern half of the province. Added to this was the fact that the major entry route for English settlers into the province was through the Lagan valley, down the Clogher valley, and into Co. Fermanagh. Settlers moving down this corridor spilled over into south Antrim and north Down but the main thrust was into north Armagh. Here in the barony of O'Neill the British population was completely dominated by English settlers, 230 households in total. English settlers were also prominent in the southern part of the adjacent barony of Dungannon in Co. Tyrone but this area was not as densely settled. This was an area which had been granted to servitors, including Sir Arthur Chichester, and 'deserving' Irish. The northern part of the barony which had been granted to Scottish undertakers was more densely settled and had 147 households, of which 103 were Scottish.

Despite the period of colonisation from 1611, the density and geographical spread of British settlers throughout the province by 1630 was limited. On the basis of these figures it would appear that the bulk of colonists were to be found in the counties of Down, Antrim, Londonderry, Donegal and Tyrone, suggesting that the point of entry was an important factor in producing the pattern of early settlement.

The period after 1630 saw the arrival of further immigrants, particularly from Scotland. This was in response to a number of severe harvest failures during that decade. It is difficult to assess how sustained this immigration was. Certainly, it had halted by the late 1630s when there is evidence of a flow of migrants in the other direction. This outward flow from Ulster was caused by a series of bad harvests in the late 1630s, the effects of which were exacerbated by the actions of the lord deputy, Thomas Wentworth, Earl of Strafford. In 1639 he required all Presbyterians in Ulster to take a strict oath of loyalty, known as the Black Oath, to the established church and king. In order to enforce this decree the army was used and local volunteers were called up, which

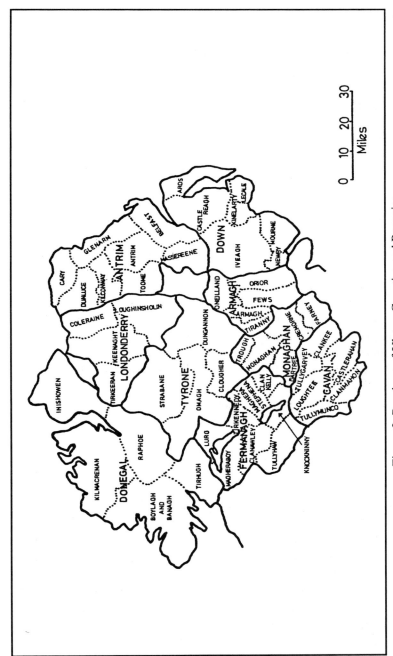

Figure 2: Province of Ulster: Counties and Baronies

took many tenants off their land at a time when they should have been in the fields ploughing and sowing. The quartering of the army on tenants at a time when grain was in short supply, due to a series of bad harvests, simply added fuel to a volatile situation. Those tenants who returned to Scotland at this time were soon joined by many others fleeing from the native Irish who revolted in 1641.

1642-1670

1642 saw the arrival in Ulster of Major-General Robert Monro with an advance force of Scottish troops. This force, to some extent, restored some order in parts of the province but was unable to defeat the Irish. This had to await the arrival of the Cromwellian forces in 1649. The 1640s, therefore, saw the destruction of many plantation settlements which, if they were to recover, required a new influx of settlers. The Scottish and Cromwellian armed forces supplied some of these settlers and the cessation of hostilities saw the return of some of the settlers who had fled in 1641. Moreover, a new influx of settlers began to arrive during the 1650s, attracted, particularly, by low rents and high wages. As in the 1630s, the majority of these new colonists were from Scotland, a country which, throughout the seventeenth century, was the major supplier of migrants to Ulster. Whilst the attraction of cheap land in the province acted as a pull factor on the Scottish migrant and the periodic occurrence of famine in Scotland often acted as the immediate push factor, there were a number of more general push factors which were also important in influencing the decision to emigrate. These were, in particular, a growing population, rent increases, and tenurial re-organisation.

Scottish population had grown substantially during the late sixteenth and early seventeenth centuries. This growth in population placed a considerable strain on fixed resources and both food prices and rents rose sharply. Although there had been considerable economic growth during the relative peace of the reign of James VI, it would appear that the Scottish economy had not expanded sufficiently to allow the country to accommodate its growing population and, throughout the seventeenth century, Scotland was ready and anxious to export people. In addition to these general factors there was one particular change in Scottish economy and society which had a considerable bearing on the decision to migrate. This related to the reorganisation of tenure on estates which was a consequence of the efforts of landlords to improve their estates. Instead of seeing their estates as the direct basis of political power in terms of the number of inhabitants it could support, they began to consider their property as a source of profit. This profit could be increased, they thought, by more efficient management of their estates. As part of the way towards achieving this efficiency, they re-organised the tenurial structure of their estates. In short this meant the removal of 'kindly tenants' (tenants-at-will with no rights to the land other than tradition) or their conversion to leaseholders at a greatly increased rent. Such a change was designed to give the tenant more of a stake in the land thereby encouraging him to carry out improvements. Unfortunately many of the poorer tenants were unable to take advantage of this offer of more security and were driven off the land. These displaced, poorer tenants could, as Perceval-Maxwell has remarked, be expected to respond favourably when offered land in Ireland. Of course the availability of cheap land in Ireland throughout the seventeenth century fluctuated in response to changing circumstances. Clearly an event like the 1641 rebellion had left much land bereft of British tenants so landlords, anxious to resettle these lands, were forced to offer good terms to attract prospective tenants. However, as the lands filled up again and the population increased, the low rents and high wages which had attracted settlers during the 1650s gave way, by the 1660s, to higher rents, static wages and falling agricultural prices. Cullen has suggested that because of these changes in rents, wages and prices, Scottish immigration, in particular, fell off temporarily during the 1660s, although he maintains that Quaker immigration from England held its own during this decade.

Economic motives, however, were not the only factors which encouraged or discouraged the prospective migrant; religious circumstances also played a prominent role. The arrival of the new Scots in Ulster under Monro had led to the establishment of Presbyterianism through the creation of the first presbytery at Carrickfergus on 10 June 1642. Shortly after this some fifteen parishes in counties Antrim and Down made applications to join the presbytery, electing elders and asking to be supplied with preachers. Under the Cromwellian Protectorate various schemes were proposed to curb the power of the Scots in Ulster, ranging from the decree that no Scots officer should be allowed to live in Ulster unless he took an oath of loyalty, to the proposal that the most dangerous Scots living in Ulster should be transplanted to counties Kilkenny, Tipperary and Waterford. Neither of these particular measures were carried out but some action was taken against ministers. In 1650 ministers were given the option of undertaking not to speak against the government or returning to Scotland. In this instance some stipends were confiscated and some ministers were imprisoned for a time. By 1654 the government, whilst not approving of the actions of the Scots in Ulster, decided not to pursue a policy of repression and this resulted in the spread of the Presbyterian religion throughout the province and, therefore, the attraction of settlers particularly from Scotland. By the end of the 1650s the original presbytery at Carrickfergus had been subdivided into four: Down, Antrim, Route (north Antrim) and Laggan in county Donegal. In 1653 it was estimated that there were twenty-four Presbyterian ministers in Ulster; by the end of the 1650s there were nearly eighty.

With the restoration of Charles II, Presbyterians in Ulster had to face further repression. This was particularly severe in 1661-3 under the primacy of Archbishop Bramhall. With the support of local gentry (a notable exception being the Massereene family of Antrim) Bramhall was able to assert the power of the established church: during 1661 sixty-one of the seventy Presbyterian ministers were expelled from their churches. A number fled to Scotland but many continued to preach in barns, houses and even open fields. Bramhall died in 1663 and his successor, Margetson, adopted a more tolerant attitude. Those who had been banished to Scotland returned and, according to Reid, in the four or five years after 1664 the Presbyterian Church in Ulster virtually recovered its former position in the province. By 1669 new churches were being erected 'for the accommodation of those who refused to frequent their parish churches, now either exclusively occupied by the Episcopalian clergy or else so ruined as to be unfit for use'. Conditions in Ulster for non-conformists continued to improve throughout the remainder of the reign of Charles II.

In many ways, despite the periodic attempts to curb Presbyterianism, religious persecution of non-conformists was less severe in Ulster at this time than it was in Scotland and England, thereby making the province very attractive as a haven from the intolerance on the mainland. Religious persecution was particularly acute in south-west Scotland, the major supply area of Scottish immigrants to Ulster. The Covenanters who inhabited this region refused to accept the religious policy of the

Restoration government and, as in Ulster, many of their ministers were expelled from their churches. Unlike Ulster, where conditions improved after 1664, the situation got worse in Scotland, leading eventually to a rising in 1666. In England the Act of Uniformity passed in 1662, which required all ministers to use the revised Prayer Book in their services or resign their livings, probably resulted in some emigration. However the fact that many English settlers in Ulster appear to have remained members of the established church, suggests that, with the possible exception of the Quakers, economic rather than religious motives were more important in influencing the decision to move.

Whatever the motives of the various immigrants to Ulster at this time they do appear to have arrived in considerable numbers. Petty, writing in 1672, was of the opinion that of the 100,000 Scots he estimated to be present in Ireland in 1672, 80,000 of them had arrived after 1650. Certainly the evidence of Pender's 'Census' and the Hearth Returns suggests a British population for the province by the end of the 1660s approaching 120,000, with the Scots forming just over 60% of the total. When these estimates for the 1660s are compared to those for 1630 we find that the British population of the province appears to have trebled in the intervening period. The Scottish population in the province had risen from something like 20,000 in 1630 to at least 60,000 and probably nearer to 70,000 by the late 1660s. At the same time the presence of around 35,000 English colonists, an increase of over 20,000 since 1630, indicates clearly that immigration during this period was not confined to Scots.

The general distribution of Scots and English colonists by the 1660s differed little from that of 1630 with the Scots dominating the north of the province, except for Co. Londonderry and the English more prominent in the south of the province, particularly in the Lagan valley and north Armagh. In Co. Armagh by the 1660s English colonists, at 80%, were still predominant and their numbers throughout the county had more than doubled to 1077 households. The barony of O'Neilland still remained the most important area of English settlement in the county. Clearly this was an area which was benefiting from the English migration along the Lagan valley corridor. The Scottish population had also doubled, but numerically they remained small, and were still concentrated in Fews and the adjacent Barony of Armagh.

In nearby Tyrone the English population had not increased to the same extent. Here, the figures suggest a modest rise of some 13%. Whilst this may have been due to inaccuracies in the available statistics it is more likely to have reflected the fact that as the distance from their port of entry increased the number of colonists decreased. The Scottish population of the county had increased by 83% in the period 1630-1666 and formed 71% of the county's total population. 72% of these Scots were to be found in the baronies of Strabane and Dungannon, and within the latter most of them were in the northern part of the barony around Cookstown and Stewartstown. The increase of Scots around Strabane and the adjacent Barony of Omagh was probably part of the influx of Scots which entered the west of the province through the port of Derry during the 1650s.

The figures for 1630 and 1660 suggest that the city of Derry did not increase its population by very much during the period 1630-1660, and exactly the same can be said of Coleraine. Most of the colonists entering the province through these ports seem to have made their way into the rural areas. In the Derry region the immigrants fanned out into Cos. Londonderry, Tyrone and Donegal. In Co. Donegal most of the Scottish immigrants made their way to the baronies of Raphoe and Kilmacrenan. In Raphoe the number of Scottish families appears to have doubled between 1630 and 1665. Of course none of these figures can be regarded as strictly accurate; at most they give some indication of those areas where immigration is likely to have been heaviest. They do suggest, as might be expected, that the more remote parts of the county such as the baronies of Boylagh and Bannagh still had a very sparse British population. The number of English colonists in Co. Donegal appears to have doubled but they were still only 25% of the total British population of the county. Most of this increase took place in the barony of Inishowen, further reflection of the fact that the immigrants were arriving through the port of Derry.

As far as Londonderry was concerned, the north of the county was much more accessible than the south. Immigrants arrived through either Coleraine or Derry. With the exception of the rural area around Coleraine and parts of the barony of Keenaght, the north of the county was dominated by English colonists. In the barony of Tirkeeran a comparison of surnames for the 1630s with those for 1663 reveals that 51% of the latter were new, and of these 71% were English. In the adjacent barony of Keenaght the corresponding figures were 54% and 62%. In the

Coleraine area the figure was just under 60% for new arrivals, with 53% of these being Scots. The fact that Sir Robert MacClelland had leased the Haberdashers and Clothworkers estates in the earlier part of the century, and had brought in Scottish tenants, created a base to which later settlers not only from Scotland but also from nearby Co. Antrim were attracted.

In the south of the county, in the barony of Loughinsholin, the English colonists were also dominant. The number of households had increased from 149 to 300, of which 221 were English. However, because of the complete absence of any Muster Rolls for the Salters' estate in 1630, the increase was not quite as great as the figures suggest. Nevertheless, surname evidence suggests a massive turnover in the population; some 75% of the surnames listed in 1663 were new. Some Scots had moved into the region, particularly in the area between Maghera and Knockloughrim, but their absolute numbers were still relatively small. As in many of the remoter parts of the province, the Irish population was still very much in the majority. The colonists occupied the new towns and villages and spread along the major natural routeways which linked them. However, their total numbers were insufficient to dominate the whole area and, although they had undoubtedly displaced many of the Irish from the more fertile lowlands, the latter were still able to occupy not only the poorer land but also the pockets of good land amidst the planter population. Indeed areas, such as Culnady and Upperlands which by the end of the century were occupied by Scots, remained exclusively Irish in 1663. South Londonderry, because of its distance from the main ports of entry for immigrants to the county, tended to receive many of its colonists, particularly Scots, from mid-Antrim.

The largest increase in the British population took place in Co. Antrim. Half of the British population of the county occupied mid- and north Antrim; 91% of this British population was Scottish. The Irish and Highlands Scots population in these areas was geographically separated from the Lowland Scots and the small number of English colonists. The other half of the British population occupied the baronies of Belfast and Massereene. The barony of Belfast had almost equal numbers of Scots and English. In the barony of Massereene there was a clear division between the northern and southern parts of the barony. The predominance of Scottish households in the northern half of the barony, reflected the movement of Scots outwards from Carrickfergus and down the Sixmilewater valley spilling as far south as the parish of Killead. Furthermore this was an area where the most important landlords, the Clotworthy family, although English, were sympathetic to Presbyterians. South of Killead, in the parishes of Glenavy, Ballinderry, Magheramesk, Aghalee, Aghagallon and Blaris, English colonists were more numerous, having moved north from the Lagan valley corridor. The estates in this area were owned by families such as the Conways who were less sympathetic to the Scots.

Despite this impression of relatively dense British settlement in County Antrim, there were many parts of the province, later to be occupied by British colonists, which were still sparsely settled at this stage. Colonisation of these areas required a further influx of settlers during the latter years of the seventeenth century. The next section will attempt to examine the extent and timing of that migration, and the religious and economic circumstances both in Ulster and in Scotland which might have acted as push or pull factors influencing migrants.

1670-1700

The early 1670s saw a dramatic worsening of the economic situation in Ulster, the most difficult period being during the Dutch wars of 1672-74. There was probably fairly widespread famine in Ulster in 1674-75. Scotland also suffered famine at the same time. By the late 1670s economic conditions had begun to improve and a period of economic growth ensued in Ulster until confidence was shattered under James II. These improved economic conditions probably led to a resumption of sustained Scottish emigration to the province. The Scottish Privy Council Register, by 1678, was referred to "sundry tenants who, of late, have gone over to Ireland". The upsurge of repression of Covenanters after the Bothwell Bridge uprising in 1679, probably helped to swell numbers crossing the North Channel during the early 1680s.

However, immigration during this period was not confined to Scots. There is also evidence of a contemporary influx from England, particularly into the Lagan valley corridor. As mentioned earlier, this area had been settled by English colonists in the earlier part of the century and Quakers had been arriving since the 1650s, and were probably accompanied by other nonconformists fleeing from persecution by the established church. Morgan's analysis of the register of baptisms, burials, and marriages for the parish of Blaris (which includes the town of Lisburn) confirms this movement and also points to further immigration, particularly in the late 1670s and early 1680s.

However, the economic and associated population growth of Ulster experienced a sharp setback in the late 1680s and early 1690s. Undoubtedly the Williamite war was an important factor but economic confidence had slumped before this, following the accession of James II in 1685. The war of itself led to some devastation but since Ulster was a theatre of hostilities for only a relatively short period of time the direct consequences of war were not as catastrophic as those of the earlier 1641 rebellion. In a sense the main economic effect was to heighten the crisis which was already in existence before war broke out. It also led to the exodus of many settlers, particularly ministers, to Scotland.

With the cessation of hostilities these refugees began to return and were joined by a new wave of immigrants from Scotland, attracted by cheap land. Landlords, with rentals heavily in arrears, were anxious to have these new tenants.According to one pamphleteer, writing in 1712:

> the church proprieters, who for some small advance in the rent of their lands, preferred numbers of those Presbyterians, who had swarmed from Scotland after the late revolution. These new adventurers were in many respects able to out-bid the old tenants, who had been in great measure ruined in the late troubles.

However, cheap land was not the only factor which caused the migration of the 1690s. As Cullen has suggested, the immigration of the early 1690s would have quickly lost impetus, as on previous occasions, had it not been boosted by a further and concentrated influx following the exceedingly bad seasons of 1695-98 in Scotland. Of all the famines in Scotland that of the 1690s is the best documented and it was also the one which burnt itself into the memory of the people much as the Great Hunger of the 1840s was to do in Ireland. It was given various titles, such as 'King William's dear years' and the 'seven ill years'. In fact the bad years lasted for five years from the harvest of 1695 until that of 1700. It appears that Ulster did not suffer from famines during this period so the province must have seemed attractive to persons wishing to run away from the horrors of famine. Estimates of the numbers involved in this migration during the 1690s vary considerably. Contemporaries estimated that 80,000 Scots had come to Ireland since the Battle of the Boyne. Whilst it is generally agreed that these estimates were exaggerated at the time, it is now clear that this post 1690 movement was substantial and made a major contribution to the figure of some 270,000 British in the province by the early eighteenth century. Table 2 gives estimates of the population of Ulster at particular times throughout the seventeenth and early eighteenth centuries.

CONCLUSION

It is now clear that without the influxes of immigrants after 1650 the Plantation in Ulster would, undoubtedly, have suffered a similar fate to the less successful attempts in the remainder of Ireland. If the Plantation had relied exclusively on its initial period of colonisation it is unlikely that by the early eighteenth century the British population in Ulster would even have reached 100,000. This figure is based on a hypothetical calculation of the 40,000 population of 1630 increasing naturally at say 0.8% per annum (a relatively high figure for a pre-industrial population). Furthermore this calculation does not take account of the disruptions caused by the 1641 rebellion. Similarly even if the 120,000 population of 1670 had grown naturally at around 0.8% per annum it would still only have produced a population of 170,000 by 1712. Thus if immigration had ceased after 1630 there would have been a shortfall in the British population in 1712 of at least 170,000 and if it had ceased after 1670 the shortfall would have been some 100,000.

Similarly, the spread of the British population in Ulster although partially controlled by the distribution of Scottish and English undertakers also reflected the basic geography of the province. Londonderry, Coleraine, Carrickfergus, Belfast and Donaghadee were the main ports of entry into the province with the Lagan, the Bann and the Foyle valleys acting as the major arteries along which the colonists travelled into the interior. In general the southern half of the province was dominated by English colonists with the Scots more prominent in the northern half – a fact which is still evident today in the very different dialects spoken in north Antrim and north Armagh.

BIBLIOGRAPHY and REFERENCES

Primary Sources:

Public Record Office of Northern Ireland

Muster Rolls, c.1630: Co. Antrim, D.1759/3C/3; Co. Armagh, T.934; Co. Down, D.1759/3C/1; Co. Fermanagh, T.934; Co. Londonderry, D.1759/3C/2; Co. Tyrone, T.934.

Hearth Money Rolls: Co. Antrim, 1669, T.307; Co. Armagh, 1664, T.604; Co. Donegal, 1665, T.307D; Co. Londonderry, 1663, T.307A; Co. Tyrone, 1666, T.307A.

S. Pender (ed), *A Census of Ireland*, circa 1659 (Dublin, 1939).

Secondary Sources:

L. M. Cullen, 'Population Trends in Seventeenth Century Ireland', *Economic and Social Review*, 6 (1975), 149-165.

R. J. Gillespie, *Colonial Ulster: The Settlement of East Ulster 1600-1641* (Cork, 1985).

G. Hill, *An Historical Account of the Plantation of Ulster at the Commencement of the Seventeenth Century, 1608-1620* (Belfast, 1877).

R. J. Hunter, 'The Settler Population of an Ulster Plantation County', *Donegal Annual*, X (1972), 124-53.

W. Macafee, 'The Colonisation of the Maghera Region of South Derry during the Seventeenth and Eighteenth Centuries', *Ulster Folklife*, 23 (1977), 70-91.

W. Macafee and V. Morgan, 'Population in Ulster, 1660-1760', in P. Roebuck (ed), *Plantation to Partition: Essays in Ulster History in Honour of J. L. McCracken* (Belfast, 1981).

W. Macafee, 'The Population of Ulster, 1630-1841: Evidence from Mid-Ulster', Unpublished D.Phil Thesis, University of Ulster, 1987.

V. Morgan, 'A Case Study of Population Change over Two Centuries: Blaris, Lisburn 1661-1848', *Irish Economic and Social History*, III (1976), 5-16.

M. Perceval-Maxwell, *The Scottish Migration to Ulster in the Reign of James I* (London, 1973) (Reprint U.H.F. Belfast 1990).

P. S. Robinson, 'British Settlement in County Tyrone, 1610-1666' *Irish Economic and Social History*, V (1978), 5-26.

P. S. Robinson, *The Plantation of Ulster: British Settlement in an Irish Landscape, 1600-1670* (Dublin, 1984).

"ON THE FIRST FAIR WIND"

by Gary J. Ford
Travel Editor "Southern Living" U.S.A.

"James Russell 300 in South Carolina"

With this brief entry, my family's life began in America. It meant my great-great-great-great-great-grandfather, James Russell, a newly-arrived immigrant from northern Ireland, received 300 acres of land in the colony of South Carolina. The entry appeared in a listing of 62 other names in the journal of the Colonial Council of South Carolina on 17 January 1771. That entry for 17 January (as well as for 10 January) appears at the end of this article.[1]

For hundreds of Irish immigrants who arrived in the port of Charles Town (now Charleston) in the South Carolina colony, their first footsteps in America are tracked across the pages of the Council Journal. The council was the governing body of the colony, and the journal a transcription of its daily business, such as recording land transactions for arriving protestant immigrants from Ireland. As such, the Council Journal provides an excellent source for genealogists picking up the trail of families who sailed to South Carolina in the mid- to late-18th century. I know, however, where my family went after James Russell crowded into the Council Chamber in 1771. When I look across the gray chop of Charleston harbor today, I want to know where his journey began. Therefore, the entry of 17 January 1771, points me east toward Ireland instead of west to America.

In this article I will describe briefly land transactions noted in the Council Journal, and how to use it and other resources in the archives of the State of South Carolina to find an immigrant's first home in the colony. Then, I will explain how I am using the entry of 17 January (and to some extent that of 10 January) to chase the ghost of James Russell east across the Atlantic and to answer the question: where was his home in northern Ireland?

1. South Carolina Department of Archives and History, Council Journal, 10 and 17 January 1771.

112

Land grants lured many Ulster families to South Carolina from the mid-1700's to the eve of the Revolutionary War. The royal government in Charles Town, anxious to fill up the fertile "back country", began offering land to "poor protestants" as early as 1731. Such land was called "bounties", authorized by the colonial government and paid for by levying taxes on slave sales.[2] Upon arrival, immigrants appeared before the colonial council and produced certificates, usually signed by a church official, stating they were of good character. Then, they petitioned for a warrant of survey. Land was granted on the basis of 100 acres for the head of the family, and 50 acres for every other person in the family. A quit rent of four shillings per 100 acres was due two years after the grant.[3] Throughout the years, the South Carolina government tempted immigrants with various schemes. In 1752, it offered tools and other provisions, as well as 5 pounds for each person between 12 and 50, and 2 pounds 10 shillings for ages 2 to 12.[4] The bounties ended in 1768, but word of the expiration was slow in reaching Ireland. For several years afterward, many poor protestants were given bounty lands once they arrived.[5]

Often, an entry of the Council Journal names the ship upon which the "poor protestants" have recently arrived. Then, it lists the land recipient – usually the head of household, but also single adult sons and daughters. Such a listing cannot be construed as a complete passenger list of a specific ship; often other colonists also appeared to receive land, mixing in with the newly arrived immigrants.

Today, the Council Journal is kept on microfilm at the Department of Archives and History in Columbia, and available for public view. Unfortunately, the volumes of the journal are not indexed by name. Still, to find the date your ancestor appeared before the council is relatively uncomplicated. Staffers show you other land records on microfilm that list land recipient names alphabetically, for which you will find surveys giving you the location of their land, dates of warrant and the date of

2. Jean Stephenson: *Scotch-Irish Migration to South Carolina*, 1772 (1971), p.6-7.
3. Ibid. p.6.
4. Ibid. p.6.
5. Ibid. p.8.

petition. That petition date is the day an ancestor's name appeared in the Council Journal. Then, ask for microfilm of the South Carolina Gazette, which listed arriving ships and sometimes the number of immigrants aboard.

When I found James Russell on 17 January, 1771, I pulled the microfilm of the Gazette for 1770-71, and found this item in the 7 January 1771 edition: "On Sunday last a vessell [sic] arrived here from Belfast with about 160 passengers on board in order to settle in this province. The same vessel put 50 passengers ashore at Georgia destined for that province." It listed the ship as the Belfast Packet, with Thomas Ashe as master. This was the only ship listed as arriving from Belfast that year.[6] "On Sunday last" would have put his arrival date around 30 December. Usually, immigrants at Charles Town were quarantined for two weeks on nearby Sullivan's Island, so around 14 January they would have been ready to apply for land. Perhaps some of those passengers applied for land on 10 January, the first entry in the Council Journal for the new year. Likely, most passenger names are listed on the 17 January entry. Only 62 names of 160 the Gazette reported arriving are listed. Bear in mind, however, wives and children (as in the case of Russell's) were not listed.

My hunch is that the 17 January entry, indeed, lists names of those on the ship with James Russell. I base that premise on the following: the ship listed in the Gazette was the only one arriving from Belfast that year; indeed, no other ship from northern Ireland sailed that year to Charles Town.[7] Additionally, the quarantine period coincides with the time of arrival and the time of appearance before the council. And finally, the language used in the introduction of both days' entries, and the ways the names were listed are quite different. They are listed alphabetically on 10 January, and introduced with words, in effect, that the lieutenant governor had "signed and sealed the following Grants for Land." Possibly, during the holiday break, the lieutenant governor had

6. South Carolina Gazeteer, 7 January 1771.
7. R. J. Dickson: *Ulster Emigration to Colonial America*, 1718-1775. Appendix E, pp.282-287.

worked his way through the grant papers, and the clerk had time to arrange his listing alphabetically. The 17 January entry, on the other hand, seems to reflect more likely the way immigrants received land – gathering in the Council Chamber and coming forward one by one in no particular order. Also the wording of the introduction "read the following Petitions for Warrants of Survey" was often used to begin land applications from immigrants.

Often, neighbors, extended families, and even whole congregations sailed to the New World together. In South Carolina, they also received their land and settled together. James Russell settled on Jackson Creek in then Cavan County (now Fairfield County) and about 10 miles from the present-day seat of Winnsboro, and approximately 138 miles northwest of Charleston. Would it not follow that many of the settlers who settled in the same area with Russell in the early 1770s would also have been from the same area in northern Ireland?

With that premise, I travelled to Winnsboro and its Fairfield County Museum, where a genealogical room is located. There, local historians have organized surname files of settlers. One-by-one, I pulled those files, and indeed, a few voices of 220 years ago began to whisper a single word: Ballymena. Most of the biographies in the files did not list specific places in Northern Ireland. But I found Richard and Thomas Gladney, who hailed from Skerry parish, just east of Ballymena. Descendants of James Russell intermarried with Gladneys. Robert and John Phillips came from Ballymena. Unlike his neighbours, John Phillips took up arms for the King in the American Revolution. Tories were unwelcome around Jackson Creek after the war, and after Yorktown, Phillips returned to his home in Ballymena.[8]

Surname files on several others on the 17 January list were located, but none specified Ireland place names. Still, Ballymena, and parishes and townlands nearby, kept cropping up in other settler files. James Russell, a stone mason, built Jackson Creek Church, where one of its founding ministers, John Logue, came from Ballymena. William Hamilton and John Gray, two names that appear on the 17 January list,

8. Frank Phillips: *The Phillips Families of Ulster and South Carolina, Familia*, vol. 2, no. 4, 1988.

are listed among the first church elders. Brothers Hugh and James McMaster of Fairfield County hailed from Drumrayer in the parish of Ballymoney, and their wives, sisters Margaret and Jane Killoch came from Killoch Mills (Cloughmills!). They were part of a fleet of five shiploads of Covenanter Presbyterians, who arrived in the colony in 1772-73, led by Reverend James Martin from Ballymoney.[9]

In April and June of 1991, I made two trips to Belfast and, after several days work in PRONI, the Linen Hall Library, and the Presbtyerian Historical Society, failed to turn up my James Russell among the scattered church, estate, valuation tables, hearth money rolls and other records pre-dating 1770.

In September of 1992, after attending the foundation's conference "Auld Lang Syne – Searching for that Elusive Scots-Irish Ancestor" I drove to Ballymena and met local historian and school master, Eull Dunlop. He kindly drove me into the lovely countryside of the valley of the Braid and the valley of the Glenwhirry. He introduced me to May Kirkpatrick of Ballycarry who took me to Broughshane Presbyterian church and to the gravesides of some of her Russell ancestry. We were not able, however, to connect our two families.

But I continued to feel more confident that most of those names on the 17 January listing indeed hailed from the Ballymena area. Mr. Dunlop, who said South Carolina was a favourite destination for emigrants from the Ballymena area, looked at the 10 and 17 January listings, and ticked off several names: "MacCardy, MacCrory-Braid"; "MacKee-Kellswater"; "Harbison-Ballymena"; "MacCord, MacClendon-Kells/Connor."

On 10 September, my birthday and my last day in Northern Ireland, I drove back to Belfast and to the Linen Hall Library, and sat down with the entire volume of the Belfast Newsletter for 1770. The only ship leaving Belfast that fall, I saw, was the Hopewell, with Thomas Ashe as master and a sailing date of 10 October. Too, I noticed the Belfast Packet cleared customs from Belfast on 25 January 1771 from Greenock. Thus, the South Carolina Gazette misidentified the Hopewell for the Belfast Packet.[10]

---

9. Jean Stephenson: p.28.
10. Belfast Newsletter, 25 January 1771.

The sailing of the Hopewell was advertised in several editions of the Belfast newspaper. On 2 October a notice was published for all those who planned to sail on the Hopewell to be in town by 15 October, for the ship would sail "on the first fair Wind after."[11]

I found a wonderful birthday present, however, in the edition of 4 September, where the last sentence in another notice for the Hopewell said: "Such persons in the neighbourhood of Ballymena as intend going in said vessel are desired to apply immediately to Robert Phillips, Jr., and William Hamilton of Ballyloughan, or to Thomas Rogers of Craigawarren, who will agree with them on reasonable terms."[12]

Thus the Belfast Newsletter identifies three names from townlands near Ballymena that would appear four months later in the Council Journal listing of 17 January. Phillips, Hamilton (later an elder at Jackson Creek Church) and Rogers were likely leaders of the group sailing on the Hopewell, and many were probably from the Ballymena area.

But was James Russell among those from Ballymena? Perhaps. I recall the stone walls and houses of mid-Antrim, and I think what a wonderful place for a stone mason to have lived. I look forward to returning to the libraries in Belfast and to renew my friendships with Eull Dunlop and May Kirkpatrick. It will take more research, but one day, somewhere in the green fields of Antrim, I will stand upon earth that was once my family's home until the day in the fall of 1770 when James Russell, and his wife and children walked down to the sea and sailed on a fair wind to Carolina.

11. Ibid. 2 October 1770.
12. Ibid. 4 September 1770.

In The Council Chamber
Thursday the 10th day of January 1771

Present

His Honor the Lieutenant Governor
The Honorable Othaniel Beak, Egerton Leigh, Thomas Shotmire

His Honor the Lieutenant Governor signed and sealed the following
Grants for Land:

	Acres	
John Adamson	100	In Craven County
William Anorumn	100	Craven County
William Anderson	100	Berkley County
George Anderson	200	Do
Margaret Brown	100	Saint Bartholomew's Parish
Robert Bull	200	Saludy & Broad Rivers
Thomas Beckham, Jr.	150	Granville County
Stephen Bull, Esq.	500	Do
Richard Blizard	150	
Isaac Barrinow	150	
Joseph Barton	200	
Mathew Brooks	300	
Joseph Burton	200	
Thomas Bosher	300	
Simon Busby	100	
Sir John Colleton	500	
Robert Cahussac	500	
Henry Cassell	100	In Craven County
Thomas Casidy	150	
Edward Conway	200	
Thomas Clark	100	
William Collins	500	
John Calvert	300	
John Cross	500	
Henry Russell	150	
Isaac Copeland	150	

John Carter	100	
Hannah Clipton	100	
Wilson Cook	500	On Little River
Daniel Coleman	200	Halfway Swamp
Mary Curry	250	Mortiss Creek
Moses Cree	100	At Four Creeks
John Donoho	150	Berkley County
Gideon Dupont	250	Saint Luke's Parish
Gideon Dupont	250	Do
Edward Dickey	100	
Paeter Doney	300	
James Dozar	100	In Craven County
Ann Dargan	200	
William Edwards	50	
Robert Ellison	150	
Robert Evans	200	Congaree River
William Flood	500	Berkley County
James Fellows	300	Craven County
Samuel Flay	727	Do
Edward Forshaw	81	Colleton County
Lewis Fallows	100	Saludy River
David Greer	100	MacGill's Creek
David Giroud	100	Purysborough Township
Moses Gregory	100	Berkley County
John Green	550	Ennoree River
Gabriel Gignalliat	425	
John Guess	100	
Mason Grumming	150	
John Green	200	
Isaac Green	200	
Arthur Graham	100	In Craven County
John Hoss, Junior	100	
Mary Hannah	200	
Thomas Hickson	150	
Robert Henderson	100	
William Harrellson	150	
John DeLa Howe	200	Granville Couinty
John Hall	100	Do

Benjamin Hawkins	100	Berkley County
John Hutto	150	Do
Isaac Huger	250	Orangeburgh Township
Joseph Hardage	100	Wateree Creek
John Irvin	200	Saludy River
Henry Jones	200	Craven County
Michael Hay	200	Granville County
Benjamin Killgore	100	Berkley County
Joshua Lucas	250	Great Peedee
Thomas Lenoir	100	
John Lewis	100	
Samuel Little	500	
Jacob Sampley	100	
John Lourman	26	3/4
Elizabeth May	250	
John Morrall	250	
John MacCord	150	In Craven County
Bryan MacClendon	100	
Charles MacCord	200	
James Melton	250	
Derrick Manning	100	
James Major	100	
Isham Moore	500	
William Mills	400	
Peter Mayroh	200	Colleton County
Jacob Martin	100	Do
William MacDowell	200	Granville County
Joshua Moore	100	Do
William Mills	100	Berkley County
John Myers	100	Berkley County
Finley MacDobb	300	Wateree River King's Bounty
David Helson	450	
Abraham Nisom	300	
Jesse Kettles	100	In Craven County
John O'Neal	26	
Richard Owen	100	Colleton County
Samuel Prileau, Jr.	(illegable)	in Charleston
Paul Porcher	150	Saint Peter's Parish

120

Paul Porcher	150	Do
John Powell	200	Beaver Dam Creek
Josias Prother	150	Berkley County
Charles Pitts	150	Do
Samuel Porcher	250	Granville County
Simon Prichard	150	
John Pamor, Esq.	500	
George Pawley	845	
Luke Polk	200	In Craven County
Isaac Porcher	1260	
Isaac Pidgeon	100	
Peter Porcher	363	
John Pamor	200	
Samuel Russell	150	
Richard Richardson	1350	
Peter Rees	200	
John Richardson	150	
John Rankin	300	Cannons Creek
Thomas Reamy	100	Saludy River
George Reed	100	Granville County
Peter Sinkler	700	Berkley County
Jannet Stuart	250	Do
William Starling	400	Granville County
Ebenatus Stevens	100	Colleton County
John Singleton	271	Do
John Sibley	300	On Mill Creek
John Starn	100	
John Smith	250	
John Smith	100	
Francis Spivey	200	In Craven County
Thomas Singleton	400	
John Timmon	100	
James Thomson	100	
Isiah Thomson	100	
Nehemiah Thomas	150	On Saludy
James Thomson	200	Edisto River
Richard Tynor	150	Saludy River
John Vought	200	

Gavin Weatherspoon	300	
Sinthia Wright	100	
John Wesler	250	
Samuel Wise	300	
Edward White	200	In Craven County
Francis Willington	150	
Gavin Weatherspoon	250	
Gavin Weatherspoon	150	
Price Willis	150	
Nicholas Weaver	200	
Jacob Wolf	150	
Jacob Witman	300	In Craven County
David Williams	250	
Robert Young	100	
Hugh Young	100	Little River
John Young	150	Do

Read the following Petitions for Warrants of Survey and certifying a platt.

	Acres	
John Daniel Hammorer	50	for a mill Seat
Philip Porcher	400	In South Carolina
Peter Mazrick	250	(illegable) for Joseph Panton

Ordered that the Secretary prepare Warrants of Survey and the Deputy Surveyor General Certify platts as prayed for by the petitioners.

In the Council Chamber

Thursday the 17th of January 1771

Present

His Honor the Lieutenant Governor

The Honorable Othaniel Beak, John Owen, Egerton Leigh, W. L. Shotmire, John Stewart

Read the following Petitions for Warrants of Survey

	Acres	
Joseph Kaine	150	
James Russell	300	
Robert Phillips, Junr.	100	
John Phillips	450	
James Cunningham	150	
Joseph Cunningham	250	
Samuel Macowell	100	
William Hamilton	250	
Elizabeth Gray	100	
Margaret Gray	100	
John Rodgers	200	
Adam Blair	150	
Robert Hull	350	
John MacBride	400	
Jane MacBride	100	In South Carolina
John MacCardy, Jnr.	250	
Thomas Morton	200	
Andrew Morton	200	
Samuel Sloan	100	
Andrew Miller	200	
William Hood	450	
David Ferris	200	
Robert Martin	450	
John Richman	100	
James Wilson	200	

Thomas Gladney	100	
John MacCurdy	200	
Mary MacCurdy	100	
Jannet MacCurdy	100	
James MacCurdy	100	
William MacKee	350	
William MacCaa	450	
Jean MacCaa	100	
James Harbison	150	
Samuel Penny	200	
John Gray	300	
John Gray Junior	100	
John MacCrory	250	
William Anderson	300	
James Potts	100	
John Arnet	150	
John Arnet Junior	100	
Alexander Arnet	100	
Margaret Arnet	100	
Ann Arnet	100	
Mary Arnet	100	
Robert Phillips	250	In South Carolina
William Hamilton	200	
Charles Hamilton	100	
Henry Henderson	100	
Richard MacCrory	100	
Margaret MacCrory	100	
Ann MacCrory	100	
George Rodgers	100	
Alexander Rodgers	100	
Thomas Rodgers	100	
Agnes Martin	100	
Jean MacCalawter	100	
Robert Ross	100	
William Graham	250	
James Rodgers	250	
Richard Gladney	100	

Order that the Secretary do prepare Warrants of Survey as prayed for by the petitioners.

RECONSTRUCTING AN EMIGRANT FAMILY
FROM UNITED STATES RECORDS

by Edward J. O'Day
Southern Illinois University

For over two centuries Irish people have looked to the Americas, and particularly to the United States, as a land where unparalleled riches are within the reach of ordinary beings and where labour is justly rewarded. Although transforming that popular image of the New World into personal reality proved elusive for many an emigrant, the dream of a new and abundant life abroad remained remarkably consistent from the eighteenth century into the twentieth. Irish-American descendants who undertake to recreate the emigrant saga of their families sometimes adopt a type of reverse-image version of that dream, imagining the rediscovery of happy pastoral Irish kinsfolk who had the good sense to stay on the island of their birth. But for those more interested in reconstructing the emigrant experience than in flights of fancy into an imagined past, the United States is still a land of great riches. Americans of Irish origin may find genealogical evidence of their families in the United States as abundant as the mother lode of California which lured many an Irish person westward across both ocean and continent.

Such American sources can open up paths to effective use of Irish records, and on occasion they may document pre-emigration events in the lives of ancestors which are nowhere else recorded. As compared to source materials extant for Ireland itself, eighteenth- and nineteenth-century records in the United States which can be used for genealogical purposes are abundant beyond measure. Virginia and the New England colonies legislated on keeping of vital records early in the seventeenth century, though local churches were left to fulfil the task, and enforcement by the state was lax until long after independence. Massachusetts in 1841 initiated the first systematic statewide reporting of vital statistics, and many northeastern states followed its example later in the nineteenth century. In midwestern and southern states, church files and privately kept Bible records (often now published by local and state genealogical or historical societies) provide workable alternatives to such state-compiled documents.

The federal decennial census, required by the constitution for

125

purposes of determining representation in Congress, though limited to naming heads of households through 1840, began listing all residents a decade later. Subsequent population counts reported significant details of family structure and social standing. These censuses, now open to all researchers through 1920, reveal occupations, ages, gender, and birthplaces for individuals; marital status and literacy levels for adults; and school attendance for children. Those from 1880 reveal the relationship of all residents to the head of the family, and beginning in 1900 reports enumerated the length of marital unions and the number of children still living. Some censuses recorded the value of taxable property and distinguished home owners from renters, while others indicated if the foreign born were naturalized, and the year of their immigration. Many states held additional censuses, usually midway between the ten year intervals of the federal census. These supplement the nationally compiled data and can be especially useful for tracing highly mobile recent immigrants.[1]

Each of these items from census reports suggests to the skilled genealogist the possible existence of other documents which may confirm, correct, or expand upon the census data. Numerous published city and county directories, compiled for commercial use, appeared regularly in major cities. Though replete with inaccuracies, such listings attempted to include domestics, labourers and boarders, as well as the rich and famous, and these directories can reveal residential mobility, shifts from rental to home ownership, and the entry of young adults into the workforce. One may deduce from them approximate dates of marriages and deaths, removals to other jurisdictions, and relationships among families of similar name. For periods between censuses or as substitutes for the destroyed 1890 census, these urban directories are invaluable.

1. All federal censuses 1790-1920 (except 1890 which was destroyed by fire) have been microfilmed and are readily accessible at regional National Archives centers throughout the nation. The most comprehensive guide to their content is the revised edition of *Guide to Genealogical Research in the National Archives* (Washington, DC, 1985).

Following census and directory leads, the historian of immigrant families must search out documentary evidence such as declarations of citizenship intent, naturalization records, voter registration data, and passenger lists for incoming vessels. Any of these may record an ancestor's age and birthplace, residence or destination, and present or past employment. Among the most rewarding American sources for the genealogist are military service and pension records, often replete with personal data about the soldier and his family. Deeds to land ownership, homesteader's claims, tax rolls, mortgages covering real or personal property, and wills or estate settlements for those who died seized of property abound in tens of thousands of probate and county courts across the United States. For immigrants whose American dream went unrealized, even temporarily, these same county repositories may also preserve detailed guardianship or orphanage records, and account books of insane asylums, prisons and nineteenth century 'poor farms'.

When public records of this type are combined with family memorabilia – reminiscences of the living as well as cherished scraps and letters by those now deceased – it is often possible to reconstruct the immigrant family and to chronicle its adjustment to the new homeland. The emigrant experience of Edmond and Bridget (Coen) O'Dea and seven of their children, all of whom ventured across the waters in the 1840s, may serve to illustrate the process of using this type of evidence. Inquiry into the family from which I had sprung initially encountered the narrow parameters of a collective memory which had preserved neither the date of emigration nor their Irish county origins. Were I to one day tell my children about their immigrant ancestors, I had first to learn the story myself.[2]

---

2. The great majority of both government and church records are still held locally or at county or diocesan levels. Locating them would be daunting task were it not for an extensive microfilming project by the Genealogical Society of Utah, carried out with the co-operation of local and state archives and genealogical societies.

My grandfather, born to immigrant parents, had worked for $26 a week in a corset factory and raised a family of four in the small Massachusetts town where I later grew up. His death in 1926 (before I was born), followed by the onset of the Great Depression and outbreak of the Second World War appear in retrospect to have severed the family's ties to its emigrant past. Local religious and ethnic prejudice against the Irish, common in the nineteenth century, had flared again in the 1920s, but not in my generation, and my O'Day family seemed secure in the positions of respect they had won in the community. Like many second generation Irish-Americans, they did not look back across the waters, and were content to 'melt into the American pot', which had finally ceased to boil around them.

My father, like his father before him, was the only male child to survive to adulthood, and I had often heard his claim that we had 'no relatives by the name of O'Day'. He showed little curiosity about his ancestry, but assisted me in sketching a family tree early in the 1960s. It had but few branches and the passage of time had obscured its Irish roots:

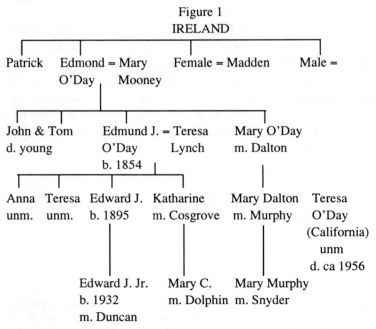

Figure 1
IRELAND

128

From my home in the Midwest I explored the unknown reaches of my immigrant past in libraries of the region, making annual visits to New England to consult relatives and local sources. The 1850 federal census, vital records, and local tax rolls quickly provided evidence of an O'Day immigrant group of larger dimensions and more generations than my father had knowledge of. Variants of the family name abounded in the documents, from an occasional 'O'Dea' (following Irish spelling), to Ody, O'Dale, and O'Day, versions more familiar to the eye or ear of the Massachusetts Yankee. The record left little doubt that an extensive clan of Irish immigrants – be they O'Deas or O'Days – had made its initial home in the United States within the confines of the west parish of Brookfield in central Massachusetts.[3]

In September 1850, when the first federal count was taken of the newly incorporated town of West Brookfield, the household of Irish-born 'Edward Ody,' aged 64, included two other males of similar name, Edmond, aged 25 and Edwin, apparently 11. Living with them were Bridget, aged 50, who might be the spouse of the eldest male, Michael, 30 and Dennis, 17, either of whom could be the progenitor of the California line which my father had mentioned. Only the young adult Edmond fits the anticipated age of my great-grandfather, and while the elder Edward might be his father, ages made it unlikely that the younger Edwin was his son. Interpreting the census taker's report on the seventh member of the household would require the powers of a seer. A youngster named Bridget, of some undecipherable age under ten, was very clearly identified as male.[4] In the nearby separate household lived Patrick and Sabina O'Day, both in their early twenties. Since no relationships were indicated for either Ody/O'Day family, the limitations of the census for genealogical research were apparent.

3. My great-grandfather's death record was entered as 'O'Dea,' as were the birth records of his children. His marriage record, naturalization papers, and land title, however, consistently rended his name as 'O'Day,' the spelling adopted by his descendants. Both forms of the name appear in the text which follows, reflecting differences in the records and the retention of 'O'Dea' among all of Michael's children.
4. 1850 Census, U.S. National Archives MC432, roll 341, frames 76-77.

Civil records of births and deaths, some filed locally, others at the county seat twenty miles distant, supplemented by Catholic church records of marriage (most of which had escaped civil registration), slowly brought the family structure more clearly into focus. Sacramental records confirmed the marriage of Edmond O'Day to another Galway-born immigrant, Mary Mooney, early in 1851 and civil records contained my grandfather's birth in 1854. Similar sources verified the unions of Patrick O'Day with Sabina Leonard and Catherine O'Day with Richard Flynn.

Poll tax records (for males over 21) in 1853 showed collections from Edman O'Dey and Edman Jr, each of whom had filed a declaration of intent to become a citizen in the Worcester County Court of Common Pleas in the previous year. These documents were amazingly rich in detail, identifying the common birthplace of both men as 'Anniedown' (Annaghdown), Co. Galway, where the elder had been born in 1786 and the younger in 1822. Both events had occurred before the keeping of the records in that parish. The declarations also included the name of their transatlantic ship – the bark *Messenger* and gave their place and date of arrival in the United States as New York, 23 April, 1849. The ship manifest which had previously eluded my search now readily provided the names of those who had accompanied them.

In another office of the county courthouse which housed the citizenship papers, probate records contained the will of Edmond O'Day the elder, written in 1857 and signed in his own hand. He enumerated and provided for six surviving children - Michael, Edmond (my great grandfather), Patrick, Catherine O'Day Flynn, Dennis and Bridget. At last there was solid evidence of family relationships at which the census had only hinted, but now a wider research arena lay ahead. Edmond O'Dea's children had begun to scatter even before he died in 1863. By the time his estate was settled in 1866, the eldest and two youngest were in California, while Patrick had moved to Connecticut after seeing battle as a Union soldier during the Civil War.[5] Of the immigrants, only my

---

5. After providing for a suitable cemetery monument and paying mortgage and other debts, the 'estate' distributed to the heirs amounted to $80. The grave, in St John's Cemetery Worcester, is marked by a small marble obelisk engraved 'O'Dey.' Cemetery files record purchase of the lot in October 1849 by Edmond O'Dea; Worcester City Deaths, Book I, 699 show that Mary O'Dea, daughter of Edmund, died in West Brookfield of consumption on October 2.

great-grandfather and his sister Catherine Flynn then remained in Massachusetts. Research had made the O'Dea immigrants no longer invisible, and the family tree had assumed a distinct shape, its Irish roots now exposed to view:

Figure 2

Edmond O'Dea   =   Bridget Coen
b. 1876 Annaghdown, Galway   b. ca. 1798 IRE
d. 1863 W. Brookfield, MA   d. 1865 W. Brookfield, MA

all born Ireland

Michael	Edmond	Patrick	Mary	Catherine	Dennis	Bridget
1819	1822	1827	1827	1828	1832	1837
			d.1849			
CA	MA	CT	MA	MA	CA	CA

Tracking the immigrant family across the vast reaches of the United States might not have been possible were it not for the assistance of a half dozen or so family members who helped open new avenues of inquiry. Treasured mementos, correspondence from long ago, and the remarkable memories of several octogenarians filled many a gap or helped me interpret what I found in the public record.[6]

My father's unmarried sister Anna had important knowledge of the female members of her father's family, a group otherwise very difficult to trace. Catherine O'Day Flynn had lived out her life within a ten mile radius of her original Massachusetts home, following her husband's moves among several boot and shoe factories which were among the area's largest employers. My aunt recalled attending her funeral in 1904 and knew of her descendants in New Jersey, Ohio, and Virginia. From

6. Those 'records assistants' deserving special mention are Anna O'Day, my father's elder sister; cousins Miriam Ashe and Gardiner Gibson (the Flynn line); Albert O'Dea, great grandson of Michael; and Annette McNeil, whose husband Harold McNeil was Dennis' grandson. All are now deceased.

her I learned also that 'father's aunt Bridget,' Mrs Michael Madden but separated from her husband, had sustained herself and a daughter by working as a domestic in San Francisco. They had lived in New England for short time after the great earthquake of 1906, but later returned to California. Bridget, the youngest of Edmond and Bridget O'Dea's children, was the only member of her generation who can be documented on both sides of the ocean. The Annaghdown parish register contains her birth date (2 August, 1837) as well as the day of her baptism (13 August); the certificate recording her death on 9 February, 1924 is filed in San Francisco City Hall.

My aunt had also maintained an irregular but unbroken correspondence since 1908 with the descendants of Dennis of San Francisco. Dennis, the immigrant teenager of 1849, pioneered the re-migration of part of the family to California in 1855. As a teamster there he profited from the gold fever then feeding San Francisco's growth, and by 1890 had sufficient income from real estate to be identified as a capitalist on the California Great Register of voters.[7] Since his descendants had made visits among New England cousins, most recently in the 1960s, renewing contacts and returning the visits during a research trip to San Francisco was not difficult. One of his great granddaughters now preserves the family Bible which Dennis and his Leitrim-born wife, Jane Meehan, brought from Massachusetts.

Wounded in the Civil War, Patrick O'Day died within a few years of the end of the conflict, and contact between his branch of the family and relatives in Massachusetts and California broke off shortly after the turn of this century. Military records in the National Archives include an unmarried daughter's petition for a federal pension, containing a complete list of Patrick's ten children by his wife Sabina Leonard. Despite such evidence, attempts to trace descendants of their two male children who reached adulthood have proven unsuccessful.

7. Great Register 11th Precinct, 29th Assembley District, San Francisco County, 1890.

Mystery still surrounded Michael, the youth Edwin, and the male youngster named Bridget. Neither my aunt nor Dennis' people knew anything; the Flynns were equally unknowing. Could I prove their relationship to one another and to me, and reconstruct the entire family, some 130 years after it had emigrated? From scanty evidence at hand, I speculated that Michael was by 1850 a widower, and that Bridget and Edwin, living in the 'Ody' household in Massachusetts at that time, were his children. Though testing that supposition took more than a decade, bits and pieces matching my speculation gradually fell into place.

Payrolls of the Western Railroad, where my great grandfather had found work in 1849, revealed that a Michael O'Dea was already employed on the railroad in 1848, a year prior to arrival of the other O'Deas aboard the *Messenger*. The passenger list of an earlier ship, the *Cushlamachree* out of Galway in March 1848, yielded the names of Michael and Mary O'Dea, accompanied by children Edwina and Catherine. If the 1850 census, the payroll and that ship manifest all referred to the same Michael, then he was a forerunner of the rest of the family. This suggestion of chain migration of the type so well known in the Irish emigrant experience, with hints that Michael's American earnings assisted the passage of others, increased my determination to discover what had become of him.

Irish records provided traces of Michael in his Annaghdown parish, where the priest recorded baptisms of Bridget (1843), Edmond (1845) and Catherine (1846), children of Michael O'Dea and Maria Shaunessy (or Shannacy). Children of those names and approximate ages had arrived on the two immigrant ships previously identified – Bridget, carried as a non-paying infant on the *Messenger*; Edmond and Catherine on the *Cushlamachree*.[8] Research strategy called for moving forward in

---

8. Though their ages are reversed on the census, Bridget and Edmond are probably the two children in West Brookfield in 1850. No trace of Catherine and her mother Maria Shaunessy O'Dea can be found in United States records other than the Cushlamachree manifest. They may have died before reaching Massachusetts.

time, to the 1860 census of San Francisco. There the enumerator of Ward 3 in July found 'Michael O'Dane,' his wife Catherine, and teenagers Bridget and Edmond, all of them born in Ireland.[9] Four younger children had been born in Massachusetts, and one month old Michael was a native Californian. The family profile fitted my hypothesis.

In search of evidence of Michael who had wed Catherine Burke at St Mary's North End in January 1852. Since neither witness to the marriage was a known relative, the church record provided nothing to associate that Michael O'Dea with my family line. The civil record, however, listed the marriage as the groom's second and identified his father as Edmond O'Day [sic]. While evidence supporting my hypothesis was mounting, caution reigned, since many a careful genealogist has been led astray by wishful thinking. No documents had yet demonstrated that the Michael O'Dea of Annaghdown, of the *Cushlamachree*, of West Brookfield, of Boston, and of San Francisco was one person. The 'smoking gun' was still missing.

The 1870 federal census for San Francisco provided the first clue that Michael O'Dea had not long survived his family's move to California. Catherine O'Day, 43, then headed a household which matched the 'O'Dane' family of 1860, but Michael was missing. All children over the age of twelve had entered the workforce, including Bridget and Edmond, the presumed stepchildren. City directories confirmed that Catherine was a widow. The task began of tracking this entire family through three generations, using later censuses, San Francisco city directories, and area telephone books (see Appendix). Without computer assistance, the effort was labour-intensive, but proved successful in identifying two of Michael's great grandsons who replied to my correspondence.

In later meetings with them, I found that neither had heard mention of the Edmond O'Days of West Brookfield, nor were they aware of any relationship to fellow San Francisco Dennis O'Day or Bridget Madden. Their Michael O'Dea was 'probably' from Co. Cork, but he was known

---

9. 1860 Census, U.S. National Archives MC653, roll 67, frame 57. The surname is indistinct, and might·be 'O'Daye,' but others have read it as 'O'Dair.' The significant of the Massachusetts born children is discussed below.

to have lived on Cape Cod (approximately 100 miles from the Brookfields) prior to arriving in California. Such claims threatened my hypothesis, shook my self-confidence, and for a time made my directory efforts seem foolish, but I nevertheless kept up the search. Following the Cape Cod lead, I turned to the Massachusetts state census of 1855. Living in Brewster, a coastal town of the Cape's Barnstable County, were Michael and Catherine O'Dea, with children Edmond, Mary and John. Edmond, born in Ireland, was seven years older than Mary, the first of two children born in Massachusetts. While this age differential could support my widower-remarriage thesis and suggested that Edmond was the 'Edwin' of 1850, the data could be open to other interpretation.

This Cape Cod family was finally linked to the O'Days of West Brookfield through vital records of the city of San Francisco. One of very few official books to survive destruction by the earthquake of 1906 included record of Michael O'Dea's death on July 28, 1869. A newspaper notice of his wake identified him as a native of Co. Galway.[10] Michael's great grandson Albert had told me about John O'Dea of the Barnstable census, apprenticed to a tinsmith at fifteen after his father died. John had become an independent plumber in San Francisco by the turn of the century, and Albert was six and living with his grandparents when the post-earthquake fire had devoured the city, destroying the O'Dea home and his grandfather's business. Exhausted by efforts to rebuild, John A. O'Dea died a few months later, of what a modern specialist might call 'post-earthquake stress syndrome.' This story relayed by an eyewitness really needed no verifying, but I nevertheless ordered copies of death certificates for John O'Dea, his siblings, and his presumed half-sister Bridget O'Dea, later Mrs Michael Caulfield.

Mary O'Dea, the first of Catherine Burke's children by Michael O'Dea, and likewise counted on the Barnstable census, had married a successful produce wholesaler in San Francisco named Thomas Burns. They were childless, Albert had told me, and since she had no

10. San Francisco City Records, Book I, 280; *Daily Morning Call*, 29 July 1869.

descendants I might have passed her by, or simply closed her file. Luckily I did not. With her death certificate, which reported the date and place of her birth as January 1853 in Brookfield, Massachusetts, I had at last struck genealogical California gold. Her birth, which numerous searches of Massachusetts civil and church records had failed to document, had occurred in the town where Michael O'Dea obtained employment in 1848, and to which his parents and the rest of the family had come in 1849. While this death certificate provided a vital tie between the Massachusetts and California families, it lacked crucial data on Mary O'Dea Burns' parents. Fortunately, the newspaper account of her death identified all her siblings, including Bridget Caulfield. Death records for John A. and Michael W. O'Dea were found to include the full names of their parents – Michael O'Dea and Catherine Burke – and the certificate of Thomas M.'s death in 1938 identified both of them as natives of Co. Galway.[11]

Ninety years after Michael O'Dea sailed from Galway, eighty after he left Massachusetts for California, and nearly two decades after his name had jumped at me from a census microfilm, Michael was invisible or unidentified no longer. The preponderance of evidence, gathered from Galway to San Francisco and points in between, finally demonstrated that Michael O'Dea, a San Francisco stevedore who died in 1869, was one of four sons named in the will of Edmond O'Dea of West Brookfield, formerly of Annaghdown. At long last the case was clinched, settled not by a smoking gun or single document, but by a mosaic of evidence which reunited on a twentieth century genealogical chart an immigrant family of the mid-nineteenth century.[12] The Appendix illustrates the seven known children and forty grandchildren of Edmond O'Dea and Bridget Coen.

11. Mary C. Burns' Death Certificate, San Francisco 35-6656 and *San Francisco Chronicle,* 13 October 1935. San Francisco Death Certificates 06-510 (John), 25-6383 (Michael) and 38-7488 (Thomas M.)
12. Unanswered questions linger about Michael's three children by Maria Shaunessy in Annaghdown. Bridget O'Dea Caulfield could not have been identified were it not for mention of her in the obituary of Mary O'Dea Burns. Her death record (24-7255) has no birth date, though it gives her father's name as Michael. Of Bridget's brother Edmond, registered voter and blacksmith in Oakland, California in States records, this one immigrant, visible in the sources for thirty years, slips from view again. All others of the immigrant generation who were living in 1850 have been accounted for.

By 1900, children of O'Dea immigrants had scattered to New Hampshire, New York and New Jersey in the East; to Ohio, Illinois and Missouri in the Midwest; and to Washington state in the Northwest. Patrick Henry Flynn, born to Catherine O'Day in West Brookfield, later became a major shoe manufacturer in Xenia, Ohio, and the only known family member to earn an entry in the *Dictionary of National Biography*. Edward F. O'Day, grandson of Dennis O'Day, a journalist and reporter for the *San Francisco Chronicle* was also a raconteur and creative writer, leaving the O'Day family name liberally sprinkled in the National Union Catalog of the Library of Congress. The less well known encompassed bank porters, shoemakers and plumbers; stenographers, governesses and Catholic nuns; salesmen, lumbermen and firemen. Amidst these successful but ordinary Irish-Americans there were individuals who married for money, and those who suffered financial misfortune; there were failed marriages, orphaned children and a few alcoholics. They were all family, and happily few were as invisible as some of the immigrant generation.

Two genealogical lessons emerge from this exercise in emigrant family reconstruction. Always follow up all members of the family, even to the black sheep or those who died without issue, in whom interest is minimal. Their lives – or deaths, like that of Mary Burns – may hold the clue to the lives of many others. Second, never neglect an Irish female, especially an unmarried one. They often know more than anyone else, and the power of their speech can be heard even from the grave.

APPENDIX

IMMEDIATE DESCENDANTS OF EDMOND O'DEA OF
ANNAGHDOWN, CO GALWAY

FIRST GENERATION

1. Edmond O'Dea/O'Day. Born, Feb 1786, in Annaghdown, Co. Galway
IRE. Died, 12 Aug 1863, in W. Brookfield MA.[1]

He married Bridget Coen, daughter of Patrick Coen and Margaret
Finnerty O'Brien, about 1818, in Co. Galway IRE. Born, ca. 1791, in
Co. Galway IRE. Died, 16 Feb 1865, in W. Brookfield MA.

Children:
  i.   Michael[2] O'Dea.
  ii. Edmond Ned O'Day.
  iii. Mary O'Dea. Born, 1826, in Annaghdown, Co. Galway IRE.
       Died, 2 Oct. 1849, in W. Brookfield MA.[2]
  iv. Patrick O'Day.
  v.   Catherine O'Day.
  vi. Dennis J. O'Day.
  vii. Bridget O'Day.

1. No Irish birth record for Edmond O'Dea is extant, but in December 1852 he declared his intent to become a citizen of the United States before the Worcester County MA Court of Common Pleas, and personally swore to the place and date of his birth. His death is recorded in West Brookfield MA Town Records.
2. Mary O'Dea's birth date is extrapolated from her age at death (Worcester MA Death Records, I, 7, No 699). A wooden grave marker in St. John's Cemetery, now long decayed, once recorded her birthplace (Flynn Notebooks, Ca. 1890, manuscript, Holy Cross College Library, Worcester MA).

SECOND GENERATION

2. Michael[2] O'Dea (Edmond[1]). Born, ca. 1819, in Annaghdown, Co. Galway IRE. Died, 28 Jul 1869, in San Francisco CA[3].

He married, first, Maria Shaunessy, ca. 1842, in IRE. Born, ca. 1822 in IRE. She died, 1849 (?), probably in Massachusetts.

Children:

    i.   Bridget[3] O'Dea. Born, 1843, in Annaghdown, Co. Galway IRE. Died, 11 Dec 1924, in San Francisco CA.[4] She married Michael H Caulfield, ca. 1875, in San Francisco CA.

    ii.   Edmond O'Dea. Born, 1845, in Annaghdown, Co. Galway IRE. Lived California 1879. Place and date of death unknown.

    iii. Catherine O'Dea. Born, 1846, in Annaghdown, Co. Galway IRE. Died, 1849 (?), probably in Massachusetts.

He married, second, Catherine Burke, daughter of John Burke, 7 Jan 1852, in St Mary's (North End), Boston MA.[5] Born, ca. 1824, in Co. Galway IRE. She died, ca. 1884, in San Francisco CA.

Children:

    iv.   Mary C. O'Dea. Born, Jan 1853, in W, Brookfield Ma. Died, 12 Oct 1935, in San Francisco CA.[6] She married Thomas A Burns, ca 1886, in San Francisco CA. No issue.

    v.   John Aloysius O'Dea. Born, Oct 1854, in Massachusetts.[7] Died, 28 May 1906, in San Francisco CA. He married Elizabeth Doyle, ca. 1877, in San Francisco CA.

---

3. San Francisco Deaths, Book I, p.280 No 12915. Michael O'Dea's obituary appeared in the *Daily Morning Call*, 29 July 1869. Neither source names his parents.
4. Bridget O'Dea's December 1843 baptism is recorded in Annaghdown Parish Records, her 1924 death on San Francisco CA certificate No 24-7255.
5. St Mary's (Boston) Parish Register. Boston City Records (1852, No 34) record it as Michael O'Dea's second marriage.
6. Though the birth was not recorded in Massachusetts, Mary O'Dea Burns' death certificate (San Francisco No 35-6656) gives her birthplace as Brookfield MA, January 1853. Her obituary appeared in the San Francisco *Chronicle*, Oct 13, 1935.
7. There is no record of John A. O'Dea's Massachusetts birth, but he was 8 months old in the household of his parents at the time of the 1855 Barnstable Co. MA census.

vi. Thomas Martin O'Dea. Born, 8 Aug. 1856, in Brewster, Barnstable, Co MA. Died, 13 Nov 1938, in San Francisco CA. He married Mary A. Doren, ca. 1885, in San Francisco CA.

vii. Hannora (Hannah) O'Dea. Born, ca. 1858, in Massachusetts. Died, 14 Nov. 1843, in San Francisco CA. She married James J Radford, Jan 1876, in San Francisco CA.

viii. Michael William O'Dea. Born, 1 Jun 1860, in San Francisco CA. Died, 4 Nov 1925, in San Francisco CA. He married Sarah Francis _____ in California.

ix. Catherine (Kate) A. O'Dea. Born, 1862, in San Francisco CA. Died, 25 Oct 1934, in San Francisco CA. She married William D. Schroder, ca. 1898, in San Francisco CA.

3. Edmond 'Ned'[2] O'Day (Edmond[1]). Born, Mar 1822, in Annaghdown, Co Galway IRE. Died, 10 Jun 1885, in W. Brookfield MA.[8]

He married Mary Mooney, daughter of Edmund Mooney and Catherine Patten, 9 Apr 1851, in St John's, Worcester MA. Born, Sep 1827, in Dunmore, Co. Galway IRE. She died, 23 Mar 1873, in W. Brookfield MA.

Children:

i. Mary[3] O'Day. Born, 15 Feb 1853, in W, Brookfield MA. Died, 29 May 1921, in W. Brookfield MA. She married, first, George Dalton, 15 Aug 1876, in St Joseph's, N. Brookfield MA; second, John H. Mullin, 10 Jun 1881. Widowed a second time, she married third, Walter Young, 1 Jul 1896, in St. Mary's, Brookfield MA.

ii. Edmund Joseph O'Day. Born, 17 Mar 1854, in W. Brookfield MA. Died, 11 Aug 1926, in W. Brookfield MA. He married Teresa M. Lynch, 27 Jan 1892, in Sacred Heart Church, W. Brookfield MA.

---

8. There is no Irish birth or baptismal record for the younger Edmond O'Dea, but his Declaration of Intention to become a citizen, in Worcester County MA Court of Common Pleas, October 1852, includes his native parish and birth month and year. The record of his death (W. Brookfield MA Town Records, I, 47) includes the names of both of his parents.

iii. John G. O'Day. Born, 2 Aug 1855, in W. Brookfield MA. Died, 11 Nov. 1859, in W. Brookfield MA.
iv. Thomas Andrew O'Day. Born, 18 Jun 1857, in W. Brookfield MA. Died, 25 Nov 1857, in W. Brookfield MA.

4. Patrick[2] O'Day (Edmond[1]). Born, Ca. 1827, in Annaghdown, Co Galway IRE. Died, 13 Sep 1869, in Manchester CT.

He married Sabina Leonard, daughter of Ellen Leonard, 26 May 1850, in St John's, Worcester MA. Born, Ca. 1828, in Ireland. Died, 28 Jul 1883, in Manchester CT.

Children:
i. Mary Agnes[3] O'Day. Born, 25 Mar 1851, in W. Brookfield MA. Died, 7 Sep 1915, in Snohomish, Snohomish, Co. WA. She married Daniel Meagher, 30 May 1875, in St. Bridget's, Mancester CT.
ii. Thomas Andrew O'Day. Born, 17 Dec 1852, in W. Brookfield MA. Place and date of death unknown.
iii. Ella Frances O'Day. Born, 30 Sep 1855, in W. Brookfield MA. Died, 6 Oct 1928, in Manchester CT. She married Michael H. Malley, 29 Dec 1892, in St Bridget's, Manchester CT.
iv. Sabina Elizabeth O'Day. Born, 30 Jul 1857, in W. Brookfield MA. Died, 1933. She married Martin Maher, Ca.1890, in Connecticut.
v. Patrick O'Day. Born, 28 Nov 1857, in W. Brookfield MA. Place and date of death unknown.
vi. Bridget O'Day. Born, 19 Nov 1861, in W. Brookfield MA. Place and date of death unknown.
vii. Anna L. O'Day. Born, 28 Feb 1864, in W. Brookfield MA. Died, ca. 1941, in Hartford CT. She married Francis H. Gribbon, 19 Apr 1888, in St. Bridget's, Manchester CT.
viii. Edward O'Day. Born, 10 Dec 1866, in Manchester CT. Died, Ca. 1878, in Connecticut.
ix. John E. O'Day. Born, 4 Jul 1868, in Manchester CT. Died, 29 Jun 1869, in Manchester CT.
x. John O'Day. Born, 2 Feb 1870, in Manchester CT. Died, 10 Jul 1870, in Manchester CT.

5. Catherine[2] O'Day (Edmond[1]). Born, 15 Nov 1828, in Annaghdown, Co. Galway IRE. Died, 21 Jan 1904, in Brookfield MA.

She married Richard Flynn, son of Patrick Flynn and Mary Callan, 9 Feb 1851, in St John's, Worcester MA.[9] Born, 25 Mar 1828, in Stradbally, Co Galway IRE. He died, 28 Dec. 1906, in Jefferson City MO.

Children:

i.   Edward F.[3] Flynn. Born, Nov 1852, in W. Brookfield MA. Died in Illinois.

ii.   Mary J. Flynn. Born, 14 Aug 1854, in W. Brookfield MA. Died, 14 Sep 1932, in Spencer MA. She married Jerome Hines, ca. 1877, in Massachusetts.

iii. F. Catherine Flynn. Born, 14 Dec 1855, in W. Brookfield MA. Died in Massachusetts. She married Patrick Cunningham in Massachusetts.

iv.   Richard James Flynn. Born, 3 Jan 1858, in W. Brookfield MA. Died, 25 Mar 1940, in Belleville IL. He married Mary Elizabeth Flynn ca. 1898.

v.   Patrick Henry Flynn. Born, 4 Jul 1861, in W. Brookfield MA. Died, 12 Apr 1934, in Xenia OH. He married, first, Elizabeth Ankeney Trebein, 20 Jun 1894, in Greene Co. OH. She died, 25 Sep 1924, in Xenia OH. He married, second, Bertha E. Trebein, younger sister of his first wife, ca. 1926, in Xenia OH.

vi.   Thomas G. Flynn. Born, 21 Dec 1865, in Spencer MA. Died, 21 May 1935, in Long Beach CA.

vii. Bridget E. Flynn. Born, 21 Dec 1865, in Spencer MA. Died, 20 Sep 1938, in Nashua NH. She married Thomas J. Ashe, 2 Jun 1887, in St Mary's, Brookfield MA.

9. St John's (Worcester) Marriage Records.

6. Dennis J.[2] O'Day (Edmond[1]). Born, 1832, in Annaghdown, Co Galway IRE. Died, 22 Jul 1989, in San Francisco CA.[10]

He married Jane Mehan, 18 Jan 1852, in W. Brookfield MA[13]. Born, 1829, in Kiltenbridge, Co. Leitrim IRE. She died, 6 Jan 1887, in San Francisco CA.

Children:

i   John F.[3] O'Day. Born, 14 Jun 1853, in W. Brookfield MA. Died, unmarried, 19 Nov 1910, in San Francisco CA.

ii.   Mary Elizabeth O'Day. Born, 14 Aug 1854, in Roxbury MA. Died, 19 Jul 1855.

iii.   Edward Thomas O'Day. Born, 25 Jan 1856, in San Francisco CA. Died, 26 Nov 1922, in San Francisco CA. He married Mary E. McGrath, ca. 1880, in San Francisco CA.

iv.   Joseph Francis O'Day. Born, 7 Oct 1858, in San Francisco CA. Died, 15 Oct 1858, in San Francisco CA.

v.   James Henry O'Day. Born, 10 Mar 1859, in San Francisco CA. Died, 15 Jun 1902, in San Francisco CA. He married Julia A. Breen, ca. 1880, in San Francisco CA.

vi.   Denis Joseph O'Day. Born, 15 Oct 1860, in San Francisco CA. Died, 13 May 1866, in San Francisco CA.

vii.   Robert Emmett O'Day. Born, 15 Jul 1862, in San Francisco CA. Died, 22 Jun 1911, in San Francisco CA. He married Hannah Leszynski, ca. 1882, in San Francisco CA.

viii. Mary Jane O'Day. Born, 12 Jan 1864, in San Francisco CA. Died, 30 May 1930, in San Francisco CA. She married Michael McNeil, 6 Oct 1887, in San Francisco CA.

ix.   Teresa Ann O'Day. Born, 2 Jan 1966, in San Francisco CA. Died, 21 Mar. 1955, in Marin Co. CA.

10. San Francisco CA Deaths, Book O; obituary in San Francisco *Chronicle,* 23 July 1898.

7. Bridget[2] O'Day (Edmond[1]). Born, 2 Aug 1837, in Annaghdown, Co. Galway IRE. Died, 7 Feb 1924, in Burlingame, San Mateo Co. CA.[11]

She married Michael Madden, son of William Madden and Ellen Shea, 18 Jan 1862, in St. William's, Ware Ma.[12] Born, 1839, in Ireland. He died, 1922, in W. Brookfield MA.

Children:

    i.   Mary 'Mayme'[3] Madden. Born ca. 1864. Died, 13 Feb 1941, in San Bernadino CA. She married, first, Hermann Rumpf, Ca. 1922, in California; second, Bill Thomas, Ca. 1940, in California.

---

11. Bridget O'Day's birth date and her parents are recorded in Annaghdown parish records. Her CA death certificate No 24-010214, includes an incorrect birth date (1848). The San Francisco *Chronicle* printed a brief obituary 8 Feb. 1924.
12. Ware MA Marriage Records, I, 62.

AN OBSERVATION ON SETTLER NAMES
IN FERMANAGH*

by Dr. Brian S. Turner
Down County Museum

It has been argued elsewhere that intensive study of the contemporary surname pattern may throw light on a past about which written history has little to say, or may indicate new directions and raise new questions to be examined in the light of old evidence. It is not the present intention to illustrate such an intensive study but merely to draw attention, using Fermanagh as an example, to the type of simple observation which can serve as a starting point for much more detailed study in which family names can be an important element.

The five most numerous names in mid-twentieth century Fermanagh are Maguire, Johnston, Armstrong, McManus, and Elliott. Looking only at these five names certain features stand out immediately. Taken in isolation it should not be surprising that Maguire occupies first place but current evidence suggests that among the twentieth century Ulster counties Fermanagh is unusual in having its principal pre-Plantation ruling family maintaining a strong numerical superiority over other common names. Not only is this the case but the Maguires are more than twice as numerous as the McManuses, the second Irish name and themselves a branch of the Maguires. Fermanagh is also unusual in that, alone among the Plantation counties, it has three settler names in the top five. These names, Johnston, Armstrong, and Elliott, also form a group with close historical associations. Although there is a great variety of names in Fermanagh, as in any Irish county, the characteristics suggested by these five names persist throughout the general pattern. On the one hand the pre-plantation names illustrate continuing history by the strong presence of Maguires and related families, while on the other the strongest settler families have relationships with each other which stretch back and beyond the shores of Ireland.

Indeed Fermanagh provides a particularly clear example of the value of taking account of surname distribution in Britain as well as Ireland. Johnston, Armstrong, and Elliott are not merely British in origin but they come from a small and clearly defined area of Britain – the western and middle Marches of England and Scotland. Throughout the sixteenth

145

century this rough border area was the home of a society whose principal characteristic was the burning, looting, and reiving by which, through historical circumstance, many of its families maintained themselves. This type of life resulted in the growth of large closely-knit family groups with intense clan loyalties and fierce feuds against others. They were known as the 'riding' or 'raiding' families.

Although lawlessness and the consequent necessity for self-reliance was a feature of the whole Anglo-Scottish frontier, the cockpit of the border and the home of its most predatory clans was Liddesdale, the valley of the Liddell Water which rises in Scotland, flows south-westwards to the border and joins the Esk in the area formerly known as the Debatable Land before entering the Solway Firth. Here the largest families were the Armstrongs and Elliotts in Liddesdale and the Grahams who lived in and around the Debatable Land. Also in this area, and on both sides of the border, lived many other riding families like the Beatties, Croziers, Kerrs, Halls, Nixons, Fosters, Bells, Hetheringtons, Irvines, Storeys, Littles and Nobles, and stretching from the border north-west to Annandale were the powerful Johnstons. It is relevant to Fermanagh to remark, without going into detail, that the exploits of these clans led both English and Scottish governments to devise special systems of authority, which, nevertheless, completely failed to alter, and even became part of, the lawless way of life which had grown up on their frontier.

Until 1603: in that year Elizabeth of England died and James VI became King of England as well as of Scotland. He had the will and the opportunity to pacify the Borders which he now called the 'middle shires' of his new united kingdom. His campaign was ruthless and sustained. In 1603 thirty-two Elliotts, Armstrongs, Johnstons, Beattys and others were hanged, fifteen were banished and one hundred and forty outlawed. The campaign continued throughout the decade, and the Grahams suffered most. They were not only a riding family of long standing but they occupied some of the best land in the west Marches. In 1605 an attempt, modified by death and escape, was made to transport 150 Grahams to the Low Countries. In 1606 124 Grahams were shipped to Roscommon, but after two years of resentment and resistance on their part only half a dozen families remained in the county. It was suggested that the Grahams scattered in various parts of Ireland should be moved to Ulster, but the Lord Deputy thought it unwise. 'They are now dispersed,

146

and when they shall be placed upon any land together, the next country will find them ill neighbours, for they are a fractious and naughty people'.

And so the Borders were subdued. In 1611 a report 'lists the names of thirty-eight who are to hang at Jedburgh and Dumfries, of others cautioned, and of about sixty still fugitive. Elliots, Nixons, Armstrongs, Irvines, Johnstones and even Grahams are among those marked for death, warning and banishment – Thom, Jok and Lancie Armstrangis . . . sall pass furth of the Kingdomes of Scotland and England, and sall not returne. . .'.

Where could they go in face of such persecution? From 1610 onwards the same government which cleared so many people from the Borders wanted British settlers for their Plantation in Ulster. Livingstone has shown that Armstrongs, Elliots, Croziers, Fosters, Grahams, Hetheringtons, Irvines, Nixons, and Storeys were all among the earliest and most widespread tenant settlers in Fermanagh. Current evidence suggests that although many of these names are well known throughout Ulster (families like the Grahams dispersed widely and strongly) they are particularly strong in Fermanagh, especially the Armstrongs and Elliotts, the main families of Liddesdale. And while the names of most of the Plantation landlords of the county have disappeared the names of their tough and tenacious tenants have stayed and multiplied to become a presence in Fermanagh stronger than that created by any similar group in any other of the planted counties.

It can be suggested that the reasons for this presence are intimately bound up with the particular circumstances and qualities of the original settlers. A desire to escape from persecution, and perhaps a last effort to avoid living under the restrictions of state authority, drove many people with Border names to Ulster in the early seventeenth century, and Fermanagh may have attracted them as being far from their British troubles and on the frontier of the new plantation. But an even more important factor in the occurrence of a large number of Border names in twentieth century Fermanagh may well have been the ability of these resilient people not only to come to the county but to stay in it throughout the troubles of the seventeenth century. Contemporary observers remarked that the Scots were hardier settlers than the English and the Borderers must have been even better adapted to life on a new frontier. Not only were they early and widespread in the plantation of Fermanagh, but in the 1659 'Census', compiled after the Plantation in most of Ulster had been overwhelmed by the 1641 Rising, the same names reappear as constituting almost all the numerous non-Irish names in Fermanagh – Armstrong, Elliott, Johnston, Nixon, Crozier, Graham, Irvine, Noble, Scott. Very few were gentry but they clearly had the art of survival. Whatever happened in other parts of Ulster the families of the original Plantation seem not to have been driven out of Fermanagh. Far from any escape back to Scotland they must have stayed either as fugitives in the open countryside, as their forebears had learned to do in the Borders, or defending themselves in the undefeated outpost of Enniskillen. And when the settlers again began to arrive later in the seventeenth century comparatively few came to the distant county of Fermanagh, leaving the descendants of the Gaels and of the earliest settlers to make of it what they could.

And so the pattern of Fermanagh evolved. The comments in this article are deliberately general, directing attention towards the value of studying family name distribution. But its methods can and should be applied to more particular problems. For example, questions have sometimes arisen about the suggested inconsistency of the fact that there is so little Presbyterianism in Fermanagh, although apparently settled by many Scots. Having located the origins of many of these 'Scots' by studying their names we can look to the Anglo-Scottish border for a possible answer to the problem. In so far as they had any religion the Borderers probably inclined towards Roman Catholicism, but the truth of the situation may be better summed up by the story of the visitor to Liddesdale who, finding no churches asked, 'Are there no Christians here?', and received the reply, "Na, we's a' Elliotts and Armstrongs.' Presumably the Borderers put up little theological resistance to accepting the Church of the other settler interests, the landlords and their English tenants. Fermanagh therefore necessitates qualification of the use of Presbyterianism as an overall index of Scots settlement in Ulster. In fact it draws attention to the origin of some settlers in an area of Britain where the distinction between 'English' and 'Scots' was very blurred indeed.

And general contentions gain depth from the consideration of local elaboration and variation. Maps of the distribution of individuals names can throw up detailed questions about the relationship of human history to the environment. Is a surname found in a particular area; on low ground; on the coast? The location of names or groups of names may relate to types of speech, farming practice, religion, and all kinds of other culture elements which may help us to understand the development of our community.

One important point remains to be made. Throughout this article I have referred to 'settler' names and families. By this I do not imply distinction between the people of present day Fermanagh. Because of the fact that each of us is heir to many surnames the terminology used in family name study must refer to the historical elements within the community rather than within the individual. Indeed family name study in Fermanagh can help to demonstrate that all its ordinary people have shown a capacity for survival in difficult times and that throughout the centuries, as their work has moulded the land, the same land has equally moulded them.

*We wish to acknowledge the help of the Clogher Historical Society in granting permission for the reproduction of this article first published in The Clogher Record Vol. 8, No. 3, pp. 285-289 (1875).

SOURCES FOR THE HISTORY OF BELFAST IN THE SEVENTEENTH AND EARLY EIGHTEENTH CENTURIES

by Jean Agnew
Ulster Historical Foundation

This article is about sources for the history of Belfast and its inhabitants from the middle of the seventeenth century: how I am using them for my research into Belfast merchants and how you can use them if your ancestors came from Belfast.

Belfast in the seventeenth century was a very small place covering only a quarter of a square mile including the castle gardens. The original settlement was on a spit of land, a sandbank between the Farset and the Owynvarra, two small rivers which ran into the Lagan. The more northerly of these two rivers, the Farset, ran open down the middle of High Street and the town dock was where it joined the Lagan. Because Belfast was the lowest point at which the Lagan could be forded there was probably some kind of settlement here from almost pre-historic times, and the castle was originally built during the period of Anglo-Norman occupation; nevertheless when the town was planned and laid out at the beginning of the seventeenth century, it was more or less on what we would call a 'green field site'.

Apart from the pioneering history of the town written in the last century by Frederick Benn, very little has been written about Belfast before the eighteenth century. Even those books which purport to cover the entire history of the town and its trade generally contain about half a chapter on the seventeenth century and their authors only get into their stride when they reach the development of the linen industry in the eighteenth century. Linen was of course exported before that date – it is a mistake to think that the industry was introduced by the Huguenots – but the quantities were very small. Quite large quantities of yarn were also exported to England, but the early prosperity and rapid growth of the town, which within a century of its foundation had become one of the major ports of Ireland, was due to its being the centre in the north for the provisions trade.

The chief goods exported from Ireland in the seventeenth century were butter, beef, tallow, leather, grain, fish and timber. The most important of these was butter which went to markets in Europe and the

150

Colonies. Until the 1660s great numbers of live cattle were exported to England to be fattened up for the London market. This was banned, largely as the result of lobbying in the English Parliament by M.P.s representing the English cattle breeders, and the short term results of the ban were severe in many parts of Ireland. However Belfast did not suffer, partly because there is no indication that the Belfast merchants were involved in the live cattle trade: the cattle went out through Donaghadee which had a more suitable harbour and offered a shorter crossing to the mainland, and partly because the ban on live cattle exports meant that more beef was available for salting.

There are of course drawbacks to a trade that is based on the export of agricultural surpluses. Irish trade was favoured for some time by the incidence of cattle plague in Europe and the poor state of French agriculture. There was a steady market in the colonies: in the West Indian islands the gradual squeezing out of small farmers, and the increasing use of expensive slave labour, led to intensive cultivation of sugar and tobacco for export and reliance on imported foodstuffs. European wars closed some markets but the Belfast merchants were adept at finding ways round embargoes and ships were frequently registered in the names of residents of neutral or even enemy countries and quite commonly carried two sets of papers. Even when goods reached their market in safety they might prove unsaleable. Provisions are highly perishable and, in spite of great care taken in salting and packing, merchants' letter books at this time are full of complaints about rancid butter and stinking fish.

Imports, which included sugar and tobacco from the colonies and wine from France and Spain, can mostly be classed as luxury goods. Tobacco is an exception – it rapidly became an essential part of life for all classes in Ireland. The market for luxury goods was limited and easily glutted. Moreover the customers were highly discriminating. In 1667 the merchant George McCartney wrote to one of his contacts in Dublin 'salt will do no good here neither will bad Spanish wine [there are] few drinkers of wine and what they drink they would have it good': claret and brandy sold best in the North. The import of wine was a chancy business because it travelled badly and was subject to very high customs duty on arrival, so that bad wine that would not sell could wipe out the profit on the goods exported on the outward leg of the journey.

In spite of the hazards of trade, the town prospered and

contemporary descriptions refer to the streets being piled high with barrels of provisions waiting to be loaded on ships. Belfast had a poor harbour. Even at high tide it was impossible to bring big ships up to the town dock and at low tide the Lagan was barely navigable: it was shallow enough to be forded just above the Long Bridge. Ships used to lie three miles away down the Lough in the Pool of Garmoyle where they were unloaded by lighters called gabards. A certain amount of embanking was carried out in the eighteenth century and new quays were built but the line of the water front remained quite a way back from the present line which was embanked in the nineteenth century.

The earliest settlers in the town were English, Scots and Manxmen. However, in the 1650s an increasing number of settlers, many of them merchants, arrived from Scotland. They were mostly Presbyterians and by the end of the seventeenth century the majority of townsmen were Presbyterians. Apart from the merchants, and of course the ships' captains, mariners and shipwrights, a great many more of the townsmen were involved in the provisions trade. There were large numbers of butchers, tallow chandlers, tanners, curriers, cordwainers and coopers, but by the 1680s there were also goldsmiths, watch and clockmakers, cutlers, a bow maker, two gunsmiths, a sugar baker, a confectioner, a stationer and a bookbinder. There was also a very large number of alesellers and innkeepers. A bye-law of 1665 forbad drinking or playing of games after 9 o'clock, and if there were public entertainments, apart from sermons, no record of them has survived other than occasional references to races between horses belonging to the local gentry on the Earl of Donegall's race course, which was thought to be much inferior to that at Lisburn. Even so, a letter of 1681 from the merchant George Macartney relating to a ship's captain, of doubtful reputation, states 'I find him not the man he ought to be, for all the time he hath been here he stayed ashore idling and debauching' which suggests that Belfast had sufficient amenities at that date to afford the ungodly a thoroughly good time.

There are advantages and disadvantages to genealogical research in Belfast. The advantages are a number of good early genealogical sources which are probably without parallel in Ulster except perhaps in Londonderry. The main drawback is a lack of continuity: many Belfast families died out or bought land and moved out of town, and were replaced by an increasing stream of immigrants.

A combination of low rents in Ireland and poor harvests in Scotland attracted many Scots settlers to Ulster in the late 1690s and early 1700s, and there was also a steady drift from the countryside to the town, which increased in volume in the latter part of the eighteenth century. The town's population which had been 8,500 in 1757 had reached 20,000 by 1800, over 70,000 by 1840 and at least 300,000 by the 1890s. This means that if you have an ancestor who emigrated from Belfast, the later the date of emigration, the less likely he is to be descended from a family who were there in the seventeenth and eighteenth centuries.

I am a postgraduate student at Queen's University and the subject of my thesis is the merchant community in Belfast from 1660 to 1707: the latter year was when the Presbyterian merchants were ousted from the Corporation and ceased to play a part in town government. I am attempting a socio-economic study of the merchant community, and apart from studying their trading methods and business contacts, I am also interested in intermarriage and other relationships between groups of families, relationships with the gentry and religious affiliations. This means that I have used all major genealogical sources for Belfast and many minor ones.

Belfast received its Charter of Incorporation in 1613. This was not in recognition of the town's importance, there were only a couple of streets at that date, but as a means of packing the Irish House of Commons with new Protestant Members of Parliament. Until the nineteenth century, Belfast's two M.P.s were elected by the Sovereign (or Mayor) and Corporation, which consisted of twelve Burgesses; the M.P.s, the Sovereign, and most of the Burgesses were nominated by Lord Donegall whose influence and patronage were paramount in Belfast as he actually owned the whole town and much of the surrounding land.

The Corporation kept their records in the Town Book but this contains little of use before the 1640s. The first lists of inhabitants of Belfast are the cess or rate lists of the 1640s. Unlike, for example, Carrickfergus, the town had no endowments of land so many extraordinary expenses had to be met by rates levied on the inhabitants. The Town Book contains cess lists from 1639-45. Since a fair number of widows are named, the names probably represent households. I have put together all the lists in print and alphabeticised them and find that there are 341 individuals named with about 237 surnames. It is hard to be precise as there are many variant spellings of surnames. The rates varied from about 1s 6d for the poorer households to 10s plus for the better-off. As the civil war progressed, the rates became more frequent and heavier. The town was occupied by Monro's army for several years and most of the payments were for food for the soldiers, fodder for their horses, turves, candles and so on. By 1651 the town was in arrears with payments and petitioned the Commonwealth Commissioners for some relief from their contributions. Several sources suggest that times were so hard in the 1640s that some of the inhabitants actually left Belfast.

Also from the Town Book, but of more use than the cess lists, is the Roll of Freemen. Freedom of the town meant a reduced rate of dues in the market and the various town courts and so was essential for anyone in trade. (Freemen did not have voting rights as in Dublin). Judging by the occupations of those listed – which include labourers and porters – it seems likely that the majority of townsmen were Freemen. The most useful section of the Freemen's roll runs from 1636 to 1682 and contains about 1280 names. The Roll gives name, occupation, date of becoming free, fee paid, and whether the Freeman had served an apprenticeship in the town. Such apprentices did not pay a fee and the principle became established that the sons of Freemen received their own freedom gratis. In addition, a number of people, mostly gentry, were also made Freemen without fee. By the 1670s the fees became fixed at 10s for ordinary tradespeople and more for merchants. (This was at a time when labourers earned 4d-6d a day). A few people were excused fees – for example in 1665 Richard Saltus, butcher, 'for his many services to the town'; some paid in instalments – for example in 1656, Black George McCartney 'paid 20s now and 20s when he is better able', and a few defaulted altogether – like Abraham Egerton, butcher, who was made free in 1671 but 'ran away and paid nothing'. The fees paid were of course an important source of income for a borough without endowments. I have indexed this Roll and the post 1723 one and interesting family groups appear. It is quite helpful for estimating ages, or at least for sorting out generations. Unfortunately no record has survived of Freemen between 1682 and 1723. By that date a considerable change had taken place. It had clearly stopped being essential to be a Freeman. After 1723, there are far more 'honorary' Freemen from the nobility and gentry; merchants and tradesmen did not become free at the beginning of their careers, and by the middle of the century, a number of children – even infants – can be identified in the roll, generally the offspring of the current Sovereign.

Despite drawbacks the Roll of Freemen is still a useful list of Belfast inhabitants.

To return briefly to the seventeenth century, the 1666 and 1669 Hearth Money Rolls have survived for Co. Antrim (including Belfast of course) and these have recently been published by the Public Record Office of Northern Ireland. The editor Trevor Carleton has put the names within parishes into alphabetical order, but if you are not sure of the parish, remember there are complete indexes to these and other Hearth Money rolls available for reference at PRONI.

If you are looking for ancestors in seventeenth century Belfast you should use all of these sources as, taken together, it is possible to build up quite a lot of information about particular families.

By far the most important genealogical source for the early part of the eighteenth century, is the Rosemary Street Funeral Register. The First and Second Rosemary Street Presbyterian congregations owned a collection of mort-cloths or palls which they hired out for funerals. This was common practice in Scotland at this date and probably elsewhere in Ulster although this is the only northern Irish hiring register which has survived. The two Rosemary Street congregations also owned cloaks and hats which were hired for the mourners. This collection of funeral equipment was used by residents of Belfast regardless of religion, and also by many of the gentry, clergy and substantial farmers as far away as counties Londonderry and Tyrone. Their use was not confined to the wealthy; the register shows that plenty of poor people used the mort cloths and that the hiring charge was often 'forgiven' by the session.

The register lists about 2,000 funerals, each entry giving the place of residence and occupation of the person involved. The entries generally name the head of the family and his relationship with the person being buried; (for example, 'Mr James Reed apothecary his child's funeral'; children and wives are never actually named and ages are not given) then follows the name of the person paying for or arranging the funeral. If this person is a relative, the register usually states the relationship. This is extremely useful: for example there are entries in August 1721 for the wife of Hugh Montgomery of Donegore who died in Peter Hill and was buried in Shankill by her son Robert Montgomery; and in August 1729, for Mr James Woods living in Malone buried by his daughter Mrs McGee of Waring Street, widow. Even where the relationship is not stated it is often possible to discover it by further research. For example,

Thomas Pottinger, the famous merchant who gave his name to Pottinger's Entry, was buried in 1715 by Mr Patrick Trail who turned out to be his son-in-law. The register was printed just over a hundred years ago. The Ulster Historical Foundation is bringing out a new edition with an index and notes.

There are no baptismal registers for the First Rosemary Street Presbyterian Church until 1757 but these are good and indexed. There is nothing for the Second Presbyterian Church, (which became known as All Souls), before 1771. The earliest baptismal registers for Belfast are those of the Third Rosemary Street Presbyterian Church which begin in 1723 and are also indexed.

For the Church of Ireland parish of Belfast, there are unfortunately no registers surviving before 1745; an earlier volume once existed (it is mentioned in the Town Book) but it disappeared at least a couple of centuries ago. The Belfast, or rather Shankill parish registers are clear, legible and indexed. The marriage register has been published. Just as there are members of the Church of Ireland in the Rosemary Street Funeral Register, so there are Presbyterians in the sections for burials in the Shankill registers; both Presbtyerians and Episcopalians were buried in the graveyard of the Corporation church (the old parish church) in the High Street. Tragically, no record of the gravestone inscriptions was made before the churchyard was cleared at the beginning of the nineteenth century; St George's church stands right on the churchyard – the site of the church is under Victoria Street. Henry Joy, the Belfast antiquarian who wrote at the end of the eighteenth century, was unfortunately daunted by the brambles and mud and made no attempt to transcribe the inscriptions, apart from 'half-remembering' the dates on one or two. But in fairness to Joy it must be said that the graveyard was by his day a most unpleasant place, being regularly flooded, and burials were forbidden there when the Clifton Street cemetery was opened. (The Foundation has published all the Clifton Street inscriptions in volume 4 of the Belfast Gravestone Inscription series).

It is virtually impossible to trace Roman Catholic families in Belfast back beyond the beginning of the nineteenth century when the baptismal register of St. Patrick's parish begins. There were in fact extremely few Roman Catholic families in the town. In 1757 there were said to be only 556 Catholics in Belfast. The earliest estimate of the Catholic population is in the census of c.1659-60 which gives a figure of 223 Irish as against

366 English (which presumably includes the Scots). This figure is probably taken from the poll tax returns and you would need to multiply it by about three or four to get the total population. These Irish are something of a mystery as there are very few names in the 1669 hearth money roll for Belfast and the surrounding district which sound Irish, and virtually none in any other records. In 1709 the Sovereign – another George Macartney – was ordered to arrest any popish priest within his jurisdiction. He reported that 'we have not amongst us within the town above seven papists'. The nearest Roman Catholic priest was Father Phelomy O'Hamol at Derriaghy. Father O'Hamol was ill but surrendered himself as soon as he was able, whereat the Protestant inhabitants offered to pay his bail as he had been instrumental in protecting the goods of some of them during the late Revolution.

Professional genealogists usually hope to use estate records where there are no church registers or where these are inadequate. Unfortunately, very little in the way of estate records has survived for Belfast for the 17th century. The entire town and most of the surrounding townlands on the Co. Antrim side belonged to the Donegall family. They had a fine house at Carrickfergus but generally lived in Belfast Castle when not in Dublin or London. In 1708 the Castle was gutted by fire, and three of the younger daughters of the Earl of Donegall died in the blaze. It seems likely, although I have not seen this stated anywhere, that the same blaze destroyed most of the estate records, as very little survives for the seventeenth century. There is of course a very large collection for the later 18th and 19th centuries in PRONI. The earliest surviving rental dates from c.1719 but includes a few names of people who had been dead for several years. It only lists 95 tenants for the whole of Belfast. The rest of the inhabitants of Belfast therefore were subtenants of these 95.

There are a fair number of deeds relating to Belfast enrolled in the Registry of Deeds from 1708 and many of these refer to earlier deeds, dating back as far as the 1670s. They are not a very good genealogical source unless you are looking for one of the more important Belfast families. Properties were sublet for terms of years rather than lives. Many deeds do mention the occupiers of adjacent properties but you would have to be very lucky to find a particular family in this way. Moreover many properties were known by the name of the original tenant and deeds as late as the 1730s may refer to Belfast residents from before the Civil War of the 1640s.

Finally, one of the best sources for Belfast genealogy is the Belfast Newsletter which was founded in 1737. It carried notices of marriages and deaths, although there are not a great many of these for the first twenty years. These entries have been extracted and indexed up to 1800 and copies are available both at the Public Record Office of Northern Ireland and at the Linen Hall Library. The period between 1800 and 1864 – when civil registration of deaths started – is covered by a card index kept at the Linen Hall. These entries, which include quite a lot of births in the nineteenth century, relate to families all over the eastern side of Ulster, not just to residents of Belfast. In addition, a major computer indexing project was carried through at Queen's University some years ago wherein all the information on the files of the *Belfast Newsletter* 1737-1800 (apart from details of the weather) was transcribed and is held on a massive data base. This will be an extremely important source of information when available.

SOURCES FOR THE HISTORY OF BELFAST FAMILIES, SEVENTEENTH AND EIGHTEENTH CENTURIES

1. Cess lists, 1639-45, printed in *The Town Book of the Corporation of Belfast*, ed. R. M. Young (Belfast 1892) (Index at the Ulster Historical Foundation).

2. Hearth Money Rolls for Co. Antrim, printed as *Heads and Hearths, the Hearth Money Rolls and Poll tax returns for Co. Antrim 1660-69*, Trevor Carleton (PRONI 1991) (Index available at PRONI)

3. Roll of Freemen 1636-82 and 1723-96, printed in *The Town Book* (Indexes at the Ulster Historical Foundation).

4. Rosemary Street Funeral Register 1712-36 (To be published by the Ulster Historical Foundation).

5. Presbyterian registers: First Rosemary Street, from 1757 (PRONI: CR4/5)
   Second Rosemary Street, from 1771 (PRONI: CR4/9)
   Third Rosemary Street, from 1723 (PRONI: MIC1P/7)

6. Shankill parish registers: index 1745-1823 (PRONI: T.679/260)
   baptisms, marriages and deaths from 1745
   (PRONI: T.679/237, 238, 256, 224, 225, 252 etc.)

7. Donegall rental, c.1719 (PRONI: D.2249/61: Index at the Ulster Historical Foundation).

8. Registry of Deeds: see article in *Familia*, Vol. 2, No. 6, 1990, pp.78 et seq.

9. *Belfast Newsletter*: indexes to births, marriages and deaths, 1738-1800 at the Linen Hall Library, and at PRONI (T.1584); 1800-64, card index at the Linen Hall Library.

IRISH EMIGRATION TO CANADA:
THE DIRECTIVE ROLE OF WILLIAM HUTTON

C. J. Houston

Erindale College

University of Toronto

W. J. Smyth

St. Patrick's College

Maynooth

For much of the first half of the nineteenth century the Irish constituted the largest immigrant group in Canada, outnumbering the English, Scottish and American settlers. In the post 1855 period the significance of the Irish waned amongst the migration stream and they became a scarcely identifiable minority. However, in that critical first half of the century the Irish settlers laid firm bases for settlements that were to retain for many generations, the distinctive cultural identity transplanted from Ireland. The nature and identity of these Canadian-Irish settlements varied in response to both the composition of the Irish immigrant community (be they Protestant or Catholic), and varied also in response to the environmental challenges posed by the different geographical regions of the huge country. Thus, for example, in Newfoundland a largely Catholic Irish community supported for the most part by fishing emerged early on, whereas in neighbouring New Brunswick the emphasis was on farming and part-time forestry. The rich agricultural lands of Ontario sustained Irish communities that were characterised by large-scale commercial farming, and further west, the mountains of British Columbia attracted gold miners, foresters and ranchers. No single stereotype of the Irish in Canada is applicable.

Of course not all Irish immigrants ended up in rural or resource-based activities. The immigrants numbered amongst them a minority of educated persons who would fill niches in the surveying and administration of the new country. Many of this elite were Protestants, often Dublin-born and Trinity-educated, and their contribution to Canada has often been overlooked. Illustrative of this class, yet indicative also of the lot of ordinary settlers, is the life of William Hutton, farmer, writer, administrator and emigration propagandist.

Recent studies of nineteenth century Irish emigration to Canada have dispensed with the notion of the exodus being a haphazard flight from poverty, lacking in forward planning and oblivious of the nature of the likely regions of settlement.[1] Rather, it has been clearly demonstrated that, with the possible exception of the Famine years, the migration was characterized by a considerable degree of advance planning and foresight. The migration was part of a process which included much more than the simple transfer of a population from one district in Europe to a new region in North America. That migration process included also a movement of information which was conveyed in the form of emigrant letters, ship advertisements, newspaper reports, and emigration pamphlets. Later in the century this information flow would be formally recognised in the establishment of Canadian Government emigration offices in Dublin and Belfast, but even in the pre-Famine era the rapidity and extensive nature of the exchange of news, information and guidance was quite striking.In 1820, for example, it was recorded that in several cabins in the Sperrin Mountains of County Londonderry . . ." we observed printed notices stuck up of ships about to sail for America, and found that a great many are going from time to time." [2]

The flow of letters back home, and indeed the growing frequency whereby remittance money or pre-paid passages directly influenced the choice of destination, meant that very strong kinship bonds and neighbourhood links evolved to span the Atlantic. As many a genealogical researcher has discovered there were close and enduring ties between particular localities in the New World and identifiable parishes and even townlands in Ireland.[3] This linkage was recognised by

1. The role of kinship links and information flows in directing Irish emigrants to specific destinations in Canada have been analysed in the writings of: Bruce Elliott, *Irish Migration To The Canadas* (McGill – Queen's University Press, Montreal,1988); Also C. J. Houston and W. J. Smyth, *Irish Emigration And Canadian Settlement*, (University of Toronto Press, Toronto 1990); Also J. J. Mannion, "Old World Antecedents, New World Adaptations" in Thomas P. Power (ed.) *The Irish in Atlantic Canada* 1780-1900, (New Ireland Press, Fredericton New Brunswick,1991) p.30-96; Also P. M. Toner, "The origins of the New Brunswick Irish" *Journal of Canadian Studies*, 23 : 1 (1988) p.104-119.
2. Quoted in Houston and Smyth op.cit. p.103.
3. This has best been emphasised in the works of Bruce Elliott, op.cit. and Houston and Smyth op.cit; also Peter Toner, "The Irish of New Brunswick at mid-century: 1851 census" in P. M. Toner (ed) *New Ireland Remembered* (Fredericton, New Brunswick, 1988) p.106-22.

contemporaries and as early as 1825 a House of Lords' committee commented . . .

> '. . .there was a colony of the friends of the Protestants of Ireland settled in America, and there was a constant coming of letters from their friends, inviting and encouraging them to emigrate. Almost every Protestant family in Ireland has his friends before him in America; they consider it as merely going to visit their own relations.'[4]

In this instance the term America really referred to British North America, i.e., Canada and the reference to Protestants simply recognised that they, not Catholics, predominated in these early movements across the Atlantic.

The volume and contents of emigrant correspondence has been commented upon in detail by recent writers[5] and for the most part these commentaries have concentrated upon the writings of the largely unidentified poorer and more simple elements of society. These letters, often with phonetical spelling, are all the more important and evocative for that. However, with some notable exceptions, such as the Carrothers and Kirkpatrick letters held in the Public Record Office in Belfast these letters do not extend over more than a few years, and it is therefore difficult to establish the evolution of society in the new land. For this reason it is now proposed to examine the correspondence of one emigrant whose communications from Canada were sustained for almost thirty years, and in whose private and public writings the whole process of migration and resettlement is commented upon in detail. That emigrant, William Hutton, had settled in Canada in 1834 and the remaining twenty-seven years of his life coincided with the period when emigration from Ireland to Canada was at its peak. He was not perhaps a typical emigrant, but through him much can be learned of the context of Canadian development and the emergence of the country to which countless thousands of other Irish were to emigrate.

4. Quoted in Houston and Smyth op.cit p.92.
5. For the most comprehensive use of emigrant letters see Kerby Miller *Emigrants and Exiles* (Oxford University Press, Oxford, 1985).

WILLIAM HUTTON (1801-1861).

William Hutton, the sixth son of a Unitarian clergyman, was born in Dublin in 1801. While his elder brothers were directed into trade and the professions William was sent by his parents to become a gentleman farmer. Having acquired the theory of 'improved agriculture' and having become acquainted with the writings of continental agricultural theoreticians such as Ricardo, the young Hutton, in his early twenties, took out a lease on a farm in County Tyrone.[6] Located on the extensive flood plain of the River Foyle near Strabane the farm at Grange Foyle contained three hundred acres. Within a few years he was to double its size by the acquisition of a lease for an adjoining property. In the early 1820s he married Frances McCrea, the daughter of a prosperous neighbouring farmer and over the next seven years four daughters and a son were born to him.

Despite his training in the theory and practice of husbandry William Hutton failed to make a success of his farming venture. He engaged in mixed farming but neither his crops nor his livestock generated much return and he continued to rely upon his parents for financial support. In 1833 he wrote to his landlord appealing to be released from the remaining years of his lease for

'We have been labouring now nearly ten years in Grange without its ever affording us a coat to our backs, but on the contrary swallowing up every shilling of our income from other sources. With this fact before us and a family of five children, we appeal to your kindness to allow us to go elsewhere.'[7]

Hutton's predicament, despite the scale of his farm, was not unlike that of many of his fellow Irish tenantry and like many before him he turned towards North America as a possible opportunity for a fresh start and future prosperity. Like so many of his countrymen also he left his wife and family in Ireland while he explored the new land seeking a place to settle.

In April 1834 he landed in New York, having probably sailed from Dublin, and spent several weeks investigating possible farm sites in

6. For the early history of Hutton's life see Gerald E. Boyce, *Hutton of Hastings*, (Belleville, 1972).
7. Quoted in Boyce, op.cit. p.5.

upstate New York in a traverse which ran from Albany right up to the Canadian border at Niagara. In his travels he had introductions to many Irish, Scottish and English gentlemen farmers who provided him with information on produce prices and the cost of local land. Unimpressed with the land quality and deterred by the high price of land (upwards of fifty dollars an acre) Hutton crossed into Canada where he stayed for some time with his cousin, Francis Hincks, who had emigrated from Cork two years earlier. 'Frank Hincks and his lady are truly kind and hospitality itself, and have an interesting lovely baby of ten months old . . .'[8] he reported to his mother in Dublin in his first transAtlantic correspondence. Little did he realize then that his cousin would, within twenty years, become the Prime Minister of Canada but in 1834, as later, Hutton displayed a keen sense of kinship and family loyalty. Much of his future progress depended upon his availing of the patronage and financial help which such connections could offer.

Following several geographical forays into the settled regions of what was to later become Ontario, William Hutton decided eventually to settle in the Moira river valley near Belleville in the eastern part of the region. Purchasing a farm of 165 acres, more than half of it already cleared, at a cost of $660 he established what was to be his home for the remainder of his life. For the next eighteen years he earned his living from a mixture of farming and petty local government jobs. Certainly, during this period he was never rich, and barely comfortable. On more than one occasion he had to turn to his family in Ireland for assistance and overall he would appear to have been a less than competent farmer. In fact his wife, Frances, would seem to have taken charge of many of the routine chores, leaving him to pursue more cerebral activities.

For the rest of his life William Hutton was to remain, in his own words, "an inveterate scribbler". He corresponded with his mother in Ireland every few weeks, outlining in his letters not only the affairs of his family but also Canadian public affairs in general. After his death in 1861 his transAtlantic correspondence found its way back across the ocean to his Belleville home where it was subsequently to form the basis of Gerald Boyce's 1972 publication, *Hutton of Hastings*. In addition to such private writing Hutton also committed many of his thoughts to print,

8. Ibid p.9.

earning in the process various prize monies in competitions at agricultural shows, as well as royalties on some of his more successful publications. He was a methodical, but not an inspired writer and kept a diary of all his travels and his observations of local conditions. Recounted subsequently in factual displays his diarist writings are, at times, obsessively detailed and flooded with statistical information on prices, transportation costs and market trends. They are, however, invaluable as insights into the functioning of Canadian society at the time.

The significance of William Hutton, however, does not rest solely upon his reputation as a writer and as a polemicist, for the young Irish immigrant eventually made his mark in the world of the public service. Utilizing to the full the patronage of his cousin Francis Hincks, Hutton was able to transcend the world of gentleman farmer and local government administrator to become in 1855 the first Secretary of the combined Bureaux of Agriculture and Statistics – the forerunner of the modern Department of Agriculture. This Bureau had as one of its briefs the task of overseeing the publishing of the 1851 Canadian census. Significantly also, it had charge of land colonization policy and through the exercise of this power Hutton was able to directly influence the Government's attitude to immigration. The policy of opening up the rocky and infertile Canadian Shield to agricultural settlement by means of Colonization Roads was largely the product of Hutton's belief in the unlimited agricultural potential of the new land.[9] Furthermore, by means of his Government sponsored emigration pamphlets Hutton sought to attract immigrants to the new settlement frontier, and indeed from his very earliest days in Canada he had served as a propagandist for the new country.

Hutton's surviving writings may be subdivided into three broadly defined groups, each reflective of either different periods of his life or of

9. W. J. Smyth and C. J. Houston, 'Limits to Growth, The Canadian Shield in Nineteenth Century Ontario', Paper delivered at University College London Conference on Canadian Studies, February 1992.

particular interests at the time. The most extensive group is composed of his published writings which concentrate for the most part upon the agricultural attractions of Canada as a potential destination for British and Irish farmers. These publications commenced in 1834 and extended into the early 1860s in the form of posthumous reprints of his later pamphlets. In a second group may be identified the personal correspondence with his mother which continued throughout his life, and the bulk of which has been republished in Boyce's biography. Finally, a collection of letters to his brother-in-law John McCrea of Co. Tyrone contain a wealth of information on both public and private matters. Collectively these writings are a good guide to the social and economic history of the period, but above all they are an excellent introduction to the whole process of nineteenth century emigration to Canada.

THE PUBLISHED WRITINGS 1834-1861

Upon his arrival in Canada in 1834, and finding himself with some free time to be spent before he could take up possession of his selected farm William Hutton proceeded to publish his impressions of the new land in a series of four open letters to his afore-mentioned brother-in-law, John McCrea. These letters, which were really essays of circa two thousand words each, were published in the *British Farmers' Magazine*, and they provide a clear account of the rational process of farm selection engaged in by Hutton as he travelled across Ontario, inspecting the soil quality, climate and transportation advantages of the different regions. In his text he also conveys important information about the cost of land acquisition for free grants of land had ceased and land purchase was now the norm. Partially cleared farms with a house and barn cost from £4.10.0 to £10 per acre, depending upon location, and even "wild land" sold for fifteen to twenty shillings per acre and cost upwards of £3 per acre to clear. Intending immigrants who hoped to acquire a stake in the New World probably required upwards of £100 to make a downpayment on a farm and provide subsistence for themselves and their families until the first crops matured. This sum could be acquired by those willing to labour for some time in Ontario where, as Hutton noted, wages for agricultural labourers were £25 to £30 per annum.

In these early writings he also provided useful information about the survey system in Ontario and the system of townships which 'are about nine miles by twelve' and which were subdivided into lots of 200 acres or fractions thereof.[10] The lots in their natural state were covered by forest which had to be cleared before farming could commence and Hutton wisely advised that 'the rapidity with which a Canadian can cut down the forest is almost beyond the comprehension of one who has never witnessed it . . . a novice can do nothing at this business'.[11] Notwithstanding these initial obstacles to agricultural settlement Hutton firmly aligned himself with the supporters of the contemporary emigration debate in Britain and argued

> 'It appears to me to be a subject worthy of the consideration of the poor law commissioners in Ireland, and of the poor rate payers in England, and in fact, of all those interested in diminishing the number of paupers in Great Britain, whether it would not, in the end, remunerate the country to send them out to Canada. It is quite clear, that in a new and not thickly-settled country, manual labour is what is most required . . . The government has many vessels unemployed, in which they could send out the super-numeracy poor at a very cheap rate. . .'[12]

It was a theme to which he was to return frequently in his later career as was his strident advocacy of Belleville as a district of great future prosperity and a most bountiful environment which was characterized by 'another great advantage, the healthiness of the climate, there having been no fever or ague here of any consequence since 1829'.[13]

William Hutton returned to themes of land acquisition and farming techniques in his prize essay, 'On Agriculture And its Advantages As a Pursuit', for which he reserved the gold medal of the Agricultural Society of Upper Canada in 1851.[14] In that work he advocated a six course husbandry of mixed farming and in so doing he was articulating the theories propagated by many other contemporary agricultural writers – theories which were largely ignored by ordinary Canadian farmers who

10. The *British Farmers' Magazine*, April 1835.
11. Ibid. June 1835.
12. Ibid. June 1835.
13. Ibid. June 1835.
14. Hutton's prize essay has been republished in Boyce op.cit. p.223-246.

concentrated more remuneratively upon cereal cultivation.[15] The publication of this essay in the leading monthly journal, *The Canadian Agriculturist*, gave Hutton considerable national prominence and within a few months he repeated his success by publishing another prize winning essay, 'A Report on the State of Agriculture in the County of Hastings'.[16] It was from this platform, and aided by the patronage of Francis Hincks, that Hutton was able to obtain a post in the Inspector-General's office,[17] and within three years he was placed in charge of the Bureau of Agriculture. His appointment to that powerful post was applauded by the editor of *The Canadian Agriculturalist* who noted

'His able reports have already favourably impressed the public mind at home [Great Britain] in favour of Canada, and his long practical acquaintance with both British and Canadian Agriculture must eminently qualify him for his new and important position.'[18]

In his new public service position Hutton was not to obscure his deeply felt views about the prospects for agriculturalists in Canada.

Thereafter his public writings may be subdivided into routine departmental correspondence and reports to the Canadian Parliament on the one hand, and officially sponsored emigration propaganda. In the former, he advocated and reported regularly upon the scheme to construct Colonization Roads linking the settled parts of southern Ontario with the unclaimed territories of the Canadian Shield. Hutton incorrectly believed that the Shield was potentially a new agricultural frontier; in reality it was an infertile wilderness whose wealth lay in timber and minerals.[19] The lack of success notwithstanding, Hutton's attempts to modernize the Bureau of Agriculture and to turn it towards a policy of actively recruiting immigrants represented a major shift in official Government policy. The accounts of it are well captured in the official Government documents of the time.[20] In a more public forum

15. For a discussion of this aspect of early Canadian farming see Kenneth Kelly, 'The Transfer of British Ideas on Improved Farming to Ontario During the First Half of the Nineteenth Century', *Ontario History*, LX111, 1971, p.103-111.
16. Hutton's prize essay, see Boyce op.cit.
17. Boyce op.cit. p.178.
18. Ibid. 194.
19. Houston and Smyth *Irish Emigration* Ch.IV.
20. As indicated by Boyce, Hutton's correspondence with the Bureau of Agriculture is in Department of Agriculture Papers (RG17), Public Archives of Canada.

Hutton articulated his ideas in the form of a pamphlet published in 1854 entitled *Canada: its present condition, prospects, and resources, fully described for the information of intending emigrants.*[21] The pamphlet was reprinted a number of times, translated into several European languages, and thousands of copies were distributed at the expense of the Government. Arising out of this policy of active propaganda the Canadian Government decided in 1859 to appoint official emigration agents in the major emigrant centres of Europe. In their initial years these agents reported directly to Hutton. Continuing this advocacy of his adopted country Hutton also challenged the allegations being made in Europe by writers asserting the superiority of the United States over Canada, and a few months after his death a treatise on this topic was published.[22] Within a few years of his death the settlement focus of Canada shifted from the Canadian Shield of Central Canada to the prairies of the West and William Hutton's writings became obsolete. In their day, however, they had been a powerful expression of a young country asserting its identity and nationhood.

HUTTON'S CORRESPONDENCE WITH HIS MOTHER

From his arrival in Canada William Hutton maintained an unceasing flow of correspondence with his mother in Dublin, communicating every few weeks and always receiving a steady stream of replies. He did in fact predecease his mother, and so the correspondence was maintained right up until his death in 1861. The letters collected by Boyce reveal that in many of the early years Hutton engaged in a pattern of cross-writing with whole paragraphs overwritten at right angles to the text on the initial page and rendering the product almost illegible. Such a measure saved on both paper and postage and was only discontinued in later years when he was somewhat more prosperous.[23] Much of the text of his letters dealt with his factual observations on the climate, vegetation and the agricultural and settlement patterns of his adopted country, all recounted

21. William Hutton, *Caird's Slanders on Canada Answered*, (Toronto 1861).
22. Ibid.
23. Boyce op.cit p.37.

in precise detail. But he also maintained a constant flow of information about his growing family and acknowledged receipt of presents such as the volumes on Shakespeare and Hume which he received in 1835.[24] In these early years he supplemented his income by school teaching and in order to equip the class he requested his mother to send a variety of the Irish National arithmetics, 'as well as my own Lexicon, Dictionary and other classical books which are somewhere about my Father's premises'.[25] As well as the books, he requested his mother to send out flannel to his wife and during the next ten or more years he requested and received a continuous supply of clothes for his wife and books and chattels for the house from his parents in Dublin. This dependence upon imported luxuries was not unusual in the pioneering era of Canadian history, but the sustained volume of gifts was perhaps unique to the Hutton family.

That generosity extended also into financing land purchases by Hutton, and probably more than one thousand pounds was borrowed from his parents, brother and uncle in the early years.[26] Much of this was in the form of interest-free loans, and it was generally invested in land purchase, drainage improvements and construction of the home. In essence, however, Hutton's method of mixed farming was incapable of generating rapid commercial returns and in addition he was but a half-hearted labourer. Much of the routine work continued to be done by his wife, a fact he never tried to hide, and the farm income always required supplementation from his teaching and local administrative jobs.

Hutton's letters also illustrate the network of social contacts which were available to him. He brought with him to Canada an introduction to the lieutenant-governor, Sir John Colborne, and managed to arrange a meeting with him in 1834. Two years later, following the appointment of Sir Francis Bond Head as Colborne's successor, Hutton wrote to his mother asking, 'Are there any of our friends acquainted with him?'[27] In 1841 he again requested his mother '. . . If you hear of any of our friends

24. Ibid. p.43.
25. Ibid. p.46.
26. Ibid. p.61.
27. Ibid. p.67.

who are acquainted either with Sir C. Bagot [the latest lieutenant-governor] or the Secretary of the Colonies, I would write to them myself if there were any at home to make application on my behalf'.[28] Ultimately, however, he was to turn to his cousin, Francis Hincks, for patronage, he having been elected in 1841 to the first Legislative Assembly of the united province of Upper and Lower Canada. Through this family connection Hutton was appointed Warden of the Victoria District of central Ontario in 1842. This close connection with the Hincks was extended in 1843 by Mrs Hincks spending a week with the Hutton family, and subsequently recruiting the young Anna Hutton as a child minder for the Hincks' children.[29] However, during the years 1843-48 Francis Hincks was relegated to the Opposition benches in the Assembly and Hutton's fortunes stagnated, only being resurrected and climaxing when Hincks became Inspector General and later Premier. In this use of patronage neither Hutton nor Hincks were acting without precedent. In the Canada, and indeed Britain, of the day patronage was viewed as an entirely ethical and appropriate method of filling vacancies: social connections were vital for career advancement. On a more humble level, the ordinary emigrants also availed of friendship, kinship and social linkages in their everyday tasks of buying and selling property and produce, and in gleaning information about emerging opportunities in the region.[30] Despite its great distance from Ireland, and the scattered nature of its population, Canada was in many ways a remarkably intimate place operating upon social values and connections directly traceable to particular situations in the Old World. Regular family correspondence of emigrants such as Hutton were at once reflective and causative elements in that complex web of interconnections which spanned the Atlantic.

HUTTON'S CORRESPONDENCE WITH JOHN McCREA, 1848-1857

The collection of letters which are lodged in the Public Record Office of Northern Ireland contain his communications with his brother-in-law, and former neighbour, in Tyrone, John McCrea. These letters pertain to a period of Hutton's life when financial security in the form of

28. Ibid. p.89.
29. Ibid. p.108.
30. Hutton Papers, 1848-60, Public Record Office of Northern Ireland.

a salaried income was finally available. The topics covered in this correspondence: the state of the Canadian economy, the price of land, and progress of the family, are similar to those referred to in his letters to his mother. They are, however, somewhat more explicit on economic and social problems than are his published works of the same period. They are also most revealing of his own personal drive and ambitions, and his willingness to avail of all opportunities for social advancement.

Introducing himself after a prolonged lack of communication, Hutton in 1848 informed McCrea that his public office as Provincial Arbitrator represented 'a high and responsible situation and is very well paid' and confessed that 'I take a good deal of interest in them [politics], and knowing personally almost every member of the Administration, I think a better day is dawning upon us.'[31] He claimed to have property worth at least £5000 and projected overall an image of a successful and well-positioned emigrant. In an unstinting manner he offered to extend to his nephews in Ireland an element of the patronage which had benefited him in Canada . . .

> 'I have often thought whether your lads would not improve their prospects much by coming out here and serving their time with an attorney or medical man. If you had any wish that way, I think I could find offices where they would receive their professional education gratis . . . If you think of sending any of your lads out here, all that I can say is that I will do everything in my power to advance their interests'[32]

In September 1853 Hutton wrote to McCrea announcing that he and his wife would be paying a visit to Ireland that autumn. This was Hutton's first, and only, return visit to Ireland and it was paid for by the Canadian Government, anxious that he publicize his recently completed emigration pamphlet in Europe. The return trip was by a steamer, The Lady Eglington, and was reflective of a new mode of travelling that was safer, more rapid and certainly more comfortable than the older sailing vessels. With such new technology return visits by many emigrants were

31. Hutton Papers op.cit. 20 Oct, 1848.
32. Ibid.

now feasible, though, in comparison with other Europeans, relatively few Irish availed of the opportunity.[33] The visit was a success and as well as seeing his relatives, Hutton managed to sell a manuscript to a London publisher for £20. The visit also strengthened the bond with McCrea and a letter the following year revealed that Hutton was now in receipt weekly of newspapers sent from Tyrone.[34]

Hutton, however, expected to avail of some help from his renewed Irish acquaintances and commented ...

> 'I wish Mr. Chambers would get the Londonderry Standard to review the Emigrants Manual if he can, and send me the paper or any other papers; a good review might put money in my pocket. The Dublin Nation has a most admirable review of it as also the Britannia and Professor Lindley's paper the (London) Gardener's Chronicle'[35]

A month later he commended McCrea for his efforts

> 'I am much obliged by your circulating a knowledge of my little Emigrants' Guide. I am glad to think that it meets very ready sale. The emigrants on board ship coming to Quebec are in possession of numbers of copies, and I have had several letters of capitalists led hither by it.'[36]

In return for such help Hutton promised to send 'a good map of our country and our railroads'.

Ever the propagandist for Canada, Hutton boasted '. . . both in minerals and agriculture we carry off the palm except from Great Britain in agriculture – excelling all other countries. I begin to think that I have not been one bit too sanguine about this Canada.'[37] Likewise, he was dismissive of the attractions of the United States and condemned its Government as 'unprincipled slave holding, grasping repudiators.' Then, as always, Hutton was a firm supporter of the British link with Canada and a strong advocate of the parliamentary system of government. In his private and public writings he continuously asserted the supremacy of the colony, and in that respect all of his writings were part of a single

33. Ibid. 17 Sept, 1853.
34. Ibid. 1 Sept, 1854.
35. Ibid.
36. Ibid. 20 Oct, 1854.
37. Ibid. 27 Aug, 1855.

continuum. His private correspondence was coloured greatly by his political views, and his public career was greatly influenced by his private views. Hutton the emigrant, had become a staunch Canadian.

CONCLUSION

The writings of William Hutton are of themselves interesting, displaying as they do the progress of one man and his family in the emerging Canadian society. However, for those interested in Irish emigration in general they are an invaluable source of insights into the whole emigration process. Not only do they provide accurate and detailed data for prices of commodities and land, but they also reveal the procedures for establishing oneself in society. Especially of interest are the insights provided into the networking of social contacts and the exercise of patronage. By such means many immigrants prospered. Oblique references to former neighbours from Dublin, Tyrone and Londonderry, as well as relatives, also provide some clues as to the reconstitution of Old World friendships in the New, and by themselves also provide some evidence for genealogical researchers. Hutton himself confessed

> 'I never was cut out for a hewer of wood and a drawer of water, and I hope I may be found useful and efficient in other more important pursuits'[38]

In his career he was immensely important to the evolution of Canadian immigration policy. In his writings he was a most efficient chronicler of events and life in his adopted country, and in these he has provided material of lasting value.

38. Boyce op.cit. p.97.

THE McGUCKINS OF DESERTMARTIN: EMIGRATION FROM THE DRAPERS' ESTATE IN CO. LONDONDERRY

by John H. McGuckin, Jr,
of San Francisco, U.S.A.

Sooner or later, every Irish genealogist and family historian confronts the Great Famine and Emigration of the 1840s. For many Irish-Americans, the migration of Irish men, women and children from famine, poverty and religious discrimination in Ireland to the greater freedom and promise of America is central to the 19th century history of our families.

Between 1845 and 1855, 1.5 million people left Ireland for the United States.[1] Many of those immigrants left few traces behind them in Ireland. This article seeks to shed a little light on the reasons several families of McGuckins emigrated from the parish of Desertmartin in County "Derry" during "the Hungry Forties". The emphasis here is not on their subsequent history in the United States, but rather on the reasons these McGuckins left Ulster.[2]

BEFORE THE FAMINE

At the time of the Plantation of Ulster during the reign of King James I of England, the Master and Wardens and Brethren and Sisters of the Guild or Fraternity of the Blessed Mary the Virgin of the Mystery of Drapers of the City of London received one of the larger proportions of the lands confiscated from the Gaelic rebels. Entirely situated in the barony of Loughinsholin and adjacent to the Salters' lands, the Drapers' Estate included 4438 acres of cultivated land and 4760 acres of bog, mountainous and wooded land in the parishes of Artrea, Ballinascreen, Ballinderry, Desertlyn, Desertmartin, Kilcronaghan, Lissan and Derryloran.[3] Living within the Brackaslievegallion Division, which contained the parish of Desertmartin, were many McGuckins.

---

1. K. A. Miller, *Emigrants and Exiles, Ireland and the Irish Exodus to North America* (New York, 1985), p.291.
2. A modified version of this essay is found in volume III of my history of the McGuckin Family, *The McGuckins: More Irish Ancestors* (1991). This and the first two volumes of this series may be obtained from the author at Two Ashbury Terrace, San Francisco, California 94117.
3. J. S. Curl, *The Londonderry Plantation, 1609-1914* (Chichester, 1986), p.191.

The McGuckins of Desertmartin

The records preserved in the Drapers' Hall in London (now deposited in the Public Record Office of N. Ireland) provide a great deal of information, albeit somewhat intermittant, about many of the McGuckins who lived in the Drapers' Estate. Much of this information is found in the periodic reports and surveys which the Drapers' Irish agents forwarded to London. If we supplement this information with the data found in parish and immigration records, extracts from the 1831 census and the 1859 Valuation Survey, we can construct some picture of the McGuckins in 19th century Desertmartin. Finally, the American immigration records and census returns permit us to follow some of the Drapers' McGuckins to the New World.

The 1663 hearth survey of Ulster indicates that Irishmen with surnames similar to McGuckin were living in the Drapers' Proportion during the mid-17th century. In Desertmartin, Tirlo McQuiggan lived in the townland of Carnecrosse and Phelomie McQuillan and Cullo McQuillan lived in Tirrigan. Other McQuiggans lived nearby in the parish of Desertlyn.[4] In these and neighbouring parishes, the McGuckin surname seems to have been pronounced rather more often with a "q" than with a "g" as it was later pronounced in Ballinderry parish. Later parish records, here and elsewhere in Loughinsholin, document the evolution of "McQuiggan" and similar surnames to "McGuigan" and "McGuchan". Thus, it is reasonable to conclude that the three Gaelic hearths in Carnecrosse and Tirrigan are the first record of the McGuckins who nearly 200 years later abandoned their homelands for America.

The 1740 and 1766 religious censuses for Desertmartin find even more variety in the McGuckin surname among the inhabitants of the parish. In 1740, nine Protestant households in the parish were headed by Irishmen with surnames similar to McGuckin: Shan McGihen; Bryan, Thomas, James, Francis, James and Michael McGurk; Bryan McGigan and John McGuken.[5]

4. D. O'Doibhlin, "Hearth Money Rolls (1663), City and County of Derry,"*Derriana*, vol. 1, no. 1, p.69 (1979).
5. Handwritten transcription of the 1740 Protestant census, New England Historical Society, Boston, Massachusetts.

A generation later, there are many other McGuckins in Desertmartin, but all were Roman Catholic.[6]

John McGuchan	John McGuchan	Laurance McCucian
Jane McGuigan widow	Francis McGuigan	Alexander McGurk
James McGucian	Brian McGurk	James McGurk
Alexander McGucian	Jane McGeechan widow	Catherine McGichan widow
Hendry McGucian	Michael McGuigan	Neal McGurk
Edmond McGurk	Hugh McGurk	William Gucian
Nicolas McGucian		

These lists prompt several comments. First, by the mid-18th century, the surname was pronounced with the more familiar "g". There are no McQuillens or McQuiggans in Desertmartin, but McGuigans, McGuchans, McGeechans, McGucians, McGukens and McGurks.

Second, the religious affiliation of the McGuckins during the Penal Era remains uncertain. The 1766 survey lists no McGuckins among the Dissenters (Presbyterians) in the parish, even though there were nine Protestant families in 1740. It is possible that, during the intervening 80 years between the 1663 and 1740 surveys, at least some of the McGuckins in the Drapers' estate converted to Protestantism and, then by 1766, returned to the Catholic Church. The Protestant convert rolls do verify that at least one Roman Catholic Desertmartin McGuckin, Lawrence McGucken, who is listed as Laurance McGucian in the 1766 census, converted to the Church of England variant of Protestantism in 1789.[7] But, what of Bryan and James McGurk, John McGuken and John McGuchan, who were Protestant in 1740, but Catholic in 1766? Are these the same men? What could have prompted such religious upheaval in this rural parish?

Again, a generation later, we have another list of McGuckins for Desertmartin parish, this time without religious affiliations. The printed Flaxgrowers Bounty Lists 1796, held in the Linenhall Library, note that eight potentially McGuckin households received the bounty of one spinning wheel for growing a quarter of an acre of flax:

John M'Guckian	Myles M'Guigan
Neil M'Guigan	Michael M'Guckian
Edward M'Guckian	Daniel M'Geehan
James M'Geehan	James M'Guckian

---

6. T. O'Fiaich, "The 1766 Religious Census in Some County Tyrone Parishes,"*Seanchas Ard Mhacha*, vol. 6, no. 1, p.146 (1960-1961); D. O'Doibhlin, "Desertmartin Householders in 1766," *Journal of the South Derry Historical Society*, vol. 1, no. 3, p.221 (1982-1983).
7. *The Convert Rolls* (E. O'Byrne, ed.) (Dublin, 1981), p.178.

These eight households, including four who were clearly McGuckins, were able to supplement their farm income with additional cash derived from the linen trade. If this additional source of income continued into the 1840s, it could become the difference between starvation and survival during the Famine.[8]

THE DRAPER'S IN 1817

The Drapers' Irish estate records now deposited in the Public Record Office of N. Ireland effectively c.1820 and list, by parish and townland, each tenant, acreage leased and annual rent. After the 1817 survey, which will be discussed below, the Drapers periodically renewed their leases with their Irish tenantry. In contrast to the Salters, who favored oral tenancies at will, the Drapers seem to have prefered written leases. Generally, dozens of leases were renewed simultaneously, on the same basic terms and conditions. The major variations would be, as expected, the size of the farm leased and the annual rent.

It was the custom, when renewing leases, to begin the lease term retroactively, so that the tenants were already well into the present term when the actual renewal was signed. This custom, which seems unusual today, was a frequent occurrence throughout the Drapers' estate and continued throughout the entire century. Taken as a series, these renewals give us additional information from which we can trace the descent of individual farms.

The First Report of the Master and Master-Warden to the Drapers Company, June, 1817, affords a detailed picture of the conditions in the Drapers' proportion at a time, coincidentally, of crop failure, bad weather and threatened famine.[9] A generation before the Great Famine, the picture was discouraging and dismal. In the Brackagh Slieve Gallion Division, which included Desertmartin, there was "no town . . . nor even any cluster of houses which deserves the name of a village."

The "very great population" of the estate lived predominantly on or near the land they farmed. The warden concluded that the "larger part of the inhabitants . . . are descended from aboriginal Irish."[10] In the early

---

8. Miller, *Emigrants and Exiles*, p.291.
9. *Journal of the South Derry Historical Society*, vol. 2, no. 1 (1984-1985); J. S. Curl, *Moneymore and Draperstown, The Architecture and Planning of the Estates of the Drapers' Company in Ulster* (Belfast, 1979).
10. Curl, *Moneymore*, p.28.

19th century, there were a few "respectable farm-houses . . . occupied by men of comparative wealth and substance,"[11] and two of the best farmers upon the estate engaged in the tanning business. As we shall see, one of these farmers was a McGuckin.

In Ireland before the Famine, 80% of the land holdings were under 15 acres in size, 50% were under 5 acres. These smaller farmers lived like agricultural laborers, selling all their produce, except the precious potatoes, to pay the rent. The Drapers' tenants failed to follow the most elementary principles of husbandry in working a farm ("if" – in the words of the warden – "a few acres of land deserve that name"). Oats, potatoes and flax were planted without any thought to rotation or future production. Only the potato crop was manured and land was never permitted to lie fallow.

"The quantity of land sown with oats, and set with potatoes, is in general regulated by the expected consumption of the family; and it is only in case of an accidental surplus that any part of either crop is carried to market."[12]

The rent was paid, not with the proceeds of any crops, but from yarn, cloth and pig sales. In addition, the tenantry was burdened with taxes and rates, including King's taxes, county, barony and Church rates, tithes to the Established Church rector (even though the McGuckins were Roman Catholic), hearth and window taxes.[13]

The majority of the 9,000 souls on the Drapers' Estate lived in misery. Their homes were "mere mud huts, covered sometimes with straw . . . and are but rarely water-tight." Smoke escaped and rain entered through a single hole in the roof. Generally, "but not universally", the hovel was partitioned so that the cattle, pigs and horse were somewhat separated from the family. By 1841, almost half the population of Ireland lived in one-roomed houses about 18 feet long by 12 feet wide.[14] The Drapers' inspectors found that the tenantry's furniture and clothing were bad, largely "patched, cast-off clothes".[15]

11. *Ibid.*, p.28.
12. *South Derry Journal*, p.80.
13. Curl, *Moneymore*, p.29.
14. D. O'Miurithe, *A Seat Behind the Coachman, Travellers in Ireland, 1800-1900* (Dublin, 1972), p.38.
15. *South Derry Journal*, p.80.

In the Brackagh Slieve Gallion Division "they are miserable in the extreme." In words which foreshadow the attitudes of many in a later generation of English and Anglo-Irish officials, the warden wrote,

"The distress occasioned by the unfortunate failure of the last year's crops . . . might have been supposed to have been the cause of the miserable appearance exhibited by the inhabitants of the Brackasliavgallon Division, if the same cause had not operated with the same severity upon the inhabitants of the Ballinascreen Division without producing the same effect. Their extremely miserable appearance, probably, may have been increased, but cannot have been occasioned by temporary causes: it must be referred to slovely habits."[16]

Not surprisingly, the Drapers' inspectors drew sobering conclusions from their depressing visit.

"It seems clear that the land, as it has been heretofore let and occupied, has not yielded to the landlord rent in proportion to its intrinsic worth; nor has it afforded to the occupiers those means of enjoyment, which, under other circumstaces, it might have yielded. Rent to the landlord, and the means of enjoyment to the occupier, arise from the same source; the same causes tend to the increase of [sic] diminution of both." These causes were simple to identify: "deficiency of capital, and the habits of the people."[17] As for the later, the future held little hope for radical change.

"They could not instantly change their habits, if driven from their cabins, beyond the Company's boundary; and from the hard subsistence which they now earn, the larger part of them must perish before they could find employment or a livelihood; and even supposing that they were got rid of, no tenants with more ample capitals, or different habits, could be found to replace them."[18]

16. *Ibid.*
17. *Ibid.* p.89.
18. *Ibid.*

HENRY McGUCKIN & SONS

The large number of McGuckins in the parish of Desertmartin becomes evident from the 1820s onward. By the time of the tithe survey 1827, M'Guckin was the most common surname in the parish. The Drapers' rent books begin as of November 1, 1820, and show a heavy concentration of McGuckin households in the townlands of "Brakaslavegallon", Carncose, Carndeasie, Craney, Cullion, Durnascallon and Tirgin.[19] We will focus on the McGuckins in the townlands of Carncose, Craney and Tirgin.

The most important fact to be drawn from the Drapers' records is that the McGuckins of Desertmartin leased significantly larger farms than most Irish peasants. Of the 18 McGuckin farms listed in the 1820 Drapers' survey for Desertmartin, only three are less than five acres in size. Three, including two leased by Henry McGuckin, were significantly over 15 acres. The Desertmartin McGuckins entered the pre-Famine era with the benefits of relatively large farms.

The most prominent McGuckin in 1820 Desertmartin was Henry McGuckin of Crany, who farmed fields in several townlands in the parish and was a large cattle dealer in England. The 1820 Drapers' rent rolls tell us that he (or perhaps his son and namesake, although this seems unlikely this early in the century) had possession of land totalling more than 105 acres in the townlands of "Brakaslavegallon", Carncose, Crany and Cullion. Of these he held the 29 acres in Carncose in freehold, an unusual tenure for a Catholic Irishman in early 19th century Ulster. James Curl indicates that the *total* quit-rent payable to the Drapers' agent by free tenants in 1817 was £10.11s.5d.[20] Yet, according to the London records, in 1820, Henry McGuckin alone owed the Drapers an annual rent for his freehold estate of £20.

The 76 acres which Henry leased from the London Company, plus his 29 acre freehold farm, comprised an extremely large, albeit scattered farm. Annually, he owed the Drapers £55 in rent. We do not know in which townland he lived. It seems most likely that he lived either on his freehold in Carncose or in Crany, where his sons and widow lived at the time of the 1831 census.

---

19. Irish placenames are spelled with bewildering variety in different documents. The spellings used here are those found in the original documents cited.
20. Curl, *Moneymore*, p.28.

Here was one of the few men of "comparative wealth and substance" in the Drapers' Proportion. Henry clearly had the capital needed to respond to the initiatives proposed by the 1817 report. It is possible that he benefitted directly from the warden's plan to enlarge farms by consolidation "whenever it can be so arranged by agreement with the occupiers, or upon other principles of humanity and justice". By encouraging modern husbandry, the Drapers sought to increase stock and capital and permit the purchase of additional, smaller and less economic farms "till [the tenant] shall have the occupation of such an extent of land as it may be deemed advisable to encourage."[21] Henry McGuckin probably benefited from this approach.

The Drapers' investment in Henry extended to his sons. In the townland of Crany, John McGuckin, who appears to have been Henry's oldest son, leased 11 more acres for an annual rent of £7.10s.0d.

We know from the Drapers' records relating to his sons that Henry died in 1824. Thus, when, in late 1828 and mid-1829, the Drapers renewed several of the Carncose leases, the tenant was Henry Jr. On December 13, 1828, the London Company leased farmland and bog for turf to Henry McGuckin of Crany for a term of seven years, beginning on November 1, 1827. The annual rent was £6, payable semi-annually in Moneymore. At the same time, his brother John McGuckin renewed his lease with the Drapers for his 11-acre farm in Crany for another seven years at the 1820 rental of £5.5s.0d, on July 16, 1829 and, then again, on August 6, 1829. The Londoners' agent clearly felt less comfortable with Henry's sons than he had with the older man. The acreage they farmed was significantly less than their father's and for shorter lease terms, a practice which was, again, consistant with the 1817 recommendation that lease terms should correspond to the level of rent charged.[22]

The surviving 1831 census confirms that Henry's widow and sons maintained their residences in the townland of Crany, rather than in Carncose, where Henry, Sr., held his freehold. In 1831, widow

---

21. *South Derry Journal*, p.91.
22. *Ibid*.

McGuckin, who was Henry Sr.'s second wife, lived in one house with three men and another woman, while her son Henry Jr. lived nearby with three other men and three women. Henry's son, John McGuckin headed a neighbouring household of three men and two women on a farm of slightly more than eleven acres with an annual rent of £7.11s.0d. All these Desertmartin McGuckins were Roman Catholic.

THE HUNGRY FORTIES

All went quietly in Desertmartin, at least as far as the Drapers' records indicate, until the potato blight and resultant famine destroyed the fabric and stability in Irish rural life. A traveller in Ireland in the early 19th century noted that much of the population lived close to the starvation level, burdened by high rents payable to absentee landlords. The role of the potato in their lives was clear.

"Their prayers are seldom offered for any heavenly favours other than God's blessing on the potato crop."[23]

When the potato blight first struck in 1845, it destroyed 30-40% of the crop throughout Ireland. There was at first little starvation throughout the island as relief measures proved largely adequate. However, the rural Irish ate most of the food they generally sent to market, sold their livestock and pawned their clothes as they struggled to pay their rents.

Conditions on the Drapers' Estate paralleled those in the country at large. With the failure of the potato crop, the Drapers' Company lost one third of its revenues. The year 1845 was especially disastrous with bad weather, famine, recession being added to crop failure to creat incredible poverty throughout the estate. The Company responded "with great leniency" by forgiving rents and other fees due and dispatched gifts of money, seed and stock. Five pounds of meal was provided to the poorer tenants. Relief work was begun throughout the estate, building roads and walls, draining land and planting hedges, to provide some wage to the poor. The Drapers carried out these public works, despite a continuing lack of revenue.[24]

23. O'Miurithe, *Travellers in Ireland,* p.39.
24. Curl, *Plantation,* p.60. See also, Miller, *Emigrants and Exiles,* pp.218, 223.

Conditions reached disastrous levels in 1846 and London began to bring pressure to bear on its local managers to deal with the crisis. The blight destroyed almost the entire potato crop and, although the blight abated in 1847, few potatoes were planted throughout the island and panic seized rural Ireland. More than 214,000 people fled Ireland for North America in 1847. The truly destitute headed the flood of emigration and the migration "bore all the marks of panic and hysteria . . ., the headlong flight of refugees." When the blight returned in full force in the summer of 1848, those farmers who had somehow weathered the earlier blights joined those who saw life in Ireland as hopeless and they, too, joined the migration.[25] In Ulster, the Drapers' agent finally began evictions in 1849.[26]

CRANY

The impact of the Famine in Desertmartin is evident in early 1847 in the correspondence of Rowley Miller, the Drapers' Irish agent. Miller was the son of John Miller, who, at the time of the 1817 report, had lived on the estate for 37 years and was then acting as the agent for Sir William Rowley, to whom the London Company had leased the estate. In its report, the warden recommended that Miller be continued as agent having "done his duty most meritoriously with reference as well to the interests of his employer as to those of the tenantry and the estate . . ."[27] John Miller named his son after his former employer and devised his position as the Drapers' Irish representative to him.

On February 10, 1847, Rowley Miller wrote to London that Harry McGuckin (Henry Mcguckin, Jr.) had sold his farm and, "It would be a great matter to get him and his family out of the country." If the Company added £10 to the proceeds of the sale of the farm, the family, which Miller felt were troublesome, would be "across the water." By the 1840s, the cost of passage to America was in the £2.5s. range, although in the famine year of 1847, the passage to New York peaked at £7 per

25. Miller, *Emigrants and Exiles,* p.292; G. O'Tuathaigh, *Ireland before the Famine, 1798-1848* (Dublin, 1972), pp.203-205.
26. Curl, *Moneymore,* p.60.
27. *South Derry Journal,* p.84.

person.[28] Nonetheless, the Company agreed with Miller and Harry was paid off to emigrate. He may be the Henry McGukan, age 40, who arrrived in New York from Liverpool on November 4, 1848, although this Henry travelled alone.

The Company had barely rid itself of Harry, when his brother Michael McGuckin of Crany demanded £115 from the Londoners. He claimed the money had been withheld by the Drapers during the administration of his father Henry's estate. Michael stated that his father had been an extensive cattle dealer in England and had married twice, having children by both marriages. The eldest son, John, had worked with his father in England and sold the cattle on hand at Henry's death at a profit. The money had been placed with a Cookstown banker who refused later to account to Henry's widow, the mother of Michael and Harry. At the time, John Miller, then the Drapers' agent, had intervened at the widow's request and John admitted that £500 of the bank deposit was his father's and agreed to pay the money to the agent's custody if the Company lent him £100 at 5% to continue his business.

All this apparently made sense at the time and probably fitted in well with the Drapers' plan to encourage rural capitalism among its more affluent tenantry. John continued to be successful in his cattle business until 1840. By that time, he was badly in debt to the Provincial Bank of Ireland for £400, the Belfast Bank in Cookstown for £250 and the Drapers themselves for £66.4s.9d in back rent. John solved his financial difficulties by running off to America, leaving his family in the lurch. His assets were seized and his stepmother was forced to pay £20.8s.8d, a fraction of his actual debts, to his creditors.

Research in contemporaneous American records indicates the difficulties in following John McGuckin of Crany to the New World. There are no John McGuckins listed in the New York City directories until the mid-1840s, after John would have migrated. Philadelphia was the destination of most immigrant McGuckins and, here, we do discover some data worth considering.

---

28. Miller, *Emigrants and Exiles,* p.294; T. Coleman, *Passage to America* (London, 1974), pp.24, 164.

John McGucken, age 23, arrived in Philadelphia with his wife Bridget, age 20, on board the *Walter* on June 6, 1839.[29] This young man arrived a little early in America and is simply too young to be John of Crany. The *Philadelphia Directory* for 1841 only lists one John with a McGuckin-sounding surname, John McGuckey, who lived at 13th Street and Fitzwater. He is at the same address in 1842, disappears from the directory in 1843 and reappears in 1844 at 11th Street, near Carpenter. He remained at this address until 1854. In 1851, he finally corrected the American spelling of his name to McGuckin and he appears that way until the last entry in 1854.

Only one John appears in the 1850 Philadelphia census returns, John McGugan, who lived in the 3rd ward of the Kensington District. This may be our absconding John; but, there are more problems than the spelling of his surname. First, John McGugan told the Assistant Marshall who polled him that he was a carpenter and 30 years old. Again, he would be too young to be John McGuckin of Crany, although he could be the 1839 immigrant John McGucken. Both men were born in Ireland, but this fact does not help with identification.

On the other hand, the census does provide one interesting fact. John McGugan's son, born in April, 1850, was named Henry. Given the Irish tendency to name children after grandparents, perhaps, we may have followed John McGuckin from Crany to Philadelphia. It is tempting to think so.

To return to Michael's petition to the Drapers' agent, we learn that Harry, Jr., Michael's full brother and John's stepbrother, had been John's partner. Consequently, John's abrupt departure for America jeopardized the family farm, which had been purchased by Henry's widow in 1827 with money borrowed from the London Company. Michael denied that he had been involved in any way with the negotiations and fraud surrounding his father's will and now demanded the money John had deposited and apparently still owed to his stepmother. To make matters worse, Michael's mother had foolishly allowed John to keep the original note.

29. Passenger Index, U.S.A. National Archives, Atlantic & Gulf Ports.

By this time, Rowley Miller was more than a little impatient with the Crany McGuckins. On March 10, 1847, he wrote to London that Michael was being "a most insolent young fellow in his language" while continually disrupting business in Miller's office in Moneymore. Would the London officials reconsider his earlier recommendation that this entire matter be resolved by shipping Michael off after John and Harry, Jr., to America?

Apparently, the Drapers had spent enough on this fractious family and rejected Miller's recommendation. Michael remained a tenant on the Drapers' Estate. In1860, at the time of the Valuation Survey, he still leased a 12-acre farm from the Drapers immediately adjacent to the farms of John and James McGuckin.

TIRGAN

By 1845, one of the two McGuckin farms in Tirgan had passed to Pat McGuckin, whom Rowley Miller identified as the stepbrother of the exceedingly troublesome Michael. A memorial in the Agents' letterbook, dated December 7, 1846, indicates that in 1845, the first year of the blight, the Drapers agreed to reduce Pat's rent from £6 to £4.10s.0d if he paid his arrears. Despite the landlord's concession, Pat claimed that he could not pay either sum "owing to his poverty together with bad crops." The agent recommended that London forgive another £10.10s.0d as the only hope of keeping Pat on the land. By court action, the rent in arrears was reduced £5 on May 22, 1846.

Pat was still on his farm in 1847, when the agent wrote to London to update his employers on the situation in Tirgan. After his rent had been reduced and £5 of his arrears forgiven, Pat had built a cottage on the land at his own expense. This was customary in Ireland, where the landlord contributed neither materials nor workmanship to tenant improvement, but garnered the benefits upon reversion of the farm.[30] Despite this, the Drapers' agent stated in a letter dated March 4, 1847, that Pat was "one of those troublesome persons that it would be exceedingly well to get rid of" and recommended a £10 donation to assist in his emigration.

30. Curl, *Moneymore*, pp.28-29.

Two months later, Pat had apparently changed his attitude and had proven himself to be more docile than his brothers. On May 1, 1847, the agent recommended an £8 grant to allow Pat, his wife and children to emigrate. He was now "a different kind of person."

This time, the Drapers apparently accepted Miller's recommendation.The United States Passenger Lists shed some light on Patrick's fate. Patrick McGoogen, age 30, and Ellen McGoogen, age 22, arrived in New York City from Liverpool on board *Judah Fuoro* on May 12, 1848.[31] Other Patricks with McGuckin-sounding surnames arrived in the United States in the early 1850s. But, Patrick McGoogen seems the best candidate for the last of the Crany family to reach the New World.

The Paul McSuigan of Crany who is listed in the 1831 census may be the same Paul McGuckin of Tyrgan, who received £10 to emigrate as a result of a recommendation from the Drapeers' agent on March 4, 1847. Rowley Miller wrote to London that the price of Paul's land would not cover the costs of passage for the eleven members of his family. If he emigrated, the Drapers could pull his cottage down and consolidate his farm with another.

Paul emigrated to America, although apparently without his large family. Paul Mcgucker, age 40, a weaver, arrived alone in New York City on *Millicete* on February 1, 1848.[32] He filed a citizenship petition in the Philadelphia Court of Quarter Sessions on October 2, 1852, although his Oath of Allegiance is not recorded.[33] Because Paul is an unusual name among the McGuckins, there is some reason to assume that all this information related to Paul of Crany/Tirgan. In 1853, Paul McGuckin lived in a tavern on Carpenter Street, near 8th, in Philadelphia. He does not appear in any other Philadelphia Directory or census return.

31. *The Famine Immigrants*, vol. 2, New York, 1846-1851 (Baltimore, 1983).
32. *Ibid.*, vol. 2, p.233.
33. Index, *Philadelphia Naturalization Records*, vol. 7.

CARNCOSE

The 1831 census provides our initial information about Charles McGuckin of Carncose, who was then the head of a family of a man and two women. He is probably the son of the Edward McGuckin who appears in the 1796 Flaxgrowers Bounty List. With his brothers Edward and John and his widowed mother ("Widow Edward" in the Drapers' records), Charles leased a farm of slightly more than 16 acres from the Drapers for an annual rent of £7.45s.0d. The Drapers' records further indicate that on May 1, 1847, Charles McGuckin sold his farm and house to pay his delinquent rent of £13.18d.7d and the costs of £2.5s.0d incurred by the Drapers' Company to eject him and his family from their homestead. The land and house brought a total price of £26.10s.0d, of which Charles netted only £16.3s.7d, which was insufficient to pay for the costs of emigration to America. Anxious to be rid of him, the Drapers contributed a further £12 for his travelling costs.

According to the Passenger Lists maintained by the United States Government at the principal ports of entry, Charles McGookin, age 70, arrived in New York City on board *Thomas H. Perkins* from Liverpool on September 29, 1848. With him were June (probably a misreading of the transcription for Jane, a more common Irish name), age 25, Eliza, age 14, Henry, age 12, and Nancy, an infant of less than one year in age.[34]

Charles McGucken filed his declaration of intention to become an American citizen in Philadelphia's Court of Quarter Sessions on April 18, 1854. His naturalization papers were issued in May, 1858, by the Court of Common Pleas.[35] These dates suggest that we are tracing the migration of Charles of Carncose, although his advanced age in 1848 is a little troublesome. Charles would have been 80 when he became a citizen. Ordinarily, this would be the endeavour of a far younger man.

On July 16, 1829, John McGuckin of Carncose leased his farm from the Drapers for £7 a year on the same terms and conditions as the other leases granted at that time. This may be Edward's brother, who lived with him at the time of the 1831 census. However, it would be unusual

---

34. *The Famine Immigrants,* vol. 2, New York (Baltimore, 1984).
35. Index, *Aliens' Declarations of Intention and/or Oaths of Allegiance, 1789-1880* (Philadelphia).

for a tenant farmer not to live on his land. On August 6, 1829, the Drapers leased to John McGuckin, farmer, additional land in Carncose townland for an annual rent of £43. The term of the leasehold was until 1851 or until all of the following gentlemen were dead: King George IV (who died in 1830); Sir George Fitzgerald Hill, Bart., Vice Treasurer of Ireland; and Reverend John Torrin, Doctor of Divinity, Archdeacon of Dublin. Such lease terms were common in English drafting of the 19th century, although one wonders how John McGuckin was to keep track of the health of Reverend Torrin in Dublin. It is interesting to note that John signed the lease "McGuckian", which is the more common Ballinderry spelling of the McGuckin surname.

THE SURVIVORS IN IRELAND

The economic depression caused by the Famine severely reduced the number of McGuckins living in Desertmartin parish on the Drapers' estate. A valuation survey done by Charles Pollock in 1857 lists only the following McGuckins in Desertmartin:

Carncose: Edward McGuckin, Francis McGuckin, John McGuckin, John McGuckin, Jr., Hugh McGuckin and Alexander McGuckin.

Cranny: Michael McGuckin (the son of Henry) and John McGuckin.

On January 2, 1860, the Drapers reviewed and renewed many of their leases in their estate. All the leases were for 21 years retroactively from November 1, 1854, for various rents. In Crany, only John McGuckin renewed his lease. Michael had died, moved or, perhaps at last, emigrated. The Drapers' archives indicate that John M'Guckin of Crany died in 1864 or 1865, leaving his widow Ellen and one minor child, Ellen.

In Carncose, only four McGuckin tenants remained in 1860: John McGuckin, Sr., and John McGuckin, Jr. (who may or may not have been father and son), Hugh and Francis McGuckin.

The tragedy of the Great Famine changed the face of Ireland. A social revolution occurred, completing the consolidation of smaller holdings which the Drapers' warden had recommended in 1817.[36] The

---

36. O'Tuathaigh, *Ireland before the Famine*, p.206.

McGuckins in Desertmartin were both victims and facilitators of that social change, but it is difficult to conclude that they were truly representative of what was happening in Ireland in the first half of the 19th century.

For example, Henry McGuckin, the cattle dealer, was an atypical tenant in the 1820s. A minor capitalist, he farmed and raised cattle on a small empire of 105 acres. He held a unique freehold tenancy and he and his partner-sons borrowed on a grand scale from the local Ulster banks. The economically advanced ideas of the Drapers, evidenced in the 1817 report, afforded Henry and his sons John and Harr, Jr., with unusual opportunities for Catholic Irishmen before the Famine.

The Famine did, however, reduce this prosperous family to the level of their Irish neighbours. John overplayed his hand, ignored the needs of his stepmother and brothers and eventually insolvent and a fugitive by 1840, undermining the family's economic stability. Thus, by 1845, the principal McGuckin family in Desertmartin had fallen on hard times. After the blight struck, matters worsened steadily. The McGuckins' rents were in arrears, farm tenancies were sold and consolidated and families were ejected as early as 1847, before Rowley Miller began actively to eject defaulting tenants.

But, even here, the history of the McGuckin families in Desertmartin parish indictes that, at least on the Drapers' estate, Rowley Miller was proactive in opportuning his employers to invest significant sums of money in facilitating emigration. Eviction was not his remedy of choice. Of course, Miller's motives were not altruistic. Many of the McGuckin tenants were "troublesome", "insolent" and, in the case of the administration of Henry McGuckin's estate, a reminder of problems perhaps mishandled by Miller's father. Eviction was not a weapon Rowley Miller lightly or frequently used during the early years of the Famine. Rather, he sought to encourage emigration with cash subsidies.

Undoubtedly, there is much more to the stories told here. But, the terrifying reality of the Famine conditions creeps into the businesslike correspondence from Moneymore to London and indicates that family historians should not neglect the rich resources found in the records of the London Companies.

I am grateful to the Education Officer of The Honourable Company of Drapers, London, for permitting me to review and quote the material which forms the basis of this article.

BOOK REVIEW

The Winters on the Wannon by Dr. Gordon Forth. Deakin University Press. 1991. 199pp. Paperback. No price.

The TV and film rights of this splendid account of how two Anglo-Irish gentry families colonised part of western Victoria, first as pioneering pastoralists and later as landed gentry Australian style, ought to be snapped up by some enterprising Irish/Australian film company. It has all the elements of a good Western and a popular Soap: from white sheep in wide open spaces to black sheep in family rows.

In a perceptive Foreword Professor Shaw of Monash University writes that the book is about two families ". . . the Winters and the Cookes, with properties at Tahara and Condah who coalesced to become the Winter-Cookes of Murndal. Basing his story on the family papers there . . . Dr. Forth has written a fascinating account of the families' decisions to leave Ireland and establish themselves in Victoria's western district. He discusses their motives for emigrating, their long indecision whether to stay in Victoria or to return home, their trials as pioneers and their relations with the Aborigines, with their labour force and between themselves. He recounts their financial ups and downs, their grievances against the Victorian government and their contribution to their community. In other words he makes the traditional generalised account of the Victorian squatters come alive by providing a detailed narrative of two families and noticing where this accords with and where it differs from the customary summarised story."

What that excellent summary by Professor Shaw does not bring out for non-Australian readers is the true novelty of this book in the context of Irish migration. For it is the story of relatively well-to-do children of Irish landed gentry emigrating from 1833 onwards and taking with them the concept of the Local Squire and the Big House first to Tasmania and from there to Victoria. It is this attitude and its practical application over a century, through three generations, which fascinates. Thus it is in stark contrast to the usual theme of deprived Irish arriving as convicts, orphans and gold diggers. The interaction of the deprived with the landed-gents is a strong theme in the story.

The main character is Samuel Pratt Winter, born on the Auger family estate in Co Meath in 1815 to a rather harum-scarum father who died in 1830. Three years later the young Winter emigrated to Tasmania as a trainee manager on an estate owned by William Bryan, a Wexford landed-gent who had emigrated in 1822. By 1833 Bryan was at loggerheads with the Governor of Tasmania as to whether (and here I over-simplify) convicts were tenants or prisoners when working for landed proprietors. Bryan was getting out as Winter arrived. This basic experience of running Bryan's estate on his own from 1834-1838 taught Winter, the hard way, what he needed to know to manage successfully a sheep-run in Victoria, after only four years in the colonies. From then on it is a success story until he died in 1878. As a bachelor uncle he then left the pastoral runs of the 1840s to his nephew: but meantime they had become a landed Australian estate: Murndal, a seat fit for a gentleman.

Winter had taken to Australia the philosophy and attitude of a liberal, paternal but conservative Irish landowner. He tried, in the 1840s and 1850s to understand and sympathise with the Aborigines whose hunting grounds and shrines were being taken for sheep runs. Something of his feelings can be appreciated by his dying wish "to be buried in the stones at Murndal where the blacks are buried" (p.45). Typically his unreliable younger brother Trevor failed to outface local white prejudice and buried him in a conventional plot: by 1878 middle class morality had replaced pioneering respect for fellow humans.

There was indeed a down side to him. Winter's snobbish search on his trips to Europe for an English landed ancestry, his commissioning of copies of family portraits to hang at Murndal and of Italian masterpieces, displays a pathological insecurity. Dr Forth writes: ". . . he was prepared to spend considerable time and money in a bid to establish that he was no rude pioneer but a gentleman of impressive pedigree and cultivated taste" (p.119). It would however be wrong to denigrate Winter: he was an extraordinary and successful man.

This book is not a biography of one man. It is the story of a family and a social class. An important aspect of that story is the light it throws on the circumstances of the children of the Irish gentry in 19th century Ireland which compelled them to depart to the colonies and how the fact that they went with a modest capital placed them ahead of their fellow deprived Irish. Winter's fear of democracy in late 19th century Victoria is revealing of the social philosophy and prejudice the Anglo-Irish gentry took with them from a growing revolutionary Irish scene.

Dr. Forth has given us not only a lively and scholarly book, but also a very readable book. He writes with a clarity and simplicity comparable to that of Professor J. C. Beckett whose study "The Anglo-Irish Tradition" (Faber 1976) provides in depth the Irish background of these Protestant gentry which still influenced them so profoundly, when they were miles from their roots, in Australia.

Kenneth Darwin

BOOK REVIEW

The Home Children by Phyllis Harrison. Watson and Dwyer Ltd., Winnipeg, Canada. 1979. 271pp. 38 photos. No price.

Some years ago the BBC screened a television play called *Swallows* by Rhydderch Jones, in which a group of Cockney children are sent to stay among adoptive strangers in a remote northern Welsh village during the blitz of 1943. The play dramatized very effectively the initial and mutual incomprehension between the rural Welsh hosts and the little urban invaders, to whom the first sight of the countryside was a novel experience. From the tensions raised by this encounter, Jones was able to air a variety of themes, ranging from racial hostility to questions of adolescence, sex and religion.

Evacuations such as this, which took place during the Second World War, are still relatively fresh in the popular memory. One has to travel much further both in distance and time to embrace imaginatively the experiences of the "Home Children" in Phyllis Harrison's book. These "Home Children" were from the many childrens' orphanages and "childrens homes" in Britain: Barnardos, Church of England Children's Bureau, the National Childrens' Homes and so on, who sent children to Canada under the British Child Emigration Movement. From 1870 to 1930 over 100,000 of these children arrived to work on Canadian farms. Travelling in groups of up to 400 they came to a land believed to offer the best hope for their future. Many of them are still living and this book is compiled from their own personal stories: some 106 letters in all. From their memories they tell of harsh conditions, loneliness, grinding hard work, discrimination and disappointment.

One gains a sharp sense of our good fortune in having access to their memories. The letters to the author of this book resulted from her appealing through the columns of some 40 Canadian newspapers. The response she had, whilst clearly based on chance, shows the powerful need there was to tell their stories. One also has a strong sense in reading these letters of the many which are lost to us and this tends to magnify the poignancy of those which are collected here.

These accounts are compelling, both as evidence of personal experiences and as unique evocations of a great country in transition. We move from the latter part of the age of Victoria when, as one letter

194

tells us, Canadian farms had no machines, through the universal trauma of the Great War and on to the grinding hardship of the Great Depression of the 1930s.

Whether or not the Home Children were lucky in their adoptive parents, and doubtless some of them were vilely unlucky, they seem to have been perfectly placed to offer a distinct perspective on the vast emerging nation of Canada that for many of them was to become a permanent home and the place for which they would come to feel first loyalty. As a result, fascinating stories like that of 'English' John Henry Thomas, who travelled extensively and at once stage was unofficially adopted by a family of Saulteaux Indians, manage to escape the limitations of a conventional history and grant the reader an enjoyment more usually associated with imaginative fiction.

Some of these letters are striking expressions of bitterness, of great pain and humiliations not forgotten: "We were the cheapest slave labour the farmers ever had. I was wondering how you even got to thinking of us. I thought we were long forgotten as we were only Home boys and it didn't matter much what happened to us. We were of no importance. (p.81).

Others have a resonance and a measured quality that seem unique to age and the reflections to which it gives rise: "I had youth and the God-given quality that only youth has. It is strange that in all the hell of Passchendalle and even in the prisoner of war camp I never feared life as I do now in easy circumstances and safety. It seems a paradise but it is not."

If the expectations of the very young Home children who awaited their new parents on the station platforms of Canada were confused and vague, those of their hosts often appear to have been clearly defined, sometimes brutally so. In many cases, these children were regarded as little more than drudges and were denied the opportunity of proper education or indulgence in pursuits usually associated with childhood. Boys who were still traumatised by separation from their parents were expected to do the physical work of young men, and girls became houseslaves and maids of all work.

There are stories here of children who were overworked, underpaid and cheated or not paid at all. Many were underfed, inadquately clothed in winter, beaten, sexually abused, and stigmatised both for being charity children and for being British. In some of these letters we find the tentative first expressions of feelings of shame, pain and solitude, literally suppressed for decades: as with the mother who tells her complaining children, "At least you don't know what it is to feel that no one cares if you live or die – and wants you only if you work hard." Some of the second-hand accounts included in the book tell of people who quite simply refused ever to speak of what they had undergone, and this conveys a harrowing impression of young hearts and minds irreparably wounded.

Nevertheless, there are other stories, of children who were treated decently and fairly, within the often harsh limitations of farm life in the Canada of the early 1900's, and many of the letters show an abiding love for, and gratitude towards the country and the people that offered them a new life. A good example of this feeling of affinity for the country is given by Allan M. Slade, one of whose experiences was to work at a lumber camp in Quebec during the "fall" of 1927: "Since that time I have seen a lot of the world, but it was that winter in the logging camp that left the big impression. To look out from our camp and see galloping deer on the lake being chased by wolves, and to look down the steep slopes to the fast-flowing Black River with its genuine sweet clear water, with the Laurentian Mountains as far as the eye could see, and the pines whistling in the breeze – that was an experience I'll never forget."

Interestingly many of the letters are complimentary and respectful towards the Barnardo Homes and the other organisations that brought the children to Canada. They seem to have combined a genuine concern for their charges with a great deal of efficiency, and one feels that it was the sheer number of children that they had to cope with and not wilful neglect, that allowed the abusers of the children to get away with their crimes. If, as Phyllis Harrison says in her Introduction, the experiences of Oliver Twist are not far behind us, we can at least take consolation in the fact that there do not appear to have been too many Mr Bumbles under Dr. Barnardo's eye.

Phyllis Harrison's achievement is a remarkable one. In the outwardly simple act of assembling together these letters, she gives us documents that are historically and sociologically stimulating, but which, rather more than that, remain in the mind as a collective testimony to a unique human experience. The 38 photographic illustrations add further life, while rather ironically conveying something of the intimacy of a family album. The excellent introduction removes even the most casual reader's excuse for claiming that he is not well-enough informed to be able to enjoy this absorbing book. There is a first rate index of persons, places and ships which is a model one wishes other authors might emulate. For it alone it would be worth Canadian genealogists buying the book.

Michael Cronin

BOOK REVIEW

Six publications of the Society of Genealogists, London

Using the Library of the S.O.G. 1991. 18pp. £0.65 inc. postage

This is a model of what a brief guide to a library or record office should be. It leaves you with a desire to go and actually use the library: with the feeling that you will be welcome. Not only does it tell you what is on the shelves by way of books and documents but there are clear floor plans of the shelving arrangements to enable you to walk straight to the volumes you require.

The contents of volumes are summarised comprehensively and information is arranged by subject, personal names and geographical area. There is a very comprehensive index to the 18 page Guide itself: a rare bonus!

Even if you can not visit the library this booklet is an admirable guide to basic genealogical material: both records and reference works. A bargain at 65 pence.

Library Sources No. 1. Parish Register Copies in the Library. 1992. 120pp. £5.65

This is the first of what promises to be a well produced run of guides giving precise details of the Library's holdings. This booklet lists 9000 places (parishes, congregations, cemeteries) in the British Isles and overseas for which copies are available in the Library, showing the periods covered and which have been printed and are therefore available for loan to members of the Society. The places range over 52 countries outside the British Isles from Antigua to Zululand including three pages on USA alone.

Library Sources No. 2. Marriage Licences: abstracts and indexes in the Library. 1991. 26pp. £2.30

This list covers England, Wales and Ireland. It is arranged by county and shows all the material in the Library and gives references to those Licences published as articles in journals. Prior to 1837 the indexes to marriage licences form a valuable supplement to the various county marriage indexes. Licences were frequently sought by people who were anxious to marry away from their normal residence, or were in a hurry to marry, or were non-conformists, or wished to marry in Lent, or without parental consent, or wished to marry someone of unequal social status or age. The Irish section provides a most useful guide to material which tends to be overlooked in the printed annual reports of the Public Record Office of Ireland and in other Irish journals and books.

Library Sources No. 3. A List of Parishes in Boyd's Marriage Index. 1992. 54pp. £3.35

Boyd's Marriage Index was compiled by Percival Boyd and his staff, at his expense, between 1925 and 1955 when he died. It has been added to by others since then. It is in essence a typescript index to ENGLISH marriages taken from Marriage Registers, Bishops' Transcripts and Marriage Licences 1538-1837. It does not cover Scotland, Wales or Ireland. It has seven million entries in 534 volumes. Some 4,300 parishes are covered in whole or part. The booklet lists the parishes and periods covered. Now that the Boyd Index is widely available on microfiche in centres worldwide this index provides an indispensable guide to a worldwide readership.

"My ancestor was . . ." Series gives guidance on records relating to particular religious, occupational or other categories and includes already: Merchant Seamen, Migrants, Baptists, Methodists, Quakers, Manorial Tenants, and 'Came over with the Conqueror'. They are priced from around £2 to £5 each. Two recent additions to the series are:

My Ancestor was in the British Army 1992. 122pp. £5.65 inc. postage.
My Ancestors were Congregationalists in England and Wales. 1992. 94pp. £4.50.

The 'Army volume' is by the indefatigable Watts brothers who also did the 'Seamen' volume. It provides a very practical and detailed introduction to the records of the British Army between 1660 and 1918. Sixteen pages are devoted to officers all the rest to other ranks. The latter are notoriously difficult to trace and the guide starts with non-army sources which may lead to the Regiment concerned or for those who cannot find this information it provides more than a dozen starting points in available records. Most of these are at the London PRO but there are further sections on other sources including those found abroad and there is a special section on World War I. There is an especially interesting section on campaign medals. This is a masterly survey which covers with clarity and in staggering detail a confusing and almost overwhelming mass of record material. It deserves a wide and appreciative readership worldwide.

By contrast the Congregational booklet is a simple list of places where there are or were Congregational churches, with dates of registers and where they can now be found: largely in the PRO in London. However contrary to popular opinion many such registers do exist outside the PRO and Mr. Clifford has gathered information about these together with information about chapels where no registers can be found. It should be noted that the list covers only England and Wales. Nevertheless it has a much wider interest for a much wider audience for in the first nine pages of introduction and explanation there is an historical treatise in its own right on Separatists, Independents, Brownists, Pilgrim Fathers and so on in the 17th century and later: down to 1972 in fact when the attempt at unity led to further separations! Packed into the Introduction is as accurate and brief a history of dissenters and their relations with the Anglican Church, the government and with themselves as you are likely to read anywhere. Mr. Clifford merits our thanks.

Kenneth Darwin

BOOK REVIEW

Girl, Name Forgotten . . . Stories from Seven Centuries of Family History, by John Oliver. Littlewood. 1991 119pp £6.95
Personalities at Popplesdorf, by John Oliver. Willaim Sessions Ltd. 1992. 189pp. No price.

Each of these volumes has as its origin John Oliver's imaginative interest in his family origins and an acute sense of being able to link his own experiences with those of preceding generations. Oliver has, in a long and distinguished career, been administrator, researcher, historian linguist and writer. These qualities are particularly evident in *Girl, Name Forgotten*. The poignantly-worded title is taken from an original document which Oliver came across as he traced his family's migration from the Magilligan area of Co. Londonderry to Canada in the 1830's. He cleverly incorporates the results of his research into a reconstructed account of emigration from his native parish, in a short story which captures as neatly as can be imagined the circumstances of the desperate pre-Famine days when there was some choice, but not much, left to intending emigrants.

The subjects in the other stories range from the fortunes of the Oliver family in the Scottish Borders in the sixteenth century to the arrival of the Olivers in Co. Londonderry in the early days of the Ulster Plantation, in a colony led by Sir Robert McClelland, and their subsequent settlement in the Newtownlimavady-Magilligan area. In addition to their value in telling a good story which incorporates historical evidence in fictional form, the stories contain a wealth of words and phrases which are typical of the idiom of rural people in north Co. Londonderry and in southern Scotland, from Wigtownshire to Berwickshire, and for which there is a useful glossary. This faithful use of dialect, as much as anything else, helps Oliver realise his professed aim 'to bring to life some of the people I had come to know so well in the distant past and to convey something of the lives they led'.

Personalities at Popplesdorf call on Oliver's wide-ranging experiences, as student, traveller and administrator, all of which are reflected in a varied and variable – though never less than entertaining – series of essays and short stories. Of these, 'Somerton Road', an account of Oliver's innocent (in every sense) role, while spending a year as a student in Nazi Germany, in the escape to Ireland of a young Jewish girl, is most evocative and skilfully handled. Anyone who has read his account of life as a civil servant in the Northern Ireland administration, *Working at Stormont* (1978), could be permitted to wonder why his experiences in, for example, the Ministry of Public Security and the preparations for the air raids which eventually came, do not feature as much as they ought. Perhaps they will in a future volume.

Trevor Parkhill

BOOK REVIEW

The McCabe List: Early Irish in the Ottawa Valley, by Bruce S. Elliott. Ontario Genealogical Society. 1991. 64pp. No price.

This Canadian publication takes its title from Ulster for the list of names and addresses and more which *The McCabe List* contains takes its name from John McCabe of Stoneyford near Lisburn: not because he compiled it, but because he discovered it. He found it among the Colonial Office records in the PRO London where it was part of papers relating to emigration (C.O. 384). There is some irony in the fact that it was already on microfilm in the National Archives of Canada but no one had noticed it there or its significance.

It is dated 5 February 1829 and is a list of 673 men who signed a petition to Lt. Col. By [sic], the Royal Engineer in charge of building the Rideau Canal at Ottawa, and relates to assisted emigration schemes from the United Kingdom to Canada. The detail of the background to this is explained in Bruce Elliott's introduction to the list of names.

But it is much more than merely a list of names for each 'Canadian' gives his name, his former address in Ireland (under county, parish and townland) and details of relations who are still in Ireland and who in his opinion would be interested in taking part in an assisted emigration scheme, plus the name of a local Irish worthy who knows them.

A typical entry runs:

"156   Gillespie William Fermanagh, Clogher, Scriby
        Has a nephew John Lindrim with a large family residing at
        Scriby near Fivemiletown and is known to Col. Montgomery of
        said place."

This illustrates a caution made in the Introduction about spelling of personal and place names. Local knowledge suggests to me that John Lindrim should be John Lendrum and the townland Scriby should be Screeby. These are however minor differences compared with several glaring errors elsewhere. For example Swaddlenbar which appears several times is clearly Swanlinbar, Co Cavan.

I would therefore be more dogmatic than Bruce Elliott in his Introduction on this point. I would say that readers MUST, not merely "may wish to", refer to the Townlands Index of the 1861 Irish Census. It was reprinted in 1984 by Baltimore Genealogical Publishing Co. Inc. and so is available. In fact one must wonder why the 1861 version of the names of townlands has not been given in the list as published and of parishes also. It would have meant some 700 checks but is that not what editorial work is about?

There is however a very good personal names index, not only of the signatories but of the relatives still in Ireland, compiled by Dr Alton Owens, which will be invaluable to numerous Irish and Canadian genealogists who will bless John McCabe and the publishers of this interesting historical document.

Kenneth Darwin

BOOK REVIEW

Murray Farmhouse Tavern Party. 2 Audio Tapes. Poricy Park, Middletown, New Jersey 07748 USA. No price.

The blurb on these tapes claims that in 1770 a Joseph Murray, a Scots-Irish immigrant built a farmhouse and barn in Middletown, 30 miles south of New York. Once a year The Murray Farmhouse Tavern Party re-creates, it is claimed, the atmosphere of an 18th century colonial tavern in this farmhouse. The tapes are recordings at the 1991 and 1992 parties. It is also claimed that the songs on the tapes were known in the 18th century and that they are performed in a style suited to the period. They are clearly and well sung: every word is distinct.

First let me say that I thoroughly enjoyed listening to them. Secondly that if it is all as authentic as the blurb claims, then the Scots-Irish were far from the straight-laced puritanical presbyterian Ulster folk we have been led to believe: in fact they must have been a pretty bawdy lot!

Some of the songs are traditional English folk songs: The Girl I Left Behind Me; Oh No John. Some are recognisably Irish: Bunch of Thyme; Bar The Door; Two Sisters; Fare Thee Well You Sweethearts and Seeds of Love. One, The Pig, was I think banned by Lord Reith from the BBC programmes pre-war under the title: The Pig Got Up and Slowly Walked Away, which is its last line. I was glad of the opportunity to hear this and am left wondering why it was banned. If he had banned several of the others I could have seen why: Home Came Old Man; Wanton Seed; Friar in the Well; The Creel; Bastard King of England and so on. They have that earthy humour which Victorian Music Halls conjure up but which in an age of Galway Bishops and Madonnas passes unremarked. These tapes would help to get your next St Patrick's Night party going again if it was flagging!

Kenneth Darwin

PUBLICATIONS FROM
SOUTH EASTERN EDUCATION AND LIBRARY BOARD
LIBRARY & INFORMATION SERVICE

NEWSPAPER INDEX SERIES

Each index contains a chronological list
of article references, indexed by person, subject and place.

County Down Spectator: 1904 - 1964	£1.50
Downpatrick Recorder: 1836 - 1886	£5.00
Mourne Observer: 1949 - 1980	£2.00
Newtownards Chronicle: 1873 - 1900 and Newtownards Independent: 1871 - 1873	£3.00
Northern Herald: Index to Co. Down and Lisburn items: 1833 - 1836	£1.50
Northern Star: Index to Co. Down and Lisburn items: 1792 - 1797	£2.50

Copies of these indexes are available for sale from
Irish & Local Studies Section
SEELB Library Headquarters
Windmill Hill
Ballynahinch
Co Down BT24 8DH
Northern Ireland

Postage charged on orders from outside Northern
Ireland

ILS/92/6